POCAHONTAS SHOW TRIAL

*The Wrongful Conviction
of an "Unpopular Figure"
in West Virginia*

BY

Will Williams

———

COSMOTHEIST BOOKS
MOUNTAIN CITY

ISBN 978-1-7336481-6-5

book design and editing by Kevin Alfred Strom
and Lana Williams

published by

COSMOTHEIST BOOKS
BOX 4 • MOUNTAIN CITY • TENNESSEE • 37683
COSMOTHEISTCHURCH.ORG

Table of Contents

Appendices

A Note to Readers

We are fortunate to be able to self-publish this book. It is doubtful that I would have been able to find a publisher for *Show Trial* if I had even tried, considering the "unpopularity" of myself and the National Alliance (NA) organization that I head.

This book will make for interesting reading for many citizens of West Virginia, especially Pocahontas and Greenbrier Counties. However, West Virginia bookstores will never agree to sell this book. Such is the state of the First Amendment of the Bill of Rights these days. One who holds unpopular ideas — like the idea that the White race is worth preserving — is considered by many to be undeserving of that Amendment's protections.

Show Trial barely touches on how our Alliance's powerful enemies have influenced numerous financial services to deny our online customers the use of credit cards, and how Big Tech companies censor us for telling inconvenient truths. Find more about these abuses at our online magazine NationalVanguard.org. This book will be available for sale at our bookstore, here: https://cosmotheistchurch.org/shop/ as well as at some other online sites.

Acknowledgments

Show Trial is self-published with my own funds — no fancy publishing house with layers of employers to polish a manuscript, just me and my wife pulling it together as best we could. She was put through the same ordeal by my accuser, my accuser's collaborators and co-conspirators, and the courts, so full credit for organizing of this book, and for prodding me to put in the hours to complete it must go to her.

Special gratitude to my long term friend and comrade Kevin Alfred Strom for copy editing and layout of this book, help with the cover and for setting up the Web site where everything that can't fit into the book is to be found.

Also thanks to those living and working on our National Alliance campus in West Virginia, Donald and Barbara MacMullen, and Ray Wolbert. Other Alliance members and supporters too numerous to mention, but at minimum, at least, friends Riley, Meredith, Mike, Jim, Josh, and Katherine — all who helped so much with Alliance-building to give me some time to work on this book.

Dedication

To my loving Russian bride of 17 years, Svetlana (Lana), Williams, who knows me best. Lana has stood by my side through thick and through thin, for better and for worse, no matter how challenging my leading an unpopular organization in these times has been.

Introduction

The story I will tell here is very complicated. The title, *Pocahontas Show Trial: The Wrongful Conviction of an "Unpopular Figure" in West Virginia*, could just as well have been *Four and a Half Years of Struggle Against Lies, Stupidity, and Cowardice — A Reckoning*, the original title of Adolf Hitler's famous book. The "reckoning" portion is my account of how I was treated in the 11th Judicial District of West Virginia, specifically the courts of Pocahontas County, and then by the West Virginia Supreme Court of Appeals.

When I accepted the appointment of the National Alliance (NA) board of directors to become chairman of that organization in October, 2014, I expected that I would be in for a struggle, rebuilding after a dozen years of mismanagement following the death of the Alliance's founder, Dr. William Pierce, in 2002. It has actually been six years of struggle as this account is being written in the fall of 2020.

It should be mentioned here, for readers who are not aware, that the National Alliance is hated by the powerful — particularly by Jewish "watchdog" groups like the Southern Poverty Law Center (SPLC) and the Anti-Defamation League (ADL); the compliant Jew-controlled mass media, and in many cases a compliant justice system. All this hate is projected onto the NA simply because it advocates exclusively for the interests of the White American majority. The maxim "the majority rules" does not apply when it comes to the shrinking majority of Americans who are White.

This book tells the story of the ordeal I experienced during this period while fighting off three civil judicial coup attempts against the NA, including a false accusation of misdemeanor criminal battery that led to my wrongful conviction and incarceration. As of this writing much of this ordeal has been documented in 70 monthly NA member's BULLETINs, numerous archived postings on Internet discussion boards, and hundreds of pages of documents generated in the courts of, mostly, Virginia and West Virginia. My residence during this period has been in Johnson County, in the extreme corner of Upper East Tennessee where the National Office of the NA has been located since I took over.

I have on occasion characterized my judicial misadventure by saying, "A roomful of Jew scriptwriters in Hollywood with the help of best-selling novelist John Grisham couldn't come up with a legal thriller as twisted as the mess I've been through."

One might ask, "What is so special about your story?" I'd say two things. One is how a false criminal charge by a clearly unhinged accuser can lead to an unquestioned wrongful conviction and incarceration. The other is how trust in the rule of law, in due process, and in a presumption of innocence can be so trampled upon by a corrupt judiciary because the accused is seen by the court as an "unpopular figure."

An attorney friend told me that what my accuser was doing with her dramatic temporary restraining order requests filed against me, her petitions for protective orders, her misapplication of tenant's rights, etc., etc., was like what that sociopath con man Carter Hayes (played by actor Michael Keaton) does to the young unmarried, middle-class, naive couple (played by actors Melanie Griffith and Matthew Modine) in the 1990 movie *Pacific Heights*. The reader should try to watch that horror film, if possible, to grasp the similarities of my real life horror experience with the actions of a Hollywood sociopath character who used many of the same tactics as did my accuser.

The name of my book could have been limited to Pocahontas County courts in West Virginia's 11th Judicial District, until I finally received the "memorandum decision" from the West Virginia Supreme Court of Appeal (WVSCA). Up until then, in June, 2020, I had held out hope that my shockingly unjust experience with the Pocahontas County courts had been a local aberration. Surely the five learned justices of the WVSCA would see in my appeal that I had been wrongfully prosecuted and convicted. I even wrote in my Petitioner's Brief:

> If [Defendant] isn't granted a reversal for his wrongful conviction by the Highest Court where he and his wife can put this experience behind them, to clear his name, he will have no other recourse, but to take the story of his shocking experience with 11th Judicial District to the court of public opinion. This is not a threat. Defendant has a voice and he will use it. Defendant hopes, though, that his experience with the Pocahontas County Magistrate and Circuit Courts is exceptional — like nowhere else in West Virginia — perhaps because the county is remote and difficult to monitor by higher authorities.

The nonchalant, unanimous affirmation of the 11th Judicial District's conviction of me by the Supreme Court justices made clear to me that injustice in the "theatre of the absurd" in West Virginia's judiciary is both deep-rooted and extensive, all the way to the top, not simply peculiar to the backwoods courts of Pocahontas County.

What little faith I still had in the judicial system five years ago — to search for and discover facts that will lead to the truth of a matter — was broken by the high court's rubber-stampers in black robes, not to be restored. As I said in the opening paragraph, this account is my reckoning.

My former employee, accuser Garland DeCourcy, who uses numerous aliases and more than one Social Security number, is a documented scam artist with a history of abusing the judicial process in at least two jurisdictions (West Virginia and Virginia). And further, before being fired by me, DeCourcy admitted to my friend, Meredith Kellar, that she had been diagnosed with Asperger's Syndrome (a high functioning form of autism with an inability to form normal social relationships). Since just 2014 De-

Courcy has been a fugitive from at least Virginia and West Virginia after getting herself into legal troubles with the courts. She is still "on the lam" from West Virginia since October, 2018, as I write this two years later, and has likely changed her name again. A private investigator friend who tried to locate her in 2019 for the purpose of my appeal reported that she is "deliberately elusive." She has covered her tracks well.

Though I don't have written proof of my accuser's diagnosis, everyone who will read the *66-page* portion of her court testimony in the transcript of my trial will see DeCourcy clearly demonstrating symptoms of mental disorder. Her lying and contradicting herself throughout her testimony is painfully apparent.

At trial my accuser clearly attempted to fool all three Circuit Court (CC) officers: Judge Jennifer P. Dent, Special Prosecutor Patrick I. Via, as well as my defense attorney Laura M. Finch, who was eventually revealed to be working against me. Those three court officers, who are supposed to be impartial, honest, and honorable upholders of the law, had been pretending not to see DeCourcy's proven lies under oath, her glaring contradictory testimony and outrageous courtroom behavior. Those court officers, including my own attorney, together "played dumb" during my trial, pretending not to see or hear my accuser's mendacity and outright whoppers.

Such a statement by me might raise the question, "Why would they do that?" I can not be certain what was in their minds, but the probable reason is either their fear of DeCourcy's poison pen criticism of them, as will be seen in the legal documents I'll include with this narrative, or prejudice against me because of my "unpopular" political beliefs, or both. Readers will see how DeCourcy "believes she is a lawyer" and how "she appeals every adverse decision" (words of two of her former landlords that I interviewed). I will show how my accuser badmouthed in writing everyone who dared to displease her. Her name is directly associated with at least a dozen court cases in just four years — all of which were mentioned in my appeal to the WVSCA and should have raised reasonable doubt of my accuser's veracity.

To detail all this in a book, along with a cohesive narrative, would take more than 1,000 pages and would be a ponderous read, so I will hit the highlights, provide an appendix of the more important court documents, as well as a Web page where complete documentation can be cited and viewed for the diligent reader. If I am describing the document that is presented in the Appendices section of this book, I will give its page number, like p. 125; if I am referring to the document on the Web site, it will be cited as exhibit number, for example, E1a.

Usually, trial transcripts make for boring reading for the layman, but not in my case. DeCourcy's trial testimony, especially her description of the alleged incident, might make the reader feel he is trying to watch a three-ring circus. Reading her hundreds of pages of written documents will give the same feeling.

The three previously mentioned Pocahontas County (PC) court officers turned their blind eyes and deaf ears to my accuser's contradictory testimony, as did the second West Virginia Assistant Attorney General (AAG) who was charged with responding to my appeal (after the first AAG who had actually been quite helpful to the *pro se* appellant and had demonstrated impartiality and professionalism, was inexplicably removed as the state's respondent to my brief just six days before his respondent brief was due). Both of these state's attorneys will be named later.

It's safe to say that the five WVSCA justices never read the carefully prepared, fact-based appeal that was presented to them by me. It is even doubtful that their clerks attentively read it. The West Virginia Attorney General's office defended the state from the appellant in *West Virginia vs. William W. Williams*, rather than diligently seeking the truth — simply repeating the impeached claims of my accuser in the state's defense. I am of the opinion that this may well be an unwritten policy of the Attorney General's office and/or the WVSCA, since to reverse lower court decisions in criminal cases could expose those courts to civil actions by the wrongfully convicted.

Though it took the three levels of the West Virginia judiciary five years from start to finish to indelibly label me a woman-beater, they made it look easy by denying my entitled presumption of innocence and due process, including a proper investigation into the original claim of battery. *During this entire period I was never once interviewed by either law enforcement or an investigator for the prosecutors' offices* — not once, despite requesting to be interviewed several times during the course of litigation.

As most court watchers know, guilt in criminal cases must be proven by the state beyond a reasonable doubt. I was not accorded the slightest benefit of that requirement. My case amounted to guilt by accusation. It was a *show trial* where my guilt was predetermined. A show trial is defined as:

> A trial conducted primarily to make a particular impression on the public, especially one that demonstrates the power of the state over the individual. Show trials are publicized as open and fair trials of a person regarded as a political subversive or ideological dissident in which a verdict of guilty is assured by means of false evidence, a false confession, etc. Especially in a totalitarian state — often associated with Stalinist courts in the Soviet Union era — the public trial of a political offender is conducted chiefly for propagandistic purposes, as to suppress further dissent against the government by making an example of the accused and gaining control of his life.

In American show trials of political opponents — which it can be argued I am, as an advocate for the interests of long-suffering White people — the verdict is rigged, as they are in so many non-political criminal trials, by the "false confession" (read: plea bargain). That is when the defendant is offered a lesser sentence than may be usual *if* he will make a guilty plea for a lesser offense. I was offered at least three different plea deals. They were all declined by me *because the alleged battery never happened* and I was not about to plead guilty to anything I did not do. For that I was punished.

Prosecutors often offer defendants plea bargains, a reduction in charges, to clear their courts' dockets. As many as 95 percent of cases are handled this way because if every defendant insisted on pleading not guilty, requiring a trial, the courts could not handle the case load. In the past I have agreed to a reduction in charges in traffic courts in order to avoid a trial and to keep my driver's license; I have also pleaded *not* guilty in traffic courts, if just to put the accusing officer on the stand to examine him and show him to be a stumble-bum. The courtroom *can be* a theater for arguing points and showing what really happened.

All three Pocahontas Circuit Court officers as well as the officers who responded to my appeal conveniently ignored my witnesses' testimonies at trial and the written, sworn affidavit of my primary witness, Fred Streed. He could not make it to the trial due to a serious health emergency while waiting to board his flight the day before at 5:30am at his Oregon airport, after I'd purchased an $800 round trip ticket for him. However, I did submit Fred's sworn affidavit with my appeal brief as well as with my post-trial motion for a new trial in the Circuit Court earlier.

After my appeal had matured, my accuser's hand-written note was found by accident in the NA's office building in West Virginia. Readers of this account will be the first to see it (appendix p. 2). It looks like the agenda for a gathering, soon after the alleged incident of 30 September 2015, where DeCourcy was to coach her "witnesses." Why would she need to make such notes, except to get her "story" of the alleged battery straight and rehearse it with her co-conspirators? By their subsequent lying testimonies the alleged incident would appear to have been a brutal beat-down, what she described numerous times as an "attempted homicide," impossible for anyone to forget.

Especially suspicious in this newly discovered document, in my accuser's hand, is the clarification directed to her landlord/roommate and co-conspirator "witness" Bob DeMarais: "Bruises take time to appear." If he was going to honestly describe what he supposedly saw right after the alleged incident why would he need coaching? It was because there never were even the slightest bruises, even in the undated, un-timestamped selfies DeCourcy took of her neck, after likely pinching herself, and that the prosecutors used as the *only evidence of a battery.*

I considered trying to make an amended motion to use the newly discovered evidence for my appeal, but abandoned the idea as superfluous. In my two briefs, especially in the reply brief, were submitted such an abundance of indisputable proofs of my accuser's obvious and repetitive lies under oath, the lower court officers' numerous violations of their professional rules and my Constitutional defendant's rights, that anything more I deemed by then to be unnecessary. If the WVSCA justices are impartial, I thought, there is plenty for them to see the obvious; if they are prejudiced and their ruling is preordained, any additional evidence will not change their minds.

Not only WVSCA, but the West Virginia Judicial Investigation Commission (JIC) and West Virginia Office of the Disciplinary Counsel (ODC) seemed to demonstrate an obvious unprofessional bias against me, or at least support for their colleagues in law, or both. In my Appeal to the WVSCA and in my four complaints against the three members of the "Pocahontas Court Club," as I refer to them now, I provided more than enough proof of serious violations of their ethical rules by all three Pocahontas court officers, including my sellout defense attorney Laura Finch. Three of the four complaints were quickly dismissed without any investigation. My complaint against Finch is still under investigation as I write this account, but I don't expect satisfaction or even an investigation after seeing how the courts look out for their own in West Virginia. The time-honored rule of law — the principle that all people and institutions, including defense attorneys, prosecuting attorneys, and judges, are subject to and accountable to law that is fairly applied and enforced; the principle of government by law — is not honored in the West Virginia judiciary, not in my experienced opinion.

An interesting Pocahontas County side note: Ms. Finch defeated longtime Pocahontas County Prosecutor Eugene Simmons for his position in the June 2020 Democrat primary. DeCourcy had Simmons disqualified from prosecuting my appeal in Pocahontas Circuit Court (CC) because she had no confidence that Simmons would prosecute me on appeal. In the first of DeCourcy's three illegal, personal *ex parte* communications to Judge Dent in my CC appeal — over 100 pages of gibberish, since sealed by Judge Dent, though exculpatory of me — she smeared Simmons as "corrupt, lazy and senile," without objection by Finch. Finch had intentionally kept me uninformed for two years about the court's sealing of those exculpatory communications, behind my back. I had been insisting to my counsel Finch to thoroughly cross-examine my accuser on the numerous insane accusations against me in those illegal *ex parte* letters to Judge Dent, "which she failed to do" by her own admission in one of her post-trial motions. I was disadvantaged, being an out-of-state defendant.

The West Virginia ODC's first response to my 12-page complaint gave me a measure of hope. It advised Finch to review several professional standards I had cited that she violated, including the Rule of Misconduct / Dishonesty and Fraud. Finch's response to my complaint was as short, weak, and sloppy as it could be. She even accidentally helped me to prove that she filed the fraudulent motion on my case. To my brief's 18 pages of additional comments Finch didn't bother to respond at all despite my numerous demands to cite proofs in the provided transcripts for each of her accusations against me. Her non-response to my citations should have meant my claims were accepted as true. My cited proof of her filing the fraudulent motion also got no response. Finch acted as if she knew in advance that the ODC would be lenient with her and cover for her.

Another thing that makes me pessimistic is that in all my complaints, wherein I documented collusion of the three Pocahontas court officers together against me, so far not a single sanction or charge has been brought against any of them by either West Virginia's JIC or ODC. If they had been, the charges would become public record. Certainly, the injustice I experienced and described in my complaints is not a desirable thing for the public to know about its court officers. So, it is my contention that those court officers have been shielded from public scrutiny and the citizens of West Virginia have not been protected by their ODC and JIC, the governing agencies that are supposed to monitor court officers' professionalism. It is a rigged system.

If and when the final outcome of my complaint against Finch becomes available, I will update readers of that result at the Web site created for this case: pocahontasshowtrial.com. My desire is for interested readers to have access to each and every document of my appeal's appendix — too voluminous for this book — including three circuit court transcripts. Interested readers will have the opportunity to decide for themselves whether or not I have been wrongly convicted of misdemeanor battery.

On that site will also be placed copies of my complaints against the three PC court officers. Readers should have enough evidence to decide for themselves if the handling of my complaints was impartial and professional.

In talking about my complaint against Laura Finch I must give her credit for helping me with the name of my book. She called me an "unpopular figure" in her response to my complaint. In this book readers will get an explanation of what could have made me an "unpopular figure" in the mind of my defense counsel. After all, it is unpopular figures, unpopular ideas, and unpopular speech that require the most vigorous defenses. Popular ideas need no defense.

I tell my story not for revenge against those who I feel did me wrong, nor to promote the National Alliance, but to set the record straight as I see it, and to clear my name of the stain of being called a convicted woman beater. I don't mean to bring harm to any of the court officers in any way. The court officers' job is supposed to be to serve justice and to follow their ethics rules. I informed all of them in my official findings that I will clear my good name that they have sullied by all means at my disposal — this book being one. That promise had no effect. Maybe they believed I was bluffing; or maybe they feel secure in their power since West Virginia judicial standards of professionalism and ethics are so low. I don't know. All they had to do to avoid their names being mentioned negatively regarding my wrongful conviction was to be fair-minded and professional during the judicial process. I will balance my criticism of the above-mentioned by complimenting those court officers who were truly professional and acted honorably during my five-year ordeal with the West Virginia judicial system.

One of the goals of this book is to notify my readers that even if a person has been upstanding and law-abiding his entire life as I have been, he is not protected against a deeply corrupted American jurisprudence system. My personal experience during the past six years has certainly shaken my faith in "our" system, especially as an outspoken heterosexual male dissident who criticizes the anti-White status quo, including government courts — a constitutionally protected right.

At least in Pocahontas County, West Virginia, any *suspected* defendant, against whom a TRO (temporary restraining order) request has been filed, can be thrown into a regional prison 80 miles away in the middle of nowhere, with no investigation whatsoever, and no hearing held to establish his possible guilt. Later, after being bonded out of jail, the suspected defendant would not be provided transportation back to where he was falsely arrested, regardless of the season and weather, lacking proper clothing, and having had all of his cash confiscated. If he is an out-of-state resident without anyone to pick him up from the jail he would have to hitchhike the 80 miles back to the remote location where he was arrested, like I had to do. This is one aspect of my first arrest in Pocahontas County that I will describe in this book.

I believe that such "anti-male" law often encourages legal abuse of men by women, just like my experienced TRO-filing accuser did. This has become commonplace in the #MeToo era when a false accusation becomes a wrongful conviction. I was sentenced by Magistrate Carrie Wilfong, now deceased, to an unprecedented *six months in jail* for my "first offense" just because, in her words, she had been abused herself and that there would be no battering of females in her county.

My accuser has a documented history of using "protective order" tactics not only against me, but against others before me — what the law calls a "pattern of abuse." Several innocent people had been her victims in Virginia and there likely will be more wherever she lands. Perhaps this book can serve to warn any of her future victims. My accuser has used at least ten known aliases. She can change her name but not her face. A photograph of that face can be seen on p. 1 of the Appendix.

Another important goal of my book is to help the people of West Virginia to learn the truth. I know several nice people in Pocahontas County who are familiar with my crazy accuser. When I was informing them about my guilty verdicts at the hands of both the Magistrate and Circuit Courts their reactions were very similar: "What else did you expect? This is the Pocahontas County." At the same time, though, some county residents might not have any idea of the shenanigans and dishonesty that are possible in their courts. This personal account of my own mistreatment may help to put them on guard should they have to deal with these same unethical court officers.

It will be shown in *Show Trial* that the WVSCA justices nearly always affirm lower courts' rulings, and unanimously. As I wrote above, I doubt that even the justices' clerks had a close look at my two extensive briefs and the close to 400 pages in my brief's appendix. I hope this story of filing my appeal *pro se* will encourage others to do more research about WVSCA outcomes before pursuing that discouraging avenue of relief. The legal system is broken, especially for anyone who is considered an "unpopular figure" by that system. I could cite numerous recent examples of other injustices toward pro-White defendants in America's courts, but that is beyond the scope of this book.

In brief, the WVSCA's handling of my appeal was a sham as were my trials in the lower courts. This will be evident to those who review the documents provided. Many defendants who appear before judges are guilty of the crimes for which they have been charged. But some are not and the appeals process should recognize a wrongful conviction.

I have never written a book and it's not likely that I'll write another after this one, but I feel that it's important to tell my side of the story since becoming National Alliance Chairman, telling the truth as I see it, including difficulties with the justice system during this period.

One of the main reasons I joined the National Alliance in 1992 was because it is an organization known for telling the unvarnished truth when so many today are telling lies. The Founder of the Alliance, Dr. William Pierce, gave up a successful career in the mid-1960s as a physicist, a bona fide rocket scientist, to pursue a career in serious truth-telling. He told difficult truths that were taboo, difficult truths that others have avoided because those truths are Politically Incorrect and made people uncomfortable. I'd like to think that one reason I was appointed NA Chairman is because I always try to follow his tradition of telling the same uncompromising truths that he told, truths that will attract the same sort of truth-tellers and truth-lovers that he attracted to our Alliance. I hate lies and liars and the experience I've had with the 11th Judicial District was having to deal with lies and liars, and, unfortunately, the liars prevailed.

My Russian wife of 17 years, Svetlana (Lana), who knows me best, has described me as a "pathologically honest truth teller." I don't know about that, but she knows I am not prone to lie about things, large or small. We've been through these legal travails together, and as challenging as they have been we have managed to keep our good humor, knowing we were truthful and right about everything we said. The accusations leveled at me, especially by my accuser, have been so outrageous at times that we and our Alliance friends have often been amused. I hope my reader will enjoy several of those humorous moments in this book.

Most of what I am writing about here is on the public record, either available in court documents or in public view on the Internet. Ordinary citizens, even attorneys, students of law, or judges might find my case and the documents in this book and on its associated Web site instructive. I hope all readers will find at least something that is useful in this accounting.

WILL WILLIAMS

What Makes Me an "Unpopular Figure"?

Imagine my surprise when my so-called defense lawyer, Laura Finch, wrote the following in her official response to the complaint I filed against her:

> Mr. Williams is an unpopular figure, and had I more experience at the time I would have certainly declined this representation.

What an odd admission for Finch to make in her written response as defense lawyer — one who has been making a career of defending clients, all of whom were charged with crimes and most of whom have been guilty of their charges. I was one client who retained her to defend against a conspiracy of lies of which I was not guilty.

What did she learn about me that had her change her opinion of me? Was I a murderer? Did I hire others to murder for me? Was I a rapist? A kidnapper, an arsonist, an embezzler? A gang leader? No, none of the above. In fact I have no criminal record. But these *are* accusations my accuser made about me in written documents submitted to the court, all easily disproved. Why did not Finch expose my accuser as a hopeless liar who, since she made these other wild and provably false accusations about me, would surely also be willing to make a false claim that I "battered" her when she wanted me imprisoned and removed as Chairman of the National Alliance? I will try to answer that question here.

What, then, did I do to be categorized by Finch as an "unpopular figure"? Did I have syphilis? Leprosy? Some other terrible communicable disease that would have her fearing to sit next to me at the defense table? No. She doesn't say why I'm unpopular or with whom, she only stated to the ODC that I'm "unpopular."

Ms. Finch is a liberal Democrat who proudly sported a Hillary Clinton for President bumper sticker on her car in 2016 and beyond. I didn't care about that. Oddly enough, Pocahontas County, according to census figures, is more than 97 percent White in a state, West Virginia, that is more than 94 percent White — yet both the county and state traditionally vote Democrat rather than Republican, even as the Democrat Party has become anti-White. Ms. Finch knew from our first meeting that I am the National Alliance Chairman and that the Alliance advocates White separatism, an extremely unpopular position with liberal Democrats and conservative Republicans alike, and, I contend, with the West Virginia judiciary. It's my contention that this is why Finch would tell the Office of Disciplinary Counsel that her client is an "unpopular figure." And this is one reason I also contend that the prosecution of me was not about any alleged battery, but was political. More about that in following chapters.

The judiciary these days, heavily weighted with liberal-minded females, takes a dim view of anyone and any organization that holds a masculine world view, especially a pro-White racial nationalist one. That is another factor that makes this defendant an unpopular figure. The liberal feminist Finch actually told me:

> Do not let the judge know that you served two tours of heavy combat in Vietnam as a young Green Beret captain because that would indicate violence.

In my experiences with male attorneys, having been a veteran of a foreign war with combat experience, leading men as an infantry officer, has always been seen by them as a positive, not a negative — and the same with male judges. It is too bad I had to put myself, my liberty, my very name, in the hands of such a defense lawyer and pay her thousands of dollars to help the court convict and imprison me on a transparently false claim. But I was an out-of-state defendant, needing a local attorney to represent me, and got locked in with her, one of just three or four attorneys in the entire county who represented criminal defendants.

Why Am I "Unpopular" in Pocahontas County?

The answer to this question goes back decades to when William Pierce decided to move the National Alliance offices from northern Virginia to a secluded location in Pocahontas County in 1985.

> The National Alliance (NA) was for decades the most dangerous and best organized neo-Nazi formation in America. Explicitly genocidal in its ideology, NA materials call for the eradication of the Jews and other races and the creation of an all-white homeland....For nearly thirty years, the National Alliance, headquartered at a rural hilltop compound outside the village of Mill Point, W. Va., was the most dominant and dangerous hate group in America. Founded and long led by William Pierce, a one-time university physics professor, the neo-Nazi group peaked in the late 1990s, when it developed a remarkably successful business model and Pierce's ideological influence stretched across much of the Western hemisphere...the group produced assassins, bombers and bank robbers, among other things....

What are people to think when they read a description of the Alliance like that by the Southern Poverty Law Center (SPLC)? "Dangerous hate group?" "Neo-Nazi?" "[T]he group produced assassins, bombers and bank robbers, among other things." The SPLC is the actual "hate group," yet it has a $500,000,000 tax-exempt endowment to fight "hate," or what it decides is hate. Not many people are aware that the publications of this quasi-official, so-called "law center" are the yellowest journalism imaginable. The SPLC does not honestly investigate and they know well how to lie and smear in their articles without risk of being sued for their lies. Their true goal is to create panic regarding the alleged danger of their targeted "hate" groups in order to generate as many donations as possible.

After being convicted in Pocahontas Circuit Court I was interviewed by the court's probation officer, Robert Tooze, prior to his sentencing recommendation. He recommended probation only. Thinking I was just another convicted batterer, unaware that I am the NA Chairman, Tooze asked me where I had lived in Pocahontas County. When I told him Mill Point, just past the quarry on Highway 39, he said, "That's the Nazi compound." I told him, "There's no Nazi compound. That's our National Alliance campus." He said, "Well, 90 percent of Pocahontas County residents think it's the Nazi compound." Could that be why Ms. Finch told the Office of Disciplinary Counsel that "Mr. Williams is an unpopular figure?"

I was born a couple of years after Germany and its National Socialist regime — the so-called "Nazis" — were vanquished in World War II. National Socialists are still arguably the most unpopular figures extant, right up there with serial murderers, 75 years after being defeated by the Allies.

More will be said in the following pages about Mr. Tooze, who always was impartial and professional. He did what the Court ordered him to do.

A few days after being arrested for the first time by Pocahontas County Sheriff's deputies for the alleged battery, and for unwittingly violating my accuser's Temporary Restraining Order (TRO), the newspaper of record for the county, *The Pocahontas Times*, published news of my arrest with the headline "National Alliance chairman arrested at Mill Point" [https://pocahontastimes.com/national-alliance-chairman-arrested-at-mill-point/]. (Appendix, p. 8) The account of my 16 December, 2015 arrest was taken almost wholly from my accuser's false claim to law enforcement, which was then reported in a sensationalistic "Chaos and Cops at the Compound" article by the SPLC, on 18 December: "Neo-Nazi National Alliance Chairman William White Williams arrested in alleged battery of female employee" [https://www.splcenter.org/hatewatch/2015/12/18/chaos-and-cops-compound].

I was never asked by the SPLC for comment before publishing this article, nor by the *Pocahontas Times* journalist for her article. My accuser was the one who immediately informed the SPLC about my arrest. She planned my arrest with law enforcement and assisted the SPLC in publicizing it and another subsequent arrest just five days later. After that second arrest I got even more negative publicity. This time, on 22 December, 2015, the terminally anti-White *Charleston* (WV) *Gazette* published the long article: "Chairman of hate group arrested twice in Pocahontas County." [https://www.wvgazettemail.com/news/legal_affairs/chairman-of-hate-group-arrested-twice-in-pocahontas-county/article_664c0770-71e5-52e2-a4da-cd-c348c2bf00.html] (E7b) More about this publicity and my accuser's scamming of the judicial process later.

Numerous other media outlets, including some TV channels, followed suit. Professional scammer DeCourcy knew full well how to generate bad publicity for me once the SPLC put the bogus story out on the Associated Press (AP) wire.

As usually happens nowadays in regard to the "unpopular" figures and organizations, neither *The Charleston Gazette* nor *The Pocahontas Times* granted to me the right of reply that I requested. In the past, fair-minded periodicals with journalistic integrity would offer right of reply — the right to correct errors — to those it had represented unfavorably or inaccurately. The *Pocahontas Times* article mentioned just my first arrest though it was published on 23 December, 2015, two days after my second arrest. That issue was probably already at their printer on 22 December and it was too late to update.

My written response to the *Pocahontas Times* (Appendix p. 9), invoking my right of reply for being characterized in that periodical with unsubstantiated claims of violent criminality by my accuser was, as I said, never published, except by me on the Internet [https://www.stormfront.org/forum/t1102767-28/], because I could. My correspondence with *Charleston Gazette* writer Erin Beck can be viewed on that same Stormfront page, as well as the color photograph of my accuser that is presented at p. 1 of this book's Appendix.

Hardly any resident in the Pocahontas County jury pool would have seen my reply on that Stormfront page, so they were likely to believe what they had read in their county's newspaper of record. As a result of this collective bias I opted for a bench trial over a jury trial because I felt any jury of my "peers" would have been tainted by the false report as well as the "Nazi" smear.

My defense attorney, Laura Finch, who resides in Hillsboro, West Virginia, was inadvertently bumped into in Hillsboro by the *Pocahontas Times* reporter who had written that account of my arrest, Jaynell Graham, after the report had appeared. Ms. Graham is also a Hillsboro resident, and was unaware at the time that Finch was representing me in the criminal action. According to what Ms. Finch told me back then, Ms. Graham told her, "That Will Williams is dangerous!" Could Graham have been biased against me in her report? Of course she was. Was Finch aware of the bias of the *The Pocahontas Times* against her client? Of course she was.

A document that was stolen from the NA's West Virginia office building by a disgruntled employee (who will be introduced later) that I had fired on 3 May 2015 will show the bias against the Alliance in Pocahontas County going back to at least 1987.

Another SPLC "Chaos at the Compound" article that was published at their site [https://www.splcenter.org/hatewatch/2015/05/20/chaos-compound] and that went out for wider distribution on the Associated Press (AP) wire on 21 May, 2015, was titled "Allegations of Embezzlement, Money Laundering and Tax Fraud Haunt the New Chairman of the National Alliance." This one article is so full of distortions, half-truths, and outright lies that it would take a book to refute them all — something I won't be doing here, but will revisit later.

One of the silliest, most fantastic things the SPLC quasi-official "intelligence gatherers" have ever published has to be the organizational chart they drew for the Alliance. (E7a) That article's author, and longtime enemy of the NA, the lesbian LGBT champion Heidi Beirich, a 20-year veteran "hate-watcher" at the SPLC (who has since moved on to head some other hate group), admits in this particular smear article that the disgruntled employee I had hired to live on the West Virginia property when I first became Chairman, scanned and stole thousands of NA documents and then turned them over to the SPLC to use against us and anyone even peripherally associated with us. The SPLC has been doing just that with the stolen items since compensating the thief for the "thousands of documents on six thumb drives" he sold them.

One stolen document from February, 1987, a letter from William Pierce to his attorney, which is protected by lawyer/client privilege, except apparently to the criminals at the so-called "law center," was Cc'd to Mr. Glen Allen, a Pierce friend at the time. A facsimile of that letter was displayed in full in the SPLC article at https://www.splcenter.org/hatewatch/2016/08/17/neo-nazi-lawyer-represents-baltimore-suit-over-wrongful-arrest-and-19-year-imprisonment. A couple of days after that SPLC article appeared, Mr. Allen was fired from his job with the city of Baltimore as a direct result of the SPLC's article, linking him to the National Alliance *30 years earlier* when he was a still a young law student. This confidential letter between an attorney and his client, copied to a law student friend, can be seen at p. 4 of the Appendix.

In that letter Dr. Pierce was relating to his attorney how he and the Alliance were being mistreated by the rogue Pocahontas County sheriff, Jerry Dale, whose campaign for that office was based in great part on his promise to county voters that he would "rid Pocahontas County of the Nazis." Some of Dale's lies about the NA that he leaked to the media, and some of his other dirty tricks, are detailed in this stolen letter. Pierce wrote of how nearly everyone else in the county, including newly-elected County Prosecutor Eugene Simmons, treated him cordially. Simmons, in fact, had helped Pierce close on the purchase of the NA's property prior to being elected the

Pocahontas County Prosecutor.

For the record, the National Alliance has always had a policy forbidding any violence or illegal activities. Neither the NA nor any active Alliance member has ever been charged with any "crime" beyond littering for placing the organizations' constitutionally-protected stickers where some overly protective, grandmotherly-type municipal or law enforcement official like Pocahontas County Sheriff Jerry Dale did not want them placed. The Alliance has no association with violent neo-Nazi, Ku Klux Klan, militia, or skinhead groups, despite being lumped with them continuously by controlled media and Jewish watchdog groups.

More will be included in the coming pages about why the Alliance and I would be considered "unpopular," and undeserving of a vigorous defense. We need to remember that it is unpopular people, their opinions, and their organizations that are what the freedom of speech clause in the First Amendment of the U.S. Constitution are all about. Again, popular people and their popular opinions do not need protecting. Unpopular opinions and unpopular people do. Fact!

The SPLC Vows to "Destroy" the National Alliance

The most powerful, well-financed, and long-term hater of the National Alliance is arguably the Southern Poverty Law Center (SPLC). They have openly stated for decades that their goal is to *destroy* the Alliance.

They use the meanest possible strategies to accomplish this goal. For many decades now, the "law center" would use compliant courts to selectively destroy any pro-White groups, usually with their specious "vicarious liability" lawsuits where, in plain language, the leader of a group would be held civilly liable for negligent actions of any member of that group though the leader had no connection whatsoever with the negligent action. I say selectively because this strategy was used *only* against pro-White groups. The leader of the Democrat party, for instance, would never be prosecuted for the actions of a card-carrying Democrat who committed a crime, large or small. Yet in 1986 the leaders of the perfectly legal White Patriot Party (WPP), based in North Carolina, was sued by the SPLC because one WPP member, in violation of a consent decree with SPLC, had threatened a Black prison guard telephonically and the group had practiced small squad paramilitary tactics. The WPP was banned by a federal court as the result of the adverse ruling.

Morris Dees, co-founder of the SPLC, boasted in the 1980s that the way to destroy "racist" (read: pro-White) groups was to use barratry: to tie them up in court and bankrupt them. This legal strategy worked for Dees and his SPLC for years. Three groups I've been involved with, the WPP (in 1985-86) the Church of the Creator (COTC) (1988, 1989) and the NA (1992-2002) were all sued by Dees and destroyed, or nearly destroyed, by those specious lawsuits. In more recent times that hate group has tended to use the Internet and Jew-controlled mass media to smear and destroy the pro-White groups they target. There are many people and groups now that have exposed the SPLC for what it is. The best-known may be FOX News TV host Tucker Carlson. A Web site called Watching the Watchdogs does a most excellent job of exposing the disreputable hate group, here: https://rkeefe57.wordpress.com/2011/02/06/splc-2011-forty-years-of-white-supremacy/. Yet lazy, crooked, controlled media still to this day use the SPLC as their go-to source whenever they need background for any story involving race.

With its extensive database and connections with courts and law enforcement, this semi-official "intelligence-gathering" agency will attempt to destroy the careers and families of anyone they can connect to the Alliance or to other effective pro-White groups. (There even used to be a link to the SPLC on the FBI's Web site, but that was removed because the SPLC's "intelligence" was so embarrassingly unreliable.)

There have been several real life examples of where the sleazy anti-White queers, Jews and other non-Whites at the SPLC, using their tax-exempt status, the courts, and especially media, have attempted to destroy or "dox"[1] patriots I know. I'll say that most of those attempts fail, especially when their targets are strong-willed, confident, and relatively secure in their positions.

The tables have been turned of late on this hate group with *all* of its founders and senior executives having been fired or "retired" under a cloud for sexual and racial improprieties that had recently come to light within the organization.

This book is not going to be about the SPLC, except tangentially for their major role in why I might have a reputation for being "unpopular" with the courts. However, for the purpose of showing SPLC's more or less bilateral relationship with our Alliance, I'll quote a large section of text from the Alliance's weekly *American Dissident Voices* broadcast of March 30, 2019, written by the NA's Media Director Kevin Alfred Strom. This piece excerpts my own commentary as NA Chairman from a monthly issue of our monthly printed BULLETIN, as well as commentary by David Sims and Franklin Ryckaert, and an entry from Metapedia (a much more reliable

---

1 dox (slang); verb — to search for and publish private or identifying information about a particular individual on the Internet, typically with malicious intent

source than Jew-controlled Wikipedia). The complete text of this article can bee seen here, with images: https://nationalvanguard.org/2019/03/chaos-at-the-compound/.

The SPLC compound that sits on Washington Avenue in Montgomery, Alabama, is one of the ugliest buildings I've ever seen. It's a cultural Bolshevist "postmodern" horror of disharmonious angles that looks like a cross between a junked 386 computer and a prison. It's a perfect place from which to make America itself an ideological prison, which is pretty much the mission of the Jewish group that styles itself the SPLC or "Southern Poverty Law Center."

Their specialty is defining any individual and any group that opposes the Jewish-led destruction of America through mass immigration and moral and cultural breakdown as a "hater" or a "hate group," and — along with their network of Jewish and leftist ideologues in the media — relentlessly using pressure tactics, such as threats to ruin businesses, or "expose" employers, housing providers, government workers, banks and other financial service providers, friends, and even family members, in order to destroy the reputations of said "haters" and all their associates who do not immediately and abjectly disavow them, and deny them employment, funding, the ability to do business, and even a place to live. The SPLC is a life-destroying, character-assassinating smearbund on a scale not seen since the Stasi and the NKVD. Financed in part through what many of their former supporters call outright mail fraud and by the ill-gotten lucre of wealthy leftist Jews, they have amassed a half billion dollars that we know about, much of it stashed in overseas havens catering to financial criminals.

And now they're imploding. Not the building. Not the compound. But the snakes inside. The snakes are attacking the other snakes in the pit, some snakes have run for cover, and no one knows who or what will come out on top. Whatever it is, it will probably still be poisonous.

National Alliance Chairman William White Williams recently wrote in the National Alliance BULLETIN about this outlaw organization, and part of this program is based on his report.

Despite all its wealth, the criminal SPLC is falling on hard times. Several damaged organizations and individuals, mostly White, who the SPLC had aimed to destroy by falsely labeling them "extremists," "haters," "domestic terrorists," "neo-Nazis," or the like, have sued the Jewish group.

The most prominent — and most promising — of these recent lawsuits, is *Glen Allen v. Mark Potok, Heidi Beirich and SPLC*. The National Alliance, the sponsor of this program, is involved in that case because the SPLC received documents which had been stolen from us and which were subsequently used to harm Mr. Allen.

On to the chaos; on to the implosion.

The Jew Mark Potok, the longstanding chief spokesman for the group, left the SPLC under mysterious circumstances last year, but was located by Mr. Allen and as a co-defendant in that action had to respond to Allen's iron-clad claim. No one on the outside knows why Potok left. It's all been kept hush-hush. But we do know that when photographs were taken of Potok's office shortly before his departure — high-resolution photos that show a lot of background detail — Potok had forgotten to take down his handwritten notes, taped prominently to the wall near his desk, documenting the decline in the White percentage of the US population from 1960 and dwindling to the much smaller fraction today. He also had a chart showing the ever-increasing non-White population of numerous European countries. This tells us volumes about the real, biological, genocidal ideas and motivations of Potok and the SPLC.

Some time after Potok's departure, in just one full week, the chaos really took hold. Beginning in late March, the SPLC's co-founder and top barrator Morris Seligman Dees, 82, was fired by the center's president, Richard Cohen, for reasons yet undisclosed, and then Cohen — who had been with the group since 1986 — stepped down himself under the growing cloud of controversy. The very next day, the Jewess "Rowdy" Rhonda Brownstein, the SPLC's legal director and a member of its senior leadership staff, also resigned, with other staffers following. Accusations have been flying that SPLC leaders have engaged in racial discrimination and sexual harassment.

Chinese-American and former First Woman Michelle Obama's Chief of Staff Tina Tchen has been brought in to clean up the Jewish snakepit at the SPLC. Ms. Tchen specializes in examining "workplace cultural compliance," especially "gender and racial equity, and sexual harassment." She just finished helping to get all the charges against the part-Jewish mulatto homosexual hate crime hoaxer Jussie Smollett dropped in Chicago. Her job will be to smooth over the racial and sexual reasons why so many SPLC staffers have been fired or quit, and present them in a way that keeps the donations flowing. It couldn't happen to a better group of Jews and perverts.

It's also a distinct possibility that there is something else going on — something beyond perverted Jews doing sexual things to young staffers just once or a hundred times too often — something beyond a rising generation of Blacks and Browns wanting their piece of the half-billion funding pie, and getting sick of multimillionaire Jews — some of them who only come in to work when they feel like it — hogging all the high-status jobs, five-figure speaking fees and high six-figure salaries. Something deeper, something much worse, something that hasn't been revealed yet. After all, the references to inappropriate sex and "racism" are what they're willing to admit to. What is it that they're not willing to admit to?

Metapedia tells us: "SPLC fundraising practices and large salaries to its leaders have been criticized. [The Combined Federal Campaign, a charity group, uncovered the fact that the SPLC] failed an audit by the Arlington-based Better Business Bureau's Wise Giving Alliance. The audit stipulated that at least 50 percent of an organization's total income should be set aside to fund its programs. Instead, 89 percent of the Center's budget went toward fundraising and administrative costs. Adding up the numbers, the Journal observed that anyone wishing to make a $100 donation to the SPLC would find that only $11 went to the Center's expressed mission of advancing civil rights. 'Not much bang for the buck there,' the paper stated.

"The Capital Research Center have revealed some of the funders [of the SPLC] — by far the biggest donor was the Picower Foundation, founded by the Jewish Jeffry Picower, the largest beneficiary of the Bernie Madoff financial swindle, to the tune of $3,813,112. Other high profile backers include Cisco Systems at $1,620,000 between the years 2000-2004, the Grove Foundation (associated with the Jewish Andrew Grove, a co-founder of the Intel Corporation) at $875,000 from 2001-2011, the Richard and Rhoda Goldman Fund (Jewish heirs of the Levi Strauss fortune) at $535,000, and Rockefeller Philanthropy at $510,000 between 2008-2010, amongst many others."

The SPLC has, like the Anti-Defamation League, been accused of being a private intelligence gathering agency. It may do activities as a private organization that public law enforcement agencies are barred by law from doing (such as keeping dossiers on people solely because of their political or religious views).

The SPLC has also been accused of using infiltrators, provocateurs, and outright fabrication of hate speech in order to discredit disliked groups and individuals.

Government agencies rely on the SPLC. In 2012, the SPLC stated "Law enforcement agencies come to us every day with questions about particular groups". This may be due to the above mentioned limitations for law enforcement agencies and may be seen as problematic by circumventing the law as well as being problematic by relying on a biased source for information.

In 2010, the Department of Homeland Security (DHS) organized a "Countering Violent Extremism Working Group." The member list also included Richard Cohen, President of the Southern Poverty Law Center. In addition, as one of the "Subject Matter Experts," it listed Laurie Wood, an analyst for the Southern Poverty Law Center and an instructor for the Federal Law Enforcement Training Center. The training center is run by the Southern Poverty Law Center. Law enforcement agencies send their personnel to these training classes to gain Federal Law Enforcement Training Center certification.

The SPLC also offers training for local, state and federal law enforcement officers by request, focusing "on the history, background, leaders and activities of far-right extremists in the United States."

The SPLC routinely tells us scaremongering stories about how "dangerous" White advocates are. Here writer David Sims talks about his actual experiences as a National Alliance insider working directly with Dr. Pierce (experiences I can confirm myself since I did the same thing): "I didn't see anyone committing crimes. If any of his employees had even suggested committing one, Dr. Pierce would have kicked him out immediately… What the National Alliance was doing was trying to build a media empire in parallel with the one the Jews already have. We were publishing newspapers, magazines, and books. … No bombs. No burning down Black churches. No beating up on minorities. We were even told to be nice to them… [They] continue to publish misleading presentations in both the mainstream media (news and fiction books and movies) about what a big threat racially conscious White people are, even as they promote racially conscious non-White groups every chance they get. You'd think that their very hypocrisy would offend every White person in America and propel them all into our arms. But, for reasons unknown to me, this does not happen.… The SPLC puts out a polished pretense of being an authority, and a bit of what they say is actually true. On the other hand, much of it isn't, and they're always quick to fill in the gaps in whatever way will invite the most opprobrium to us, or will instill in the public a wariness about the very groups that would save them, if only they could.… White people have been denied the equal protection of the laws just for buying a book from a White nationalist organization and then being "reported" for doing it by an infiltrator who stole the customer database for the book store owned by the organization"

What Mr. Sims says about someone buying a book and then being "reported" is precisely what the criminals at the SPLC did to Mr. Glen Allen. We should all be supporting the case of *Allen v. SPLC* — the cause is just, the attorney (Mr. Allen himself) is one of the most competent in the country — and the timing, coinciding with all the chaos at the compound, is platinum-plated perfect.

It's rather ironic that the most ethnocentric, "racist" people on Earth — the Jews — would create and fund the richest and most aggressive of all the "anti-racist" organizations since the fall of the Soviet Union. But how Jewish is the SPLC? Franklin Ryckaert writes: "Of the twenty-two (22) SPLC senior program staff members, fifteen (15) are Jews. This is a numerical representation of 68%. Of the thirteen (13) SPLC directors, eight (8) are Jews or have Jewish spouses. This is a numerical representation of 62%. Jews are approximately 2% of the U.S. population. Therefore Jews are over-represented among the SPLC senior program staff members by a factor of 34 times (3,400 percent), and over-represented on the SPLC board of directors by a factor of 31 times (3,100 percent)."

And are these nice Jewish people at the SPLC and their fine employees just "criticizing" those with whom they disagree? After all, no one should be immune from criticism, right? Listen to the words of SPLC spokesman Mark Potok himself: "Sometimes the press will describe us as 'monitoring' hate crimes and so on…. I want to say plainly that our aim in life is to destroy these groups, to completely destroy them." The SPLC's Heidi Beirich (so far, one of the survivors of the chaos at the compound) has said much the same thing. [Note: Miss Heidi "retired" from SPLC earlier in 2020, after 20 years there as a top "hate" expert, in order to start a new hate group. — W.W.W.]

A great deal of what the SPLC does is already against the law. Let's hope that Glen Allen's lawsuit does much to make them pay for at least some of their crimes. Support that suit to the maximum of your ability.

But, you know, everything the SPLC does ought to be against the law. Do you think it's legal in China to demonize the Chinese? To work to bring in hordes of non-Chinese to replace them? To criminalize any resistance to that replacement? To destroy the lives of any who complain? To keep a chart of your success in making China non-Chinese on your office wall? To collect half a billion dollars to promote such genocide and stash half of it foreign accounts where no one can keep track of it? Hell no, that isn't legal there.

And it shouldn't be legal to do the same thing to White Americans here in the country we founded a quarter millennium ago. Free speech, yes, for all among our own people who want to express themselves and seek truth and make our society better for the coming generations. Yes indeed. But we can't have such free speech unless we have our own society, free of alien manipulators, corrupters, and traitors whose very purpose is to take our freedom of speech away from us as a prelude for eliminating us and destroying everything we care about. There should be no "freedom" to genocide us. No freedom of action for those who work against our very existence as a people and against our right to be captains of our own destiny. Any alien group which does that or which works toward that goal should not be here. Not leaving — and not ceasing such activities — would be regarded by a National Alliance government as an act of war. It *is* an act of war. Working in concert with such genocidal aliens, or working toward their goals of diminishing our presence and our power in our own homelands, would be a capital crime under a National Alliance government, and punished accordingly.

Glen Allen vs. SPLC, Mark Potok, and Heidi Beirich

One of the best examples to cite about the Alliance's most aggressive enemy is Glen Allen's lawsuit against his sleazy tormentors at the SPLC. As expected, the SPLC has never informed its followers about this case, which is still working its way through federal courts. The masterful 82-page complaint, *Glen Allen vs. SPLC, Mark Potok, and Heidi Beirich,* can be seen as our E6a. The federal judge assigned to hear the case, Catherine C. Blake, a Bill Clinton "liberal activist" appointee, sat on it for six months before dismissing all nine of plaintiff Allen's carefully drawn claims. At this writing *Allen v. SPLC et. al.* has been appealed, awaiting word from the Fourth Circuit Court of Appeals about oral arguments. For those who aren't inclined to read the entire 82-page Claim, here it is described by plaintiff Allen in a nutshell:

My complaint, filed in the federal District Court for the District of Maryland, alleges nine causes of actions — nine claims — against three defendants. The three defendants are the Southern Poverty Law Center, Inc. ("SPLC"); Heidi Beirich, Director of the SPLC's Intelligence Project; and Mark Potok, former editor in chief of the Intelligence Project's publication *The Intelligence Report.*

I allege three federal claims:

• For a declaratory judgment that the SPLC has contravened the requirements imposed on 501c3 nonprofits to be eligible for this favored tax status

• A Racketeer and Corrupt Organizations Act ("RICO") claim under 18 U.S.C. 1962(c) against Beirich and Potok

• A RICO conspiracy claim under 18 U.S.C. 1962(d) against Beirich and Potok.

I allege six state law claims:

• Negligent training and supervision claim against the SPLC

• Tortious interference with prospective advantage, namely, with my employment with the City of Baltimore, against all defendants

• Tortious interference with contract, namely, with a confidentiality agreement, against all defendants

• Aiding and abetting breach of contract, namely, the confidentiality agreement, against all defendants

• Restitution claim against the SPLC

• Defamation claim against all defendants.

I seek compensatory damages of $1.5 million, for the loss of my employment and damage to my reputation as an attorney. I also seek treble damages as to my RICO claim and punitive damages as to three of my state law claims.

I must say, I had very little direct contact with Mr. Allen as he prepared his case since it is likely that I would be deposed by the "law center" and communications between us might be subject to discovery for the SPLC to make a case that the "Nazi lawyer" Allen and the "Nazi hate group" National Alliance were close when we were not. However, I and the Alliance support his lawsuit and for good reason. A proof that we are not close is Mr. Allen's misstatement in his claim that I hired the above-mentioned disgruntled employee Dilloway to do accounting. "Some bookkeeping," mentioned once, was the only reference to accounting; his job description was more about cleaning, making order, maintenance, and some landscaping, but mainly just having a presence on the Alliance's 400-acre West Virginia campus — monitoring phone messages, picking up mail, etc. More about that later.

More Examples of SPLC Perfidy Against the Alliance

In every SPLC smear article the "law center" makes sure to mention the NA's Media Director Kevin Strom — father of four and a great patriot for nearly 40 years — as some kind of "kiddie porn enthusiast." Kevin had been targeted and wrongly convicted by the corrupted judiciary for his uncompromising and effective racial politics. For those who are interested, his side of his travails with the courts is here: https://www.kevinalfredstrom.com/2018/01/kevin-alfred-strom-fast-facts-you-need-to-know/. Of course, SPLC knows full well the trumped-up circumstances of Kevin's wrongful conviction and incarceration. In 2015 Heidi Beirich contacted the parents of Kevin's then-fiancée (now his wife), her employer, and even her elderly grandmother, now deceased, terrorizing them with lurid statements such as, "Are you aware your daughter/employee/granddaughter is dating a Nazi child molester," or something similarly shocking along that line to try and break up Kevin's relationship with the future Mrs. Strom, now mother of their baby daughter, born in 2020. Beirich sent a long email to the future Mrs. Strom advising her to "run" from Kevin. It didn't work, but that's a good example of the extent of sleazy "doxxing" Beirich and her SPLC associates will go to break up families and destroy the employment and careers of their critics.

Renowned Canadian free speech advocate Paul Fromm explains how free speech and property rights took another hit at the hands of the Supreme Court of Canada in not hearing the appeal in the McCorkill inheritance and free speech case, in which scholar, scientist, writer, and National Alliance member Dr. Robert McCorkill willed his considerable estate to the Alliance to further the ideals and moral principles in which he believed. Jewish groups intervened in the case and were able to get a biased lower court judge and corrupt judicial system to invalidate the will for political reasons. More here, about how the U.S.-based SPLC intervened in that Canadian matter, along with other Jewish groups, to deny the Alliance the considerable bequest of Dr. McCorkill: https://nationalvanguard. org/2015/04/the-mccorkill-legacy-can-bequests-be-overturned-for-ideological-reasons/.

This case is still ongoing at this writing, 16 years after Dr. McCorkill died. The determined SPLC discovered and tracked down Dr. McCorkill's sister Isabelle and used her to challenge her estranged brother's will *nine years after he had died.* At that time she did *not even know he had died.* Isabelle's attorneys have consumed much of the estate by dragging the case on for years. Such is justice in Canada that Jewish groups like the SPLC, working with the Canadian Jewish Congress and corrupted judges, can overturn a man's last wishes because they do not like the beneficiary. In another instance, reported at this Web address, https://nationalvanguard.org/2018/02/the-disturbing-fliers/, National Alliance member Jim Mathias was targeted by the SPLC, in cahoots with the controlled media and churchmen in eastern Iowa, along with law enforcement and the local judiciary in a conspiracy to deny Jim his liberty and the National Alliance the right to distribute our literature. Here's part of an anti-NA hit piece, "National Alliance member arrested while distributing white supremacist fliers," published by the SPLC on 24 January, 2018:

> In early August of last year, Davenport residents were shocked to discover white supremacist fliers on their car windshields and posted in a local neighborhood. The fliers imitated missing persons posters, but what they declared missing was "a future for white children," an echo of the racist neo-Nazi "14 words" catchphrase coined by white nationalist terrorist David Lane.... Mathias's arrest [took place] while distributing racist flyers at a high school stadium parking lot....

That SPLC article is rife with errors (at one point Dr. Pierce is ludicrously referred to as the "figurehead" of the National Alliance, for example), but the most serious — and doubtless intentional — falsehood in their piece is that Mr. Mathias was arrested while distributing our fliers. On the contrary, he was never arrested.

He discovered online on 20 January that local law enforcement had issued a felony warrant for him in October for a bogus "weapon on school property" charge, based on a conversation he'd had with an officer a couple of weeks earlier while fliering in September. Jim had not been informed about this warrant for three months!

Jim retained a bondsman and an attorney, turned himself in, and was released within 20 minutes. It may help Jim's defense that there are no schools near where he was supposedly on "school property," while discreetly placing our inoffensive "They Hate Us" fliers under windshield wipers in a stadium parking lot. See that supposed "hate" flier at Appendix p. 3. It helps Jim even more that he's a man of his race who will not be intimidated by race-denying, tin-horn bureaucrats who draw up and misuse local statutes to keep us from distributing our perfectly legal, truthful material to our people.

SPLC sent an emissary to eastern Iowa to train and work with a group of LGBT freaks, Jews, and other non-Whites, led by an anti-White activist, a rabbi Karp, to oppose Jim Mathias and other NA activists in their pamphleteering. This group of anti-White busybodies, working with the SPLC, local newspapers, TV stations, social media, and online blogs, have been harassing Mr. Mathias for going on five years now, but they can't discourage him from carrying out his activism every day for the National Alliance. As in my own criminal case, despite evidence in his favor Jim was convicted in an Iowa circuit court and appealed his wrongful conviction to the Iowa Supreme Court of Appeals where, again, like my case before the WVSCA, the lower court's ruling was affirmed. Jim is still working to clear his name with Iowa's highest court at this writing.

An interesting twist in Jim's criminal trial was when his attorney, the prosecutor, and judge retired to the judge's chamber for a private *in camera* powwow to secretly conspire and strategize against Jim. I say conspire because their little closed-door gathering involved more than one person working to convict another. Oddly enough, again, unlike in my West Virginia trial in which my attorney, the prosecutor, and the judge met *in camera* to convict me, in Iowa, during Jim's trial, there was actually a stenographer recording the out-of-court dialog among the court officers. Jim procured the transcript of that meeting wherein the biased prosecutor is quoted as calling Jim, "this racist Nazi guy." It is amazing that the prosecutor would foolishly show his bias like that on the record. See that part of the transcript here: E7c. That one slipping by Jim's prosecutor shows that Jim's trial was in fact a political trial, though the regular courtroom transcript would not reveal that it was. What I would give to have a transcript of the private, off-the-record conspiratorial meeting of the Pocahontas Club — Finch, Via, and Dent — during my first sentencing hearing. More details about that secret powwow in my trial will follow.

For 15 months during 1988-89 I had been employed by Ben Klassen, founder of the Church of the Creator (COTC) as his Executive Officer and editor of his Church's monthly tabloid, *Racial Loyalty*. The COTC, like the Cosmotheist Community Church (CCC) that William Pierce founded, is not merely one church but a religion. Both were founded independently of each other by these two men. They were acquainted, mostly through correspondence and the reciprocal exchange of their periodicals, but their approaches were considerably different. Klassen's religion is known as Creativity, Pierce's is Cosmotheism. What I'd learned from Mr. Klassen while working closely with him every day for well over a year — primarily the need for a belief system, a non-Abrahamic religion, if you will, for the

White race — prepared me well to go to work with Dr. Pierce a couple of years later. These religions for Whites are popular with many White loyalists who hold dim views of Christianity, which has Middle Eastern / Jewish roots, and is unsuitable for European peoples. Creativity and Cosmotheism are "unpopular" with Jews and many Christians, which may be one of the reasons my defense attorney Laura Finch told the West Virginia Office of Disciplinary Counsel that I was an "unpopular figure" in her response to my Complaint against her. Finch is a regular Christian churchgoer.

Ben Klassen encountered trouble from busybody Anti-Defamation League (ADL) intervenors, as did Pierce, when they had each applied for tax-exempt status for their churches, identical to the exemptions granted to every other church.

Additionally, Klassen was sued by the SPLC in a convoluted vicarious liability lawsuit when one of his church's ministers killed a hothead Negro in self-defense, after the Black had threatened him with a weapon in an argument over a parking space. SPLC then sued the COTC on behalf of the dead Negro's family. Klassen committed suicide prior to the case going to court, but not before settling his affairs. He named a successor to head the COTC and sold his property, including the church buildings, to Dr. Pierce. The SPLC got a $1 million default judgment because Klassen's successor did not defend the lawsuit. Pierce had no knowledge of the *SPLC vs. COTC* lawsuit when I told him that I'd heard Klassen was going to list that church property with a local realtor and that he should make him an offer to purchase it, which he did. Klassen accepted. The SPLC then went after Pierce to collect its million-dollar judgment, claiming the real estate deal between the two men was some sort of scheme to avoid the SPLC's collecting on its ill-gotten, court-ordered spoils. Dr. Pierce had to spend nearly $150,000 to defend against the barrator Morris Dees's "law center," and the Court ordered Pierce to pay the SPLC $85,000, the profit he would have enjoyed when he sold the COTC property, but not the $1 million the SPLC had hoped for. The SPLC had hoped to destroy two prominent so-called "hate groups" with its barratry but both are still around, while it is the SPLC that has nearly imploded. More about the SPLC's sordid history can be found here:

https://en.metapedia.org/wiki/Southern_Poverty_Law_Center

My History with the National Alliance

I didn't know that when Dr. Pierce invited me to come work with him in 1991 that he had been observing how I had built the COTC up from a nearly defunct organization to a relatively successful one. In the 15 months I'd worked with Klassen as his Executive Officer I put out 14 monthly issues of *Racial Loyalty* as its editor, each issue more polished than the previous one. We sent Dr. Pierce a copy of each issue and he reciprocated by mailing us each issue of his monthly internal members' BULLETIN and copies of the Alliance's intermittently published but very impressive *National Vanguard* print magazine, both of which influenced me significantly through both their content and their professional style. After Dr. Pierce had invited me to come work with him and I had accepted, he made me the Alliance's first Membership Coordinator, essentially his Executive Officer. He wanted me to build up the Alliance's membership as I had done for Klassen's COTC. At the age of 44, that would turn out to be the most satisfying job I ever had, and I had enjoyed some great jobs. I learned more about what is truly important in life from Dr. Pierce in the two years I spent as the National Alliance's Membership Coordinator than I had learned in four years of college and four years in the Army combined. He was a very patient teacher with his inquisitive mentee.

I worked hard at recruiting, organizing NA Local Units around the country, and general Alliance-building. On my watch in West Virginia, Alliance membership expanded from approximately 200 members to approximately 600 members in the two years I worked daily for Dr. Pierce. That may not sound like many, relatively speaking, but those could be considered the glory days for Alliance-building. In 1992 I had doubled Alliance members' minimum monthly dues from $5 to $10, so that was like quadrupling our revenue stream, and from a more committed membership. Even including the time when the Internet became available to us starting in 1995, it took another nine years for membership to double again to 1,200 members in 2002 when Dr. Pierce died.

I took it as a compliment when one day he told me, "Will, I don't know exactly what it is that you do, but you are the best at it that I've ever seen." Ha! I believe it was mainly a matter of my setting achievable objectives, then making things happen, using our members to meet those goals. We had so many serious, dedicated people to work with and the Local Units competed to outdo one another. It was an exciting time. When I had put in the two years in West Virginia I'd promised I'd give him no matter what, I moved back to Raleigh, North Carolina, and became the Alliance's first Regional Membership Coordinator to put into practice in the Carolinas what I'd learned about Alliance-building at our National Office. Erich Gliebe, the Cleveland Local Unit Coordinator, was made Regional Coordinator for Ohio at the same time since he deserved it as an outstanding mid-level recruiter and organizer. Our regions competed and worked well together to motivate other members and Local Units to participate in activism. This was still prior to having the Internet.

Gliebe took on the dual roles of Regional Coordinator and editing *Resistance* magazine for Dr. Pierce after he had purchased the Resistance Records music label around 1999. Resistance Records and the magazine catered mostly to skinheads and their "White power" music. When Dr. Pierce died in July of 2002, Erich lobbied hard with the NA's Board of Directors to be named his replacement — and was so named by that board within a week or so. Knowing that oftentimes organizations do not survive the deaths of their founders, many members thought that the Alliance's board should have managed the corporation for a time, rather than name a successor so quickly. Gliebe's eventual refusal to be directed by Dr. Pierce's hand-picked board did not end well. He ran off each of the three remaining board members as well as almost all of the permanent, on-site full-time staff of approximately 15 people. The National Alliance never recovered, though it limped along for several years, mostly on the reputation of its founder.

I had officially resigned from the Alliance a couple of months prior to Pierce's death because I didn't approve of the direction that the organization was taking, with an overabundance of undisciplined young skinheads beginning to influence the group — rather than the reverse, which Dr. Pierce had hoped for. Most of these skinheads did not grasp the fundamental Cosmotheist[2] spiritual aspect of the organization — what set the Alliance apart from other belief systems and other pro-White organizations.

Nevertheless, I continued to work with Alliance friends, mostly using the Internet, to promote the NA and try to steer White loyalists in the direction Dr. Pierce had envisioned. It took 12 years, Gliebe's selling Resistance Records, and the loss of all but 24 Alliance members, before I could

2 Cosmotheism is the world view developed by Dr. William Pierce, beginning in the earliest days of the Alliance back in the mid-1970s. Some will describe it as his philosophy, others his ideology, and others his religion. This book is not about promoting Cosmotheism, but, after all, I am Trustee of the Cosmotheist Community Church that was founded by Dr. Pierce, and suppose that, for that, I am "unpopular" also, as was he, since Cosmotheism is not based on the Christian bible. It is not a universal religion as is Christianity, nor does it worship the Jew's tribal god Yahweh aka Jehovah. For those who want to explore Cosmotheism, do a search for it at the Alliance's online magazine nationalvanguard.org, or visit cosmotheistchurch.org, or listen to Dr. Pierce's foundational speech, "Our Cause" on the National Alliance's Bitchute video channel, here: https://www.bitchute.com/video/8zl3YvBRQA6b/

finally take control of the National Alliance from Gliebe and slowly begin the rebuilding process of the Piercean Alliance we have today, six years later. Having lost so many members was unfortunate and our Alliance's reputation had suffered from compromises made under Gliebe's mismanagement, but it was beneficial to some degree because I had a "clean slate" to work with and could get back to promoting Cosmotheist fundamentals.

In 2013 it didn't appear that Mr. Gliebe would ever be stepping down to let someone else try to reverse the destructive downward spiral of what Dr. Pierce and many of us had carefully built over a 32-year period. As early as 2005 Gliebe had already done away with the fundamental policy that named Christianity as an opposed ideology to that of the Alliance — a major blunder — in a misguided attempt at a Christian-friendly broader outreach, a "big tent" approach like the one practiced by the Democrats and Republicans. By 2013 he had also altogether done away with the Alliance as a membership organization and had decommissioned the *National Alliance Membership Handbook* in a lame, failed attempt to make the Alliance more popular (there's that word again). Gliebe's doing that was the *coup de grâce* for the National Alliance I had known and that had attracted so many good people and had made us the premier American racial-nationalist organization. A disaster!

At this point I approached old friend Kevin Alfred Strom, who had been a loyal Alliance member and close friend of Dr. Pierce since 1982, and who had been on staff with us in West Virginia in the early 1990s. Rather than lament the death of the NA we had embraced and worked so hard to build together with Dr. Pierce and others, we decided to build a new NA, a membership organization based on the *Membership Handbook* he and I had helped Dr. Pierce write in 1992-'93. Kevin produced our new NA's first *American Dissident Voices* (ADV) radio show the last week in December 2013 and published it on our nationalvanguard.org Web site, and has been producing and hosting a weekly ADV broadcast every week since. We were on our way to rebuild a new National Alliance.

As it turned out, a week later, on 2 January, 2014, a grouplet of six of Gliebe's former members, calling themselves NARRG (National Alliance Reform and Restoration Group), who had all formally resigned in 2012, filed a $2 million lawsuit against Gliebe and his two other NA board members, demanding that Gliebe step down and turn remaining Alliance assets over to them. Gliebe was on the spot and didn't know how to defend against such a suit, especially since he lived in Cleveland, Ohio. One of his board members resigned and NARRG's aggressive attorney was going to tie Gliebe up with discovery, depositions, and multiple harassing motions in a Virginia court, the state where the Alliance is incorporated. NARRG openly boasted that they were willing to spend $50,000 to force Gliebe to do as they demanded.

I learned that Gliebe was selling off some of the NA's West Virginia assets, but that was not something I could control. When I heard he was attempting to sell Dr. Pierce's extraordinary private research library, however, I contacted him and began negotiating with him to buy it myself for our new NA. I managed to scrape together enough cash to buy the library in March of 2014, a month before NARRG filed a lien against him that they thought would prevent him from selling off more assets that NARRG hoped would accrue to them after having a judge dissolve the Alliance. I moved approximately 13,000 of Dr. Pierce's books to the new NA headquarters building I had built on my property in Upper East Tennessee prior to NARRG's lien taking effect. I scraped together a few more thousand dollars of my own funds and in August of 2014 purchased an even larger, very well-collected library that a deceased NA member and old friend of Pierce's, Dr. Gerrit Daams, had stored on the West Virginia property. Gliebe was desperate for funds to defend against NARRG's lawsuit and I knew these books should belong to our new NA, not just sold to the highest bidder.

Gliebe still did not have an attorney, so I found one for him in Virginia and arranged payment for his services. By then Gliebe was ready to throw in the towel. He did not want to turn anything over to the NARRG plaintiffs, so he and the remaining board member agreed to add me to the Alliance board, then he nominated me to be the new Chairman; we agreed and he stepped down, resigning from the Alliance. That was at a straightforward board meeting in my motel room just minutes prior to a *NARRG v. NA* hearing in a Gloucester, Virginia, courtroom.

The NARRG plaintiffs and their attorney were shocked when Erich told them in court that he had stepped down as Chairman and that the board had named his successor. There was a mulatto SPLC reporter there for that as well as an Asian photographer, hoping to get a big story. The candid photograph of me on the cover of this book was surreptitiously snapped by this fellow with his telephoto lens from a good distance away. Don Terry, the SPLC writer, supposedly a Pulitzer Prize winning *New York Times* journalist, had lowered himself to work as an SPLC hack. He left the SPLC soon after to sink even lower and work for Jesse Jackson's Rainbow Coalition. He wrote an article for the SPLC soon after I'd taken over as NA Chairman, "Triumph of the Will: Will Williams and the National Alliance," linked here: https://www.splcenter.org/hatewatch/2014/12/17/triumph-will-will-williams-and-national-alliance The article is full of inaccuracies, but I won't get into them. Like I said, the SPLC's stated mission has been for years to "destroy" the NA.

Enough said about the NARRGsters for now, except that their lawsuit finally was dismissed in July 2016 after I'd battled with them and their buddies at the SPLC and spent nearly $50,000 in the fight. As I knew all along the NARRG plaintiffs did not have standing to sue NA. It was shown that they had "unclean hands" for going along with Gliebe's decade of destroying NA, while foolishly driving away 98 percent of the membership by the time I took over.

My accuser in the misdemeanor Pocahontas show trial that led to my incarceration, Garland DeCourcy, was working with both NARRG and the SPLC, along with her handful of other coup-plotters, to unseat me as Chairman. She succeeded in turning several former Alliance members against me in her failed judicial coup attempts. It was a kind of war; they were casualties of the war. All through it, though, our Alliance was slowly rebuilding with new, loyal members. That story will be told in the following chapters.

Kissing the Toads

The National Alliance attracts many of our race's best, racially responsible people, but it also has attracted a few who might be considered to have defective personalities — who want to be associated with winners, hoping it will rub off on them. It takes a good deal of effort to distinguish the sincere, serious members from the hobbyists and talkers, especially with a limited staff to evaluate Alliance aspirants, and with our members scattered around the country. We do it though, as best we can, with the cream naturally rising to the top. Dr. Pierce told me he had to "kiss a lot of frogs to find his prince." Readers may recognize that phrase from the Grimms' fairy tale about the Frog Prince. It's a good metaphor for the challenging process of cultivating idealistic, mostly unpaid, volunteer leaders.

While trying to save and restore National Alliance I had to "kiss a few toads" myself before finally getting reliable, trustworthy NA members to relocate to remote, rural West Virginia to live and work on our property there (which we call "The Land or "the campus," rather than repeat the foreboding description used by our enemies and the controlled media: "the compound").

The first toad I dealt with may have been Gliebe's so-called business manager, the thief Patrick Martin. While moving Dr. Pierce's library from the rooms adjacent to Dr. Pierce's former office, Martin did what he could to obstruct the move, though I had paid for the library and was not going to take any lip from him. Rather than being helpful, he would sit around and smoke cigarettes while others did the heavy lifting, boxing thousands of books and loading them into the 26-foot U-Haul truck. I thought it might come to blows between us because of his sour disposition and sloth, and told Gliebe he needed to fire him. He was fired the next day, never to return. Later, after becoming Chairman, and looking through Alliance bank statements, I saw how extensive Martin's thievery was. In one month, for example, October 2010, from receipts of timber sales on The Land, he paid himself $32,000 in what he called "back pay." Gliebe's "back pay" was caught up then also, but nowhere near to that extent. Our Alliance could have used those proceeds. I couldn't prosecute the thief for grand theft because that would require a prosecutor to indict him. I did think, for a while, that the IRS might independently go after him while I was required to deal with that agency to pay for the Alliance's income tax arrears that I'd inherited, but I never heard that they did. I had to pay tens of thousands for debt incurred by Gliebe's mismanagement, and with my own money since there was zero income from book sales and very little in members' monthly dues. It's difficult to sue someone for mismanagement and I had enough problems to deal with without that.

Then the SPLC, under the byline of their attack dog Heidi Berich, published their article about us titled "Chaos at the Compound." Here's just the subtitle and first sentence:

> *Allegations of Embezzlement, Money Laundering and Tax Fraud Haunt the New Chairman of the National Alliance*
>
> After spending months documenting evidence of embezzlement, money laundering and more than two million dollars in unreported income, the accountant hired by the National Alliance (NA) called police earlier this month after being threatened by one of the headquarters staff....

They also published a similar piece in their printed quarterly journal misnamed *Intelligence Report*. This slick magazine is mailed to tens of thousands of law enforcement agencies, media outlets, and others. That's what a tax-exempt, so-called "civil rights organization" can do when it has $500,000,000. Like I said, it's war with these bastards, and the war is not symmetrical. It does help that we have truth on our side and that we're dealing with well-documented, perfidious liars.

I'll get into more about my war with the SPLC later, but for now, this article provides a good segue to say more about my second toad: the alleged "accountant hired by the National Alliance," Randolph Dilloway, as well as the third, the toadette Garland DeCourcy. I never kissed either of these toads and never would, but wouldn't put it past Miss Heidi.

My second toad, Dilloway, had volunteered to help me move Pierce's library after I'd purchased it from Gliebe. I had encountered him on a couple of Internet discussion boards and he followed me around on them like a loyal puppy dog, reinforcing everything I wrote, unsolicited. I had some help lined up to unload the trucks back here in Tennessee, but needed to find help loading them up in West Virginia, a four-hour trip away. My old friend John McLaughlin in Illinois volunteered as did Dilloway. Gliebe was there to assist but was not much help; his toady "Business Manager" Martin was even less help. Dilloway is a big strong fellow and was actually quite helpful. He was impressed by what he saw on The Land, especially by the facilities that William Pierce had built. It was a million dollar campus with nine buildings on nearly 400 lovely, secluded mountain acres. What was not to love?

I hired Dilloway tentatively in mid December, 2014, when I was desperate to get someone on the property just to have a presence there. The NARRG plaintiffs were pressing me, mad as a nest of agitated hornets that I had outmaneuvered them to get legal possession of the Alliance as the duly appointed Chairman. Three of them had even trespassed on The Land in my absence, poking around the prize they were fighting me for, soon after I'd taken possession. Lacking anyone who could relocate to remote West Virginia with winter coming on fast, I invited Randolph to take the job. He accepted and was able to relocate there before the new year (2015).

I drew up an eight-page employment contract, E2a, setting out his terms of employment for a minimum term of one year, that included my giving him a 4x4 pickup truck since Sad Sack had no vehicle at the time. The agreement was renewable if things worked out between us. Things did not work out, however, and he was fired by me for insubordination and theft on 3 May — a little over four months later. Dilloway's job description from that contract will be quoted a little later. It was mostly cleaning and maintenance work.

In subsequent frequent trips between West Virginia and Tennessee prior to Dilloway's arrival I had moved not only books, but file cabinets that held Alliance records including some old, but sensitive, membership and financial documents, and whatever else for which I had room in the new National Alliance headquarters building in Tennessee. The severe winter of 2014-'15 was as tough on Dilloway as it was on me, but we managed to make it to spring.

Before getting to the toadette, my accuser Garland DeCourcy, I should tell a little more about Dilloway. I used the term "Sad Sack" to describe him. "Sad Sack" was a character in the funny papers, created during WWII and which ran through the 1950s and 60s — his name was a euphemistic shortening of the military slang expression "sad sack of shit." Sad Sack has come to mean an inept person or inept soldier and is kinder than "fuckup."

Dilloway was born out of wedlock to a 13-year-old mother and a ne'er-do-well, adult father, given up by the mother to her father when she couldn't take care of him. He was near deaf since birth. His birth grandfather also couldn't deal with the little tyke and gave him up for adoption. His adoptive parents, the Dilloways, raised him in a more or less stable home. If I were him, I would keep such an unpleasant fact to myself, but Sad Sack doesn't mind telling of his illegitimate start in life.

Dilloway seemed well-intentioned but I found him to be incompetent and unable to do anything very complicated. He would never be successful in life, though he thought he could do anything. In fact when told how to do something, anything, he would say, "You don't have to tell me how to do this. I've been doing this for 30 years." Always 30 years, doing everything since he was a teenager. When he was changing oil at a Honda dealership in Louisiana he was, in his words, a "fluid engineer." He worked as a laborer for several different people who I gathered had exploited his Sad Sackness. But he styled himself a "forensic accountant," something I never believed, though he bragged often of his schooling and about how he had worked as an accountant for Negro bosses in the mayor's office in Detroit, Michigan. Heidi Beirich apparently believed him, though, or she wouldn't have put his tall tales of "documented evidence" of embezzlement, money laundering, and more than two million dollars in unreported income in print. I doubt that Beirich actually took Dilloway and his fantastic tales seriously, but when trying to destroy the Alliance — and in the process, generating big donations from suckers to "fight hate" — anything is fair.

Just prior to moving to our campus, Dilloway told my wife Lana, "You and Will will soon see all of Pocahontas County is going to love me." I told him to keep to himself and keep some mystery about him. Defiant of my instructions to keep a low profile, he soon went to the West Virginia State Police barracks and introduced himself as — it's impossible to know for sure, but the National Alliance's accountant perhaps? What an idiot. He spent a great deal of time trying to make friends with everyone he encountered — the Hillsboro postmistress, the lady at the grocery store in Marlinton, etc. — instead of staying on The Land, securing the place, keeping to himself, and working on the tasks I'd assigned. He has self-esteem issues and apparently "needs" everyone to know how important he is and to love him.

A typical story from Randolph: When one day I'd noticed small splotches on the front of the sweatshirt he was wearing that looked like tiny Clorox bleach droplets I asked him what caused them. He said with a straight face that when he left the Honda dealership in Louisiana to come work for me, the girls that worked there gathered around him, telling him how much they would miss him. It was their tears that had permanently stained his sweatshirt. I laughed. When I asked him later to tell Lana how his sweatshirt became stained, he repeated the same story to her with the same straight face. We got a kick out of that, and also when he claimed he could forecast weather a month in advance. The problem was, he believed his own tall tales. The entire time I knew Sad Sack, he never had a girlfriend, or mentioned any past girlfriends. There were other similarly ridiculous claims by

Dilloway, but that one about those girls' tears on his chest is enough to get the point across. He never married, but I don't believe he's queer, just a Sad Sack who craves affection wherever he can find it. He probably thinks his Faceberg "likers" sincerely like him.

When Dilloway was fired on 3 May, 2015 and escorted off of Alliance property by three law enforcement officers, one item that didn't make it out the gate with him for some reason was a 14-page hand-written letter in pencil (approximately 300 words per page, or 4,000 words) to his mother. The almost 50-year-old brags to his mom about every little insignificant detail of each of his days on The Land, and of all the people he has made friends with in the county. What the letter revealed to me was how little he was actually working, how much he exaggerated about what he was doing and how important he considered himself to be — such big plans for how he was going to do this and do that, none of which materialized. Page 6 of this letter — dated 10 March, less than three months into his tour — reveals how deluded "Uncle Randy" was when he wrote:

> I hope you are saving my letters. When [nephew] Nolan becomes 16, I want him to know that his uncle Randolph has more contacts than his great-grandpa Dilloway could ever dream of. Nolan want to study in Europe? Name the country and I will have someone there to watch over him. A trade? We have many [NA] members who will be honored to train my nephew. College? That will be a bit difficult, but in ten years time, I will know enough professors to steer him to the right university in any state. We have many members in Michigan.

This one page can be seen as E2b. The other 13 pages of this otherwise private letter are just more of the same and not worth republishing.

I believed at first that Dilloway was sincerely idealistic, but eventually came to see that his personal ambitions were much higher than his ideals. He seemed to enjoy the solitude of being by himself on The Land, enjoying the private mountainside retreat, making order, reading, and watching old video tapes. Some people would consider this necessary job for the Alliance to be an ideal assignment. I couldn't make the 8-hour round trip often, but when I did it wasn't long before I could see that Randolph wasn't working out. He was uncooperative, even defiant, not doing the simple tasks I had hired him to do. As with the overweening self-importance of what Uncle Randy could do for his nephew Nolan, he was delusional. He considered himself the boss and practically the owner of The Land. When I did visit for a day or two at a time I let him know that I wasn't pleased with his progress and would give him a punch list of things to do and check off as he accomplished them — mostly simple cleaning and making order. But rather than cooperate with the Alliance's Chairman to keep his ideal job, he would complain and argue as if only he knew best what was needed.

By the end of February I could see I needed to replace Randolph with someone who would be appreciative and cooperative rather than argumentative and insubordinate, but none was available at the time. Unfortunately, a few more "toads" were ahead of me until I finally found a "prince."

My less-than-pleasant experience with toad number two Dilloway was a prelude to dealing with the even more problematic toadette, Garland De-Courcy.

I found later from the SPLC's "Chaos at the Compound" article — a collaboration between its writer Heidi Beirich and her paid informant/thief Dilloway — that the latter had attempted to file a complaint against me for an alleged assault on him, but when it came time for him to file the formal charge, the West Virginia State Trooper wrote that the complainant "refused to cooperate." And as will be shown soon, the same thing — refusing to cooperate with law enforcement for over two months "for fear that [I] would murder her" until she actually filed her complaint — happened with "victim" number two, toadette Garland DeCourcy, or as she affectionately came to be called by us, Garlic DeCrazy. Here is what Miss Beirich tells us in her article mentioned above:

> The wheels started to come off the wagon earlier this year, when Williams' allegedly assaulted Randolph Dilloway, his accountant on the compound. After grabbing him and allegedly threatening to throw him off the roof of the NA headquarters building last April, Dilloway, homeless and without any friends or family nearby, went to the West Virginia state police asking for help. The Trooper on duty filed an assault report over the April 1 incident, which reads in part, "The victim continued, Mr. Williams then grabbed him at the shoulder and at the right side waist and jerked him forward like he was going to throw him off the roof."

> But when Dilloway was advised by the state police that Williams would likely be charged with assault for the alleged attack, he evidently became fearful. The report reads: "[The victim] did not want to pursue charges of any kind at this time, and believed it would only make it worse. At the writing of this report, the victim has refused to cooperate."

> Though he remains in hiding, Dilloway has spoken extensively with federal law enforcement, the IRS and the SPLC over the past few months. He said in an email this week that he is not at all surprised that Williams finally got arrested for attacking someone on the compound.

Here is my side of the "roof "story just to give my readers a better idea of what a lying piece of work and toad Randolph Dilloway was and still is. An Alliance friend and I were removing a heavy flagpole base that had been added by Mr. Gliebe or by his sidekick Shaun Walker to the front of the Alliance's West Virginia office building roof at its apex. It was not only unnecessary to have this poorly designed flagpole, but it had undermined the roof and was causing a serious leak into the studio space on the second floor. It had to go. It was a slow process to remove this base, but we were taking care of the task just fine. Just fine, that is, until Dilloway decided he needed to climb on the roof to "supervise" us. Being nearly deaf he tends to talk very loud and started barking orders, telling my helper, "Bring me some paper towels," and such. I was on the underside of the roof in the studio, up on a ladder, turning nuts with a socket wrench while my helper on the roof was holding the other ends of the six or eight bolts that were securing the contraption. I heard Dilloway yelling at my helper, then stomping around on the metal roof like Jumbo the elephant. I yelled up at him to quit stomping, but he persisted. Maybe he couldn't hear me. I quit my task, went up on the roof and told Dilloway to get off the roof. He decided instead to argue with me. I was standing on the edge of the roof with my back to the open ground below. He looked like he wanted to fight. I said, "Come on." He could have pushed me off the roof but decided better, thinking maybe that I'd take him with me, or that I might land on his chest with my knee when we hit the ground (or some such scary scenario). He scurried down the ladder and we went about finishing the job of removing the offending pole mount, then repaired the roof so it would no longer leak. There was no physical contact, no grabbing Sad Sack "by the shoulder and right side waist and jerking him forward." It was a matter of the boss telling his insubordinate hireling to leave, to go away. If Dilloway didn't have to be terminated before, it was clear he had to go after that incident.

I take it from Heidi Beirich's account, based on what Dilloway had told her, that this was on 1 April, 2015. I needed to go back to Tennessee that day or the next and still had no one who could replace him and secure the property while I was out of state. By now, according to Miss Heidi's, "Chaos" article on 21 May, Dilloway, instead of doing what he was instructed to do, unbeknownst to me, had already started going through every cabinet and drawer in the office building, scanning old letters, invoices of old book sales, old bank records, etc. Heidi Beirich described it like this in her smear article:

> For five months, Dilloway organized, examined, and in many cases copied key documents and data files among tens of thousands of pages of sales receipts, donation records and ledgers.

Really? Dilloway had not been on the property for five months, and by his own admission he had started scanning the documents he eventually stole in late February, so it was more like two months.

Sad Sack desperately needs to feel important. He couldn't perform the job he had with the NA so he flipped and went to the SPLC where he could help them "destroy" the organization, get back at me, and be very important indeed. What a fool. His ploy didn't work because in nearly everything he told Heidi there is hardly a word of truth. I mentioned above the alleged Alliance organizational chart that the thief provided to the SPLC (E7a). It is as ridiculous as it could possibly be. Of the 21 names on it, once my and Kevin Strom's and our wives' names are removed, the names that are left and the positions they are claimed to hold are all figments of Dilloway's bizarre imagination. That shows how little knowledge about the Alliance the dorky traitor actually had and how loose he plays with the truth, even with his new SPLC friends. Yet "hate expert" Heidi published that contrived nonsense from her vengeful informant as "fact." Also, in Heidi's words:

> [Dilloway] gradually compiled and copied dues statements and donation records on approximately 8,000 former NA members thought suitable for a recruitment letter.

What a whopper! "8,000 former members?" I wish. Try to imagine how long it would have taken the thief to scan 8,000 records for the SPLC, the IRS, the FBI, or whoever. There were never anywhere near that number of Alliance members in its entire history. I inherited just 24 stalwart members in good standing in 2014 and Dilloway had no access to their names or to their records, nor did he have any access to any new records on my watch. SPLC got mostly old book sales invoices and they used them to try and "prove" that some book buyers that were then entered into their "hate" database, thanks to their paid thief, could then be exposed as "Nazis" in an effort to ruin their lives. Dilloway apparently thought that the more scanned documents he supplied to SPLC, the more they would pay him. I don't know how much he was paid by SPLC for our stolen records; Glen Allen makes the case in his lawsuit against the "law center" that it was at least $5,000. If so, that is small recompense indeed for becoming a traitor. Dilloway had to be expecting more. He actually believed that he would be paid a considerable reward — a percentage — from some IRS whistleblower program for exposing what he claimed were "millions of dollars" that were allegedly "embezzled" by the NA; for alleged non-payment of taxes and for something the Alliance never did but which the SPLC has actually been proven guilty of: hiding millions of dollars in offshore bank accounts. Another fantastic pipe dream by the sad sack o' shit traitor, er, uh excuse me, the Sad Sack.

What would the SPLC gain from publishing records that they knew were stolen? They figure that anyone considering joining the Alliance would be scared away by the idea that their personal information would not be secure, especially if their records were kept by this hated new target: me.

The SPLC, with its half billion dollar war chest and with the controlled media and the courts on their side, thought this latest anti-NA campaign in 2015 would finally destroy our perfectly legal organization. But which organization is relatively successful five years later, and which has practically self-destructed, the NA or the SPLC? And where is the SPLC's "whistleblowing" thief/informant Dilloway? Is he in a "protection program" as Ms. Heidi claimed? Protection from whom?

As a matter of fact even Gliebe understood the importance of keeping Alliance members' data secure. He withheld nothing from me during our transition. All important information was kept on the one dedicated laptop I got from him. Lana was the only person who reviewed the thousands of names of former members/supporters/magazine subscribers and book purchasers recorded on the laptop. Resistance Records was sold by Gliebe in 2013 — thank goodness — along with its sales records and inventory. Beirich even quoted Lana's email to Dilloway in her article:

> Out of 8500 DB [data base] I filtered 2500, we mailed [our] 1st Bulletin to them and got at least 500 of them returned to us.

Excuse Lana's 2015 broken English. Russian is her first language. To repeat, Randy "Fingers" Dilloway scanned and stole mostly old sales receipts, letters, etc., and sold them to a powerful, sleazy enemy that he knew would use what he sold them to try and destroy the lives of good people. His was grand theft that should have been prosecuted by the county prosecutor, but wasn't. He actually stole much more than has been presented so far — to be explained later.

So, by the first part of April, 2015, there was little doubt that the ambitious Sad Sack despised my guts and already sought revenge against me. This heightened after 3 May, 2015, when he was fired and escorted off of Alliance property by three law enforcement officers. I had known for a couple of months before Dilloway was actually fired that he needed to go, but as I said already, it was becoming exceedingly difficult to find someone trustworthy who would agree to relocate to our very rural Mill Point, West Virginia, property amid the controversy with the SPLC and the NARRG lawsuit.

It has been more than five and a half years since Dilloway was required to leave. Fortunately I have retained much documentation from that period so that I can reconstruct for this book what happened back then, leading up to my experiences with the 11th judicial District of West Virginia. The next few pages may seem disjointed to the reader, with "flashbacks" out of sequence like in a Hollywood movie, but bear with me. I'm no writer but will try to bring the facts together here in a way that makes sense. I'll return to what happened on 3 May, but first, on 21 May, the SPLC's Beirich admitted that she had received "a handful of thumb drives" from Dilloway on 6 May. I had no knowledge that Dilloway had any previous contact with the SPLC hate group prior to 6 May, but suspected that he may have had. I do not believe he was "planted" into our organization by the SPLC or by anyone else, but flipped to work against us some time beginning in March 2015. Perhaps "cabin fever"[3] had something to do with his traitorous transformation from idealistic White racial nationalist to paid informant for the anti-White, Jewish "law center."

Dilloway told me in a parting shot on 3 May, "I will destroy you and

---

3 The term "cabin fever" describes the psychological symptoms — feelings of restlessness, irritability, anger, boredom and loneliness — that a person may experience when he is confined alone; in Dilloway's case, snowed in during a brutal winter in a remote location for extended periods.

bankrupt the National Alliance." I knew within a few days what he meant by that, when I received an email from Heidi Beirich herself, informing me that she was preparing an article for the SPLC that would be dealing with "financial improprieties" at the Alliance. Rather than ignore Heidi I answered her inquiry with a short, measured response. She used part of my response in her 21 May "Chaos at the Compound" article:

> Williams went on to state, "I've been managing the Alliance as Chairman for more than six months now and can say with confidence there are no current improprieties with our finances, other than our having to deal with one individual, an extremely unstable employee who stole proprietary financial records when he was fired recently."

Beirich knew exactly who the unnamed, unstable thief was who stole proprietary financial records and was foolish enough to use my quote anyway. By quoting my response from the email to her, Beirich admitted in her published smear article that the SPLC had been informed that the records were stolen. Yet she and SPLC tried to make an excuse:

> Dilloway had also signed a non-disclosure agreement, or NDA, written by Kalamaros, which prohibited him from discussing his findings outside of the Alliance. As a result, he was unable to consult with other accountants or tax preparers he knew in the industry who might have been of some help.... Regardless, Dilloway knew the NDA did not apply when it came to specific knowledge of fraud or criminality.

There had been no fraud nor any criminality on my part. None whatsoever. The NDA was three and a half pages of a standard employment agreement, E2a, that my attorney friend Tim Kalamaros had helped prepare for me as employer, and Dilloway as employee, to sign.

Proving Dilloway was paid by SPLC for his theft and how much will require discovery and depositions that may come from Glen Allen's lawsuit against the SPLC, Beirich, and Mark Potok that is under appeal as this is written.

Meanwhile, Dilloway and his cohorts were attacking me and the Alliance all over the Internet with the most outrageous and libelous accusations. A notorious anti-NA discussion board, "Vanguard News Network Forum" or just "VNN Forum" (VNN) was facilitating my enemies by publishing their accusations. From 2015 to January 2017 Dilloway was banned from VNN for something else in his past. He supposedly made a request to be allowed back on, but VNN's owner, Mr. Linder, made a condition that he had to tell about his deal with the SPLC for his theft of Alliance records first. Dilloway finally responded to Linder on 19 January, 2017, in a post he made here: https://vnnforum.com/showthread.php?t=235917&page=156:

> To answer Alex Linder's question last May - I was never paid for that SPLC interview. I only accepted a relocation fee from a non profit organization who helps those who want to get out of the movement. I had no choice, Willie stole nearly everything I owned and I had no where [sic] to go. Made myself a new life on my own. Willie never ruined my life, but I am about to ruin his.

Dilloway did not want to admit that he received money for the records he stole, but had no problem admitting being compensated in kind.[4] Being compensated in kind only is not plausible, since Dilloway desired to be compensated with money, and not just for travel and other expenses. "Relocation fee?" How much and by which "tax-exempt organization that helps those who want to get out of the movement"? That can be disclosed in discovery. There have been a number of former White nationalists, usually skinheads, who for one reason or another were "helped" by the SPLC or the ADL to "get out of the movement." These reformed "haters" have been given profitable ghost-written book deals by such groups, and have been toured around the country, receiving fees for speaking to audiences of the groups' supporters. I know of no books in the works by Dilloway, nor any speeches given by him about the evils of White racial nationalism. He's not a good candidate for doing either.

Beirich went so far as to travel from SPLC headquarters in Montgomery, Alabama, to Howell, Michigan, to visit and have dinner with former "Nazi" Dilloway and his mom. After this friendly tête-à-tête Dilloway described Beirich online as "a nice German lady." Beirich didn't exactly return his compliment when she quoted from an email that I'd sent to her informant, that he foolishly turned over to her. From her "Chaos" article:

> Williams himself acknowledged this in a July 2012 email exchange with Dilloway when the two were discussing building an organization... Williams wrote, perhaps prophetically, "Frankly, Randolph, I can't attract the core I have in mind if you are the one in charge."

I needed to work with who I had at the time, not with who I wished I had. It doesn't matter how many times Dilloway's SPLC handler repeats the lie that I hired her thief/informant as an accountant; the truth is in our Employment Agreement under "2. Job Title and Description":

> The Employer agrees to employ the Employee as a maintenance/repair[man]. The Employee will be expected to perform the following duties: Building repair, maintenance and cleaning, landscaping, as required. Some bookkeeping.

Period. Nothing about "forensic accounting." Nothing about prowling through cabinets for old letters and book sales invoices and scanning them, or dealing with the IRS, FBI, or other federal agencies as Beirich reported he did. He was required to keep receipts for any petty cash purchases. That was the extent of his bookkeeping duties.

I will get more into the arrival of toadette DeCourcy on The Land in mid-April, two weeks prior to Dilloway's departure, but it's instructive here to show how she had ingratiated herself to me early on, when on 3 May she included this description of Dilloway to Lana in an email that same day:

> He is a terrorist, criminal, had this planned for a while, & in his wallet I found a 3*5 card in his handwriting with the IRS criminal hotline phone numbers & email to get us busted & had this land seized [!] understand. HE has been an infiltrator, back

---

4 In kind — compensation consisting of something such as goods or services other than money.

stabber, criminal, thief, nutbag, insane, unstable, hobbyist, who has access to WAY too much for way [to] long with no leash.

DeCourcy butchers the English language, but the point is made to Lana that DeCourcy "will be on my side" against Dilloway. Actually, she and Dilloway would soon become allies against me and the Alliance. Again, in Beirich's 21 May "Chaos" article, she wrote:

> The accountant hired by the neo-Nazi National Alliance (NA) called police earlier this month after being threatened at gunpoint by one of the headquarters staff [DeCourcy].... A scrappy, chain-smoking former NA state organizer who carries a pistol in her purse. DeCourcy wrote on a survivalist blog in 2013 that citizens should kill police officers if they raid the home of an innocent family. "The thing is, if a cop is scared then BACK THE F—- OFF!" she wrote.

DeCourcy had never been a local Alliance organizer, much less a "state organizer," any more than Dilloway had been hired as an "accountant." But SPLC agents figure that if they repeat a proven falsehood often enough as if it is self-evidently true, then the lie will be believed. This tactic is also known as the Jewish "Big Lie" technique, as described by Adolf Hitler in chapter 10 of his book, *Mein Kampf.*

DeCourcy became another SPLC asset by September 2015, if not sooner. The SPLC's 18 December 2015 article, calculated to be their *coup de grace* against me as NA Chairman, was about my 16 December arrest for an alleged battery of DeCourcy. "Chaos and the Cops at the Compound" was without Beirich's byline, instead purporting to be written by "HateWatch Staff." It described DeCourcy this time as

> a fearless little middle-aged woman answering the phones and raising vegetables and chickens... smart and funny.

Poor innocent "victim."

After becoming the "poor innocent little victim"'s puppet and tag-team partner, forgetting all the awful things she had written about him earlier, my self-styled archenemy Randolph Dilloway would now be actively promoting my accuser DeCourcy and their co-conspirator Bob DeMarais (the West Virginia neighbor, living adjacent to The Land, who will be introduced soon) as "the good people" who should be in charge of the National Alliance instead of me. At the same time, according to Dilloway's interview, granted to the SPLC in May 2015:

> Dilloway described DeMarais, the NA's former business manager, as "two-faced" and suspected he was reporting his daily activities to Williams.

Dilloway and DeMarais hated each other's guts until their hatred of me united them. Reporting daily activities? I recall once Dilloway told me he had been making trips from the gatehouse where he resided to the office building a couple of hundred feet away. Upon hearing about that from me DeMarais informed me that couldn't be true because there had been no footprints in the snow between the two buildings for several days. An employee's lying to me ranks almost as bad as an employee's stealing from me.

48

Why not simply tell the truth?

In late October 2018 when DeCourcy decided to flee West Virginia rather than have me, the accused, confront her, my accuser, in open court — as I was entitled to do and had made clear in open court that I would do at my first sentencing hearing — who did she call to come help her move out of DeMarais's house? None other than Randolph Dilloway. He admitted to this in a three-hour Internet radio interview/rant he did on Thanksgiving Day, 2019, with a nutty Christian Identity preacher, Martin Lindstedt. He stated that as they were leaving Mill Point, DeCourcy told him, "Bob [DeMarais] is no good." Bob DeMarais had put DeCourcy up in his home rent-free for three and a half years, "witnessed" a "battery" for her though he wasn't present to witness anything; paid thousands of dollars to hire lawyers for her, paid for all of her food and cigarettes and cat food (she had 11 cats at one time), etc.

In his blustery but feckless anti-Williams campaign Dilloway openly wrote:

> Yes, my motive is to now shut down Will Williams... my mother received a threatening hand-written letter from Willy.

That "threatening" hand-written note will be presented soon so the reader can decide for himself whether it is threatening or not.

Dilloway had briefly been a National Alliance member on Gliebe's watch, years before I encountered him. It is remarkable to me how so many former, supposedly idealistic Alliance members turned against the Alliance and me: the six NARRG co-plaintiffs, DeMarais, Linder, DeCourcy, and a few more to be named later. Why were they against my and Kevin Strom's resurrecting the Alliance to conform to its founder's vision? Where are they all now? I'll try to explain why and where.

No Good Deed Goes Unpunished

Now we will get into the "champion toad," or toadette, whom some call Garlic DeCrazy, and how she wormed her way into my and Lana's lives and our resurrected Alliance. I should have recognized her mental issues earlier and predicted the trouble she would bring. However, the problem is that DeCourcy does make a fairly good impression at first meeting. She talks way too much for my tastes, interrupts and talks over people, but she's halfway intelligent and I thought she would appreciate my giving her sanctuary and something productive to do for the cause, away from her "calamitous" life of alleged abuse back in Virginia. I figured and hoped early on that she might replace toad number two, Dilloway, and buy me some more time to reorganize the Alliance without bringing too much baggage of her own. Oh, my! Talk about baggage. She brought to The Land three box-truck loads of her hoardings, not to mention a truckload of mental and emotional problems.

On meeting DeCourcy again for the first time in 25 years or so, I was unaware of her self-admitted diagnosis of Asperger's Syndrome (AS), a high-functioning disorder on the autism spectrum. I learned soon enough that two symptoms of AS are an extreme obsessiveness and a focus on a particular issue or person — lucky me: I became her obsession within a couple of months after her arrival at our West Virginia campus.

In the early 1990s Garland Corse (her birth name — not DeCourcy) was an NA member in northern Virginia. I met her a couple of times, but did not know her very well. I believe she may have still been married to the first of her three husbands at the time. She had a pleasant enough speaking voice before becoming a chain smoker, so she did a pre-recorded introduction for the Alliance's weekly *American Dissident Voices* radio program that we used for year or two in the 90s.

On 13 April, 2015, less than two weeks after Sad Sack's "roof incident," the "new" DeCourcy left a cryptic comment under an article posted on our online magazine, *National Vanguard*, the previous day, 12 April, as "Aryangar." The article is a friendly interview with me by the British nationalist magazine *Heritage & Destiny* entitled "Will Williams: Taking the Hard Line," and can be read, here: https://nationalvanguard.org/2015/04/will-williams-taking-the-hard-line/

> Aryangar: 13 April, 2015 2:55 pm
>
> So glad you are doing well Will. This is a great article. Please call me ASAP to catch up. I have left msg in the contact national alliance links with my contact info. I have some urgent matters and many things to donate to NA to help the future endevours [sic]. Time is of essence so please call.

I don't want to get too far ahead of myself at this point, but after a little over two and a half years of reflection following Aryangar's reintroduction to us, I posted my own comment under hers at this same linked interview.

> Will W Williams 17 December, 2017 11:59 am
>
> [...] By the way, the comment above by anonymous ARYANGAR, was the first attempt by mentally-unhinged Alliance enemy Garland Corse aka "DeCourcy" to make contact with me in more than 20 years. This "battered mother-of-three" had "many things to donate to NA to help the future endeavors," was being evicted from her house and desperately needed sanctuary from an abusive husband, etc., etc. We gave the allegedly "battered" former NA member temporary sanctuary, which turned out to be one NA's worst nightmares. Not only did she immediately move in with neighbor Bob DeMarais, but the both of them then conspired to have me jailed, kept off of Alliance property with bogus temporary restraining orders, and take over the NA from its rightful Chairman and board of directors. They were working not only with the NARRG co-plaintiffs, but with the Southern Poverty Law Center "hate" watch-

dogs, and using the courts, filing two additional frivolous civil suits (both eventually dismissed) and filing criminal charges against me — one already thrown out, the other (what else? "Battery"), will finally be proven false also more than two and 1/2 years after the alleged incident.

Moral: No good deed goes unpunished.

The Alliance's Media Director, Kevin Strom, who is the administrator of nationalvanguard.org, sent me "Aryangar"'s email address since "time [was] of the essence." I still didn't know who Aryangar was at that point, but after making contact by email, hearing back and remembering her from more than two decades previous, then hearing her tearful sob story in which she told me that she had contemplated suicide because of her desperate situation, I offered her sanctuary on The Land. Could she be the person who could replace toad number two Dilloway? That certainly crossed my mind since she would be living there.

I was back in Tennessee when my accuser-to-be arrived on The Land. I had a helper, Mike, make two trips in a box truck to help bring the hoarder's junk from her last home in Virginia — the one from which she was going to be evicted within a couple of days. Before DeCourcy arrived on The Land she called our house in Tennessee to report some trouble with her truck, and Lana gave her the above-mentioned neighbor Bob DeMarais's phone number. In just a couple of days after her arrival he would become her landlord/roommate, and within three months her co-conspirator against me. All of DeCourcy's stuff was secured in our big two-story barn. Dilloway may have helped to unload her truck into the barn. I was not on site and don't recall. DeCourcy slept in a room in our office building, but moved almost immediately into an extra bedroom in the basement of DeMarais's house, after complaining about some mold in the office building.

DeMarais didn't like Dilloway and the feeling was mutual, but Lana and I had considered DeMarais a friend and helpful neighbor at the time. After all, he'd been Dr. Pierce's Business Manager for five or six years and served on the Alliance's board of directors until Gliebe and his sidekick Shaun Walker ran him off. Soon after DeCourcy arrived I traveled back to West Virginia to meet her and help her get settled. She had already moved into DeMarais's basement bedroom.

Two weeks after she arrived as "Gael Dempsey" (she asked us not to refer to her as DeCourcy, or as her birth name Corse, or any of her three married names), I fired Dilloway. She was very appreciative, upbeat and helpful at first, but as I wrote earlier she "turned out to be one of the NA's worst nightmares." Within five months she was claiming the National Alliance's barn where I'd let her store her junk was actually *her* barn, and that the entire Alliance was hers as well. The Jews have a word for this level of brashness and gall: *chutzpah*[5].

Since most of the buildings on The Land had been practically shuttered for several years and there was a slight mold issue in the office building room that DeCourcy slept in when she first arrived, it was all right with me that the life-long confirmed bachelor had offered to take her in. At that point I had no idea that DeMarais was, as Dilloway had claimed, as two-faced as he could be. He did not want the National Alliance to rebuild and succeed. I found out soon enough that DeCourcy and he would be working against me and the Alliance, determined not only to see us fail, but to have me incarcerated to make *sure* we failed. I had never treated DeMarais with anything but respect and had actually donated $500 to him ten years earlier when he was sued by the above-named Shaun Walker in a bizarre plot to take his house from him through a ridiculously expensive and mean-spirited lawsuit paid for with Alliance funds. That lawsuit eventually failed when Walker was imprisoned for some politically motivated trumped-up charge in his home state of Utah — a story not worth retelling here.

DeMarais knew I needed money for the Alliance to pay Gliebe's debts that we had inherited. He let me know that he had approached Gliebe and asked him to sell him the Alliance's nice two-story barn and the even nicer two-story National Vanguard Books warehouse (both adjacent to his house), plus the adjoining two and a half acre pasture across from our office building, plus another three acres above the four acres on which Fred Streed had built a nice A-frame cabin. Gliebe had agreed to sell this prime property to DeMarais at the fire sale price of $52,000.

Fred Streed was arguably Dr. Pierce's closest associate in our founder's final years. Fred had worked on The Land for 11 years (1992-2003) as a Jack of all trades (and master of many) and had built the barn, the warehouse, and had made practically every other improvement to The Land during that period. He was named by Pierce as president of the NA's board of directors — and to this day is the executor of the estate bequeathed to the Alliance that has been blocked by the SPLC and their allies. The deceased testator, Dr. Robert McCorkill, died 16 years ago and, thanks to the Tribe, still has not been settled. It is a long story that is beyond the scope of this book. See here, if interested: https://nationalvanguard.org/2016/07/implications-of-the-jewish-theft-of-the-mccorkill-fortune/

I tell you about Fred and his cabin because I learned that DeMarais had his sights set on purchasing Fred's cabin also. Fred, like DeMarais, had been foolishly run off by Gliebe as he was consolidating his power over all aspects of the Alliance ten years earlier. Gliebe did not want to answer to the board Dr. Pierce had appointed, so he replaced that board with his own

---

5 *Chutzpah* is a Yiddish word for shameless boldness or arrogant impudence.

directors that he could control.

As badly as I needed funding for Alliance-building, I had to do what was best for the National Alliance in the long run. DeMarais was gently pressuring me to follow through on the sweetheart deal he had made with Gliebe. The property he coveted had been surveyed, the closing paperwork had already been drawn by his attorney, and all I had to do was agree to sell — since, as chairman of the Alliance, and trustee of the Cosmotheist Community Church, I had that authority. What was best for the Alliance in the long term was to *not* sell that prime property. As a former builder and general contractor I knew, after reviewing the construction file on just the two-story warehouse building, that replacement costs would be well over $100,000. No sale!

The NA and CCC needed that land and those buildings. In fact, after I finally received the inheritance from my mother's estate — she had died on 31 December, 2014 — I purchased Fred and his wife Marta's cabin in September, 2015, so DeMarais couldn't. Had he purchased that, he would have not just ten prime acres and three nice buildings in the heart of our campus, but a deeded right of way across a large portion of CCC property that ran with the cabin. I needed to keep the integrity of our entire tract. I knew that, for the good of the Alliance, this is what Dr. Pierce would have wanted.

So, by denying the two-faced DeMarais those prime properties I had become his bitter enemy and he would conspire with DeCourcy and others, including Dilloway, to "destroy" me. My friend Mike, who had graciously volunteered to help desperate DeCourcy move her junk from Virginia soon learned how ungrateful the woman could be. After moving and unloading two of her borrowed box-truck loads, including the challenging replacement of two flat tires along the way, it wasn't long at all before DeCourcy started badmouthing Mike and anyone else who was helping me. She did this without any reason, and began conspiring diligently with DeMarais against me. DeMarais was the first of four primary co-conspirators she managed to turn into Williams-haters. DeMarais was easy to turn; he already had it in for me for queering his pennies-on-the-dollar sweet deal with Gliebe.

For a couple of weeks until Dilloway was fired, he and DeCourcy had to work together. Even though I was in Tennessee for most of those two weeks I could tell they didn't care for each other. Dilloway was not happy and could probably see the handwriting on the wall as Lana and I were then communicating mostly with DeCourcy rather than with him. He no longer had The Land to himself and his freedom to do as he pleased had been sharply curtailed. When I explained to Dilloway that DeCourcy was hired by me like he had been, as a contract worker, he insisted on describing her as "our guest."

Police Escort "Sad Sack" from The Land

On the first or second day of May 2015 I traveled to West Virginia for a "meeting of minds" with DeCourcy after she had settled in there. She seemed eager to work, doing whatever was needed. Dilloway, who had been living in the gatehouse for several months by then, was holed up there for the most part, sullen and aloof. I had no idea at the time that he had been "collecting evidence" to destroy the Alliance, or that he had some hare-brained scheme to collect a reward from the IRS for blowing the whistle on financial improprieties that didn't exist. I sensed that things were fast coming to a head with him, but couldn't figure out how to terminate him without giving him a 30-day notice to vacate the property — 30 days to continue creating problems and be insubordinate. He made getting rid of him without delay easy, late in the day on 3 May.

Sad Sack approached and said that he wanted to meet with me at the gatehouse. He had a list of things he wanted to discuss. I finished what I'd been doing with DeCourcy and she accompanied me to the gatehouse. We were on the covered front porch, the width of the house, me in the porch swing, Dilloway a few feet away in a chair, and DeCourcy sitting on the steps between us. I let Dilloway start reading his list, mostly grievances he had about the way he was treated. He didn't get far into his list before DeCourcy butted in and started running her mouth as she is wont to do. Dilloway was enraged. He jumped up from his chair, yelling at DeCourcy, "God dammit, you interrupted my train of thought."

I don't remember much of the brief conversation after that. I stood up also and approached him so DeCourcy was no longer between us. He came toward me, spitting mad. I held out my arm to halt him, touching his chest. He said something like, "Now you've done it. You touched me!" We stood there for a few seconds face-to-face, but no blows were exchanged. Remember, this employee had gone to the State Police a month earlier wanting to file an assault claim against me. I had no knowledge that he had done that and can only imagine what had been going through his scheming brain during the month since the alleged "roof incident."

So, why waste a good confrontation to bring things to a head? With my right hand that was at my side, I whipped it up in a quick motion and knocked his cap off of his head and out in the yard. I was careful not to touch his head, just his cap — sort of like "throwing down the gauntlet," or glove, issuing a challenge. What will you do now, big man? What he did was start screaming about how he was going to destroy me and the National Alliance. I never saw his list of grievances.

He ran past me and jumped off the end of the porch behind me, head-ed toward the office building. There would be no physical fight. That was good — but me, being me — I jumped off the porch after him in pursuit. He broke into a run, as did I after him. I was five days shy of 68 at the time; he was 49 and a good bit larger and faster. He made it to the unlocked office front door first and slammed it behind him as he went through, but didn't lock it. As I came through the door I could see he was going through the open space to the back of the building. When I got there I could hear him stomping up the stairs. He did lock that door at the bottom of the stairs. I didn't want to break the locked hollow-core door, but beat on it telling him to open it. He ignored me. I went back outside, met DeCourcy who had caught up, told her to call the police. I went over and moved the truck that psycho Dilloway had been using behind some trees and kept the keys so he couldn't drive off with it, then went to the gatehouse and started moving his junk out on the porch for a few minutes as I was figuring how to handle him. I heard DeCourcy calling for me and went back to the office building where I learned from her that Dilloway had come back downstairs, and had confronted her in the front office where the telephone was. He wanted to call the cops but she wouldn't allow him. He yelled something at her about "obstructing justice," or some such nonsense. That's when she "brandished" the pistol from the purse that was in her lap, after unplugging the phone from the wall. I was proud of her for handling him that way.

He departed on foot since I had hidden his truck. With all the commo-tion DeCourcy had not had the chance to call law enforcement yet by then. She informed me that he had come back downstairs with a briefcase and the laptop I had purchased for him to use, then took off through the woods down towards the hardtop highway. So, after checking upstairs to see what possible damage he may have wreaked up there, and briefly assessing again what he had been doing in the gatehouse, I was figuring out how best to handle the unsettled situation.

I walked back to the office and listened some more to DeCourcy's de-scription of her confrontation with him, then told her again to call law enforcement and report that a severely unstable employee by the name of Dilloway had threatened her physically, stole our property, and needed to be detained. I got on the phone with Trooper Brock of the West Virginia State Police (WVSP) and he told me, "I know exactly where he is. He just called me from Boyd Thompson's house wanting to report an assault." The cops went to Thompson's house, detained Dilloway, and got an earful of his side of the story. Meanwhile, I went back to moving his junk out of the gatehouse onto the front porch. It took a while for the cops to arrive back on the property with Dilloway. They left him in the vehicle while they talk-ed to me at the gatehouse. I told them that he was so volatile that he needed to be escorted off our property immediately. They agreed after hearing me out and listening to DeCourcy express her fear of him. They determined that to defuse the confrontation, no 30-day notice was needed for him to be required to vacate, nor should his departure be temporary, as in asking him to go somewhere else overnight to cool off. They agreed with me that he needed to leave immediately and permanently!

As consideration for Dilloway's leaving immediately, I told the cops I was willing to sign over to him my 4x4 Nissan pickup truck that he had been driving — a small price to pay to resolve the situation. As per our employment contract, he was entitled to ownership of the truck only after a full year of successful employment, but he had only worked for us for a little over four months. The cops brought Dilloway in the house to supervise the removal of his stuff. I stood by closemouthed except to occasionally say, "No, you're not taking this book, or that book," whenever he claimed Alliance property was his. A cop was impressed when one of the books Dilloway was claiming was his had my name in the front of the book in my distinctive handwriting.

I needed to draw up a hand-written agreement, allowing him to have the truck in exchange for de-assing the premises. That simple agreement, (p. 007) drawn by me, was limited to one page. Unfortunately, motormouth DeCourcy, who styles herself an attorney, was yammering unnecessary legalese in my ear as I wrote it out. I made a scrivener's error at one place, writing the word "employee" when it should have read "employer." But fortunately, I was citing and quoting a clause from a copy of our original employment contract:

> As per paragraph 31 of 1/1/15 Employment Contract, Employee acknowledges and agrees that all rights, title and interest in any Confidential Information will remain the exclusive property *of the Employee* (my emphasis added).

Of course, in the original 8-page typed employment contract from which I was copying, it's typed correctly, "... will remain the exclusive property of the Employer." (E2a)

Nearly all of Dilloway's stuff had already been loaded into that Nissan pickup truck when the time had come for employer and employee to sign and date the new agreement. The pigheaded fool refused to sign for some reason. I said okay, and instructed the cops to please unload everything from what was still my truck, put it in their truck — a West Virginia State Police pickup they had driven there, oddly enough — and take the sack o' shit to the bus station. By then the cops were fully on my side and Dilloway knew it. He read and signed the agreement I had just drawn. It contained an admission that "Employee, in violation of paragraph 31, deleted or destroyed all content of Employer's laptop. Employee knew full well he was destroying proprietary records of Employer in violation of Employment Agreement & with criminal intent" — a signed confession. After we'd both signed and dated the agreement DeCourcy ran to DeMarais's house, and made two copies — one for Dilloway and one for the cops. I retained the original.

To be fair, I present the account of the thief and SPLC paid informant's 3 May ordeal written by his handler Heidi Beirich on 21 May, 2015. Note there is no mention of his being escorted off the property by law enforcement: https://www.splcenter.org/hatewatch/2015/05/20/chaos-compound:

> [T]he accountant hired by the neo-Nazi National Alliance (NA) called police earlier this month after being threatened at gunpoint by one of the headquarters staff. The accountant fled the NA compound in Mill Point, W.V., and ran almost a mile to a nearby residence, where he called 911. He was eventually escorted back to the Alliance compound by West Virginia state troopers to recover his belongings. Randolph Dilloway, 49, an accountant with almost a decade of experience, was secretly hired by Alliance Chairman Will Williams in December to conduct a forensic audit of the organization's bank statements, member dues documents and federal income tax filings. The May 3 altercation has left him shaken and concerned for his safety. Dilloway has since been interviewed by the FBI's Joint Terrorism Task Force and he is now seeking federal protection under IRS Whistleblower statutes. Terrified of his former employer, Dilloway contacted the Southern Poverty Law Center (SPLC) on May 6.

Sergeant Barlow, the State Police shift supervisor who was helpful in de-escalating the volatile situation, had had enough lip out of Dilloway by the time he was to exit our gate for the last time. He told him, paraphrasing, "If one piece of the stuff on the back of that truck flies off on the road, you're going to jail. Now get out of Pocahontas County." It was a hostile situation that required level-headed law enforcement supervision and authority. Did Dilloway tell that part to the SPLC or to the Joint Terrorism Task Force? That SPLC paragraph alone is loaded with distortions, half truths, and outright lies, and is not worth rebuttal. It's this book that will finally set the record straight on what took place that day — not Heidi Beirich or her paid informant.

DeCourcy, earlier, had rushed to get Lana to email us from Tennessee the copy of the employment contract as well as the receipt for the laptop that Sad Sack was claiming was his. Barlow was shown my receipt for the laptop; he ordered Dilloway to hand it over or he would be arrested for theft. Dilloway complied, but he didn't want to provide the password to open it. Again, he was ordered to provide the password which didn't help his position at all since his password was "FUCKWILL." DeCourcy opened the laptop and saw that it had been wiped clean while he was at the Thompson's house, in anticipation of having to turn it over.

In the gatehouse where the thief resided we discovered a printer and two scanners belonging to the Alliance, and indications that Dilloway might have mailed or intended to mail boxes of National Vanguard Books inventory. The Hillsboro postmistress, by policy, would neither confirm nor deny that he had mailed packages of books, so I didn't pursue that further. I could not control him from Tennessee and had no other choice at the time but to trust that he would not steal from me or the Alliance.

I've mentioned above that Sad Sack tried to claim that the laptop, some books, etc. belonged to him when they did not. As quoted earlier, Dilloway projected his thievery onto me on the anti-Alliance "VNN Forum": " Willie stole nearly everything I owned." As a matter of fact, the thief and traitor did manage to leave some inexpensive items in the rush: some documents, a few clothes, some flash drives, and extra hearing devices. I had considered mailing them along with the truck title to his mom's address until I learned about him going over to the SPLC.

So, in summary, I fired Dilloway for insubordination and for lying to me before I had even learned about his thievery and treason. Had I not gotten him to sign that one-page agreement to vacate on 3 May I could possibly have had to allow him 30 days to vacate our gatehouse residence because of (questionable, in my view) "tenant's rights." For Dilloway to have scanned all of those "thousands" of stolen documents and put them on six thumb drives prior to 3 May showed his malice aforethought and criminal intent to harm me and the National Alliance. Had I not fired and expelled him from our property that day, being an absentee boss down in Tennessee I would have had a bigger mess on my hands with him "doing his thing," unsupervised, on our West Virginia property.

As I said above, my struggle with defectives had been continually documented here and there. Since, back then, my memory of 3 May was much fresher, I'll provide my contemporaneous post made on the Stormfront discussion board under the topic title "The National Alliance Endures a Soap Opera," that was created right after SPLC published its first "Chaos at the Compound" article," https://www.stormfront.org/forum/t1102767-11/:

...the WV cops sided with good guys — us — when Dilloway stole our property, and their incident report reflects that. They have a copy of his signed confession of "criminal intent," not just his extremely egregious civil breach of the page and a half, strict, non-disclosure clauses in our Employment Agreement, which I required of him before allowing the thieving nutjob drive away with my 4x4 pickup truck. I told them I didn't want him arrested; I wanted him gone and escorted out of the county. He said he wouldn't sign it, until, that is, I instructed the cops to unload my truck, put his crap in their pickup and take him and all of it to the bus station. He then stupidly signed the confession, with three state cops and pistol-packing Garland as witnesses. We had no idea he had been gathering "proof" to give to the IRS and SPLC at that time. He reportedly didn't get up with SPLC until three days later, 6 May. The only phone calls he'd made from our phone in the previous month was to his mother in Howell, MI. He had no cell phone, no laptop, and hardly any steering fluid when he drove out the gate for the last time, giving Dr. Bob [DeMarais] the finger. The head cop told me he'd follow him and arrest him for the most minor violation — like a piece of plastic flying off the back of the truck — if he didn't head out straight out of Pocahontas County, WV.

3 May was a long intense day. E2c will show that Lana, not knowing the full extent of the intense situation with Dilloway, tried to ameliorate things from Tennessee by sending Dilloway what she thought was a reasonable email in an attempt to reason with him. Lana reminded Dilloway of her previous friendly emails to him where she had tried to help him avoid being fired by advising him to work on his insubordination. She explained to him, like she might to a child, that despite his problems with me, if fired he will get his 4x4 pickup truck almost free, etc.

As would become clear later, DeCourcy always needed to be at the center of everything and get credit for everything. Having only been on site for two weeks, she wasn't a mere clerk; as will be seen later, she was the self-styled "Executive Administrative Assistant" and "Legal Liaison" for the National Alliance, and "Secretary" of the Cosmotheist Community Church. She did not appreciate Lana's temperate email to Dilloway and let her know it. At the same time, in her long email to Lana she gave a rather detailed description of that day and her own extremely dim view of Dilloway's true nature. The incident when she "obstructed justice" by denying him a phone call to law enforcement, by unplugging the telephone from the wall, was described by him to his handler, Ms. Beirich, as "being threatened at gunpoint by one of the headquarters staff." DeCourcy's and Lana's email exchange on 3 May can be viewed and compared at E2d.

On that day my supposedly new comrade DeCourcy was full of what seemed like reasonable advice to me about computers and about what I might do in the way of damage control with Dilloway. She talked like she was a lawyer with experience in conflict resolution. Little did I know then that her legal experience was in "resolving" her own convoluted personal conflicts.

One thing that made sense, however, was that she advised that I should write a letter to the Yahoo copyright agent to attempt a block of Dilloway's access to his email address which he'd clearly been using for illegal purposes. I arrived back home to Tennessee close to midnight on 3 May, but still wrote that letter (E2e). Lana tried to submit this letter on the special Yahoo customer support page, but was unable to for some reason. The next morning we called on a friend who was much more "tech savvy" with computers than we were, and he provided us with a Yahoo customer support phone number. We called it. Due to the urgency and our failure to double check, however, we had the wrong number for the wrong people. We experienced some short term setbacks from the mess, but eventually resolved the situation with no loss of any records or money, nor any consequences beyond a lot of criticism from the usual niggling detractors for having hired such a weak, defective fool as Dilloway in the first place. What we gained was a valuable lesson learned, with more to come to be sure.

I am not embarrassed to admit and joke that I am "electronically challenged," to say the least. I recognize that computers are useful tools and that the Internet has been incredibly valuable to the National Alliance since 1995 for getting our message out to many more of our people than previously. I also accept that I do not have the aptitude for things electronic and am not inclined to want to know how cloud servers or Internet browsers work. That's not in my job description. I've never been on any social media beyond using discussion boards to spread our Alliance message, and do not even own a cell phone, thank you. I like having people around me who are proficient with Internet technology while I focus on Alliance-building, our organization's long term goals and the "big picture."

We would still encounter more toads along the way, besides Dilloway and DeCourcy, while seeking our prince — ultimately my suitable replacement.

Once Dilloway was gone from The Land I could begin to assess in more detail just how much damage he had done to the organization. I was back in Tennessee, still trusting DeCourcy and having her prepare a spreadsheet with all of the books, CDs, and other National Vanguard Books (NVB) material, with the values of each, that Dilloway had purloined from our warehouse without permission. His gatehouse residence was full of new books in which he had extensively highlighted portions with his ubiquitous yellow marker, rendering them worthless for sale. Some pages of books had every word of every line foolishly highlighted in bright yellow. What does that indicate about him? See photos of at least two piles of books and CDs found in the gatehouse, as well as the spreadsheets prepared by DeCourcy at E2f.

I needed an attorney, a local attorney who would not only help me make a criminal case against Dilloway for theft, but a civil case against the Alabama-based "law center" for purchasing stolen NA documents and records from thief Dilloway. There were no suitable criminal defense attorneys in Pocahontas County — genuine "backcountry" with a population of less than 9,000 residents that is surrounded by a large wilderness region. This may be why Dr. Pierce chose to relocate there.

My Indiana attorney friend Tim Kalamaros contacted a few attorneys in adjoining Greenbrier County for me who he had deemed were "conservative" and not one of them was interested. Then he interviewed Paul Detch in Lewisburg, Greenbrier's county seat. Mr. Detch is about my age, has since retired, but was willing to talk with me. He is not conservative at all, but a very liberal "country lawyer," as he described himself to me. That didn't matter to me at the time since he was the only attorney who would consider taking a case like mine. I didn't think that it should matter to him that I'm Chairman of the National Alliance since I had a strong case against both Dilloway, who had stolen our documents "with criminal intent," and against the SPLC, who bought those documents knowing they were stolen, and intended to use then to harm the NA and anyone they could associate with the NA. Detch accepted a $500 retainer and went to work with what I provided him. He wrote a couple of letters, maybe several, to the SPLC, but provided me with just the first one, found here, E2g. As a true follower of the work of the "law center," he writes in the first letter to the SPLC, dated 16 September, 2015:

> I have been prevailed upon by Will Williams of the National Alliance to contact you in order to request the return of certain properties stolen from his organization in West Virginia. I believe I was chosen by them, not only because I was a local attorney but because I have a long history of fighting for the rights of minorities. I am sure that you would agree that the law needs to be applied equally to all. I'm sure that you would agree with the premise that though the majority can rule that there are minority rights. National Alliance has prevailed upon me as an *unpopular* minority seeking fair treatment in the courts...

There's that word again, unpopular (my emphasis). Paul Detch by his own admission to me carried on a back-and-forth correspondence with a writer at SPLC named Ryan Lenz, but when I asked to see that correspondence he refused to show it to me. Later, when I was sitting in his office, he pointed to a couple of objects on his mantel — one was a Christmas card from Barack and Michelle Obama, the other was a "Certificate of Appreciation" from none other than Morris Dees, co-founder of the SPLC. Detch amused me with his naive statement, "They [SPLC] *are* a law center, after all." His talk about "fighting for the rights of minorities," especially "an unpopular minority," must have gotten a good chuckle out of the hate watchers around the water cooler at the "Poverty Palace" down in Montgomery, Alabama. (By the way, here is the link to one of Ryan Lenz's articles about me and the Alliance: https://www.splcenter.org/hatewatch/2014/01/07/former-army-special-operations-officer-attempting-relaunch-notorious-neo-nazi-group) How about that? I paid my counsel Detch to work for me against the SPLC, and instead he was secretly communicating with that enemy, who he admired, behind my back. Detch had never provided me with any response from the SPLC to his above-quoted official letter to them. Having no other choice of representation I had to stick with Detch, who turned out to be another member of the "Pocahontas Court Club." He did, however, come in handy in another matter later.

Back to the rest of May and June. I was working with Senior State Trooper Damon Brock who was present on 3 May and had witnessed Dilloway's unhinged demeanor and had seen what he had stolen from our Alliance prior to escorting him off our property. His shift manager, State Police Sgt Barlow, and a Forest Ranger, had accompanied Brock that day. The following letter that I'd sent to Brock a couple of months after the 3 May incident with Dilloway puts things in context:

> Dear Trooper Brock, I was encouraged by our discussion on 7/1, especially since we were able to get an opinion then from assistant prosecutor Keith McMillan by speakerphone. I'd been researching WV theft law and consulting with other legal experts since then so Mr. Detch didn't have to do so much of the "legwork" in preparing his letter to you. Then got a letter from him the other day where he confirmed what I'd learned: the elements for felony theft/grand larceny in WV, according to § 61 appear to be met in this case. Theft is "grand larceny" in West Virginia if the value of the goods or services stolen is $1,000 or more. It shouldn't be difficult to prove the value of our stolen property easily exceeds $1,000 in actual damages. I've answered Mr. Detch's letter, adding what he had asked of me. He'll be using some of that in his letter to you. Stolen laptop ($500+) and stolen Alliance files/records aside, Dilloway looted/stole lots of books and CDs, which you and Sgt Barlow witnessed were in his quarters. Like with a shoplifter, just because we recovered the stolen items doesn't mean they weren't stolen. I'll be sending a list of all those items we recovered and their retail prices to Mr. Detch to help make our grand larceny case.

The extensive spreadsheets prepared by DeCourcy, itemizing what Dilloway had stolen or ruined, amounted to over $10,000 retail value. Even considering wholesale value at one half or one third of that figure, the amount stolen or ruined by the thief and SPLC informant far exceeded the threshold for grand theft, a felony in the state of West Virginia. I personally handed a CD with the extensive spreadsheets, prepared by DeCourcy, to both Trooper Brock and to Assistant County Prosecutor Keith McMillion. McMillion suggested to me that I should sue SPLC civilly. He also said to his boss, County Prosecutor Eugene Simmons, in my presence that perhaps a grand jury could be convened in the possible felony grand theft matter. Like I told Brock, I was encouraged. Regardless, Simmons' Office decided not to prosecute Dilloway's theft for some reason. A conviction for theft by the SPLC's paid informant would certainly have helped with a civil case against the "law center." It had already been established by Detch that I am "unpopular." Perhaps that was why the matter was dropped?

Enemies Inside the Gate

As I wrote above, those who are diagnosed with Asperger's Syndrome reportedly have trouble getting along with others, but their intelligence is usually higher than average and they often have good memories. DeCourcy seemed smart and well read at first, but in time would show herself as a motor-mouthed, paranoiac conspiracy nut. This can be seen in some of her court documents that will be provided. One of her favorite subjects involves federal agencies and what they will do to dissidents. It seemed unusual to me that Garland Corse had changed her birth name to Garland DeCourcy and that she insisted on being called "Gael Dempsey" when she came to West Virginia. She gave some explanation for using that alias and we went along with it — since she claimed that some people in Virginia were "after her." At the time I had no idea what a pathological liar this woman is. DeCourcy can juggle dozens of lies, and has a real talent for recalling, revising, and explaining them. But that can only fool some of the people she tells lies to, and only for some of the time. What a twisted talent, when it's so much better to simply tell the truth! That talent did serve her well, however, with the easily deceived Pocahontas court officers — or did it?

At first, my new independent contractor DeCourcy demonstrated enthusiasm and a willingness to be helpful to me and our Alliance. She appeared to be industrious and had office skills. I was surprised to discover that she apparently had an unusual aptitude for the law and for computers. As I realized later, it wasn't accidental. It was a part of her skill set as a scam artist and practiced abuser of the judicial process. But she is not nearly as smart as she thinks she is.

Soon it became nearly impossible for me to communicate with the chatterbox. She would talk over me, interrupt and change the subject to another of her conspiracy theories. The toadette assured me early on after she was living in DeMarais's house that he "had the FBI on speed dial." She had seen it. I said, "Prove it!" She couldn't. Her badmouthing of DeMarais didn't make much sense because he was being so kind to her, letting her stay in his home rent-free. At the same time, this troublemaker was badmouthing *me* to *him*, trying to get him as her ally against me. I came to discover, from interviewing a couple of DeCourcy's former landlords in Virginia, that this is her nature, her *modus operandi*. One called her a "sociopath," the other a "psychopath." They both independently told me in telephone interviews that she is a hoarder, that she thinks she is a lawyer, and that she took them to court constantly and appealed every adverse decision. That same sorry pattern continued in West Virginia. The Pocahontas Court Club, however, was not interested in her former pattern of behavior; playing the innocent victim, abusing the judicial process, filing requests for protection, etc.

I needed somebody else on The Land again, or at least someone between her and me. Someone I could communicate with reasonably. A trustworthy, easy going Alliance member, Michael Oljaca, had been very helpful to me transcribing old *National Vanguard* magazine articles for a blog that I had gotten a computer-savvy friend, Hadding Scott, to set up. This was prior to my becoming Alliance chairman. We called it the *William Luther Pierce Legacy* blog, and once these valuable articles were digitized — more than 100 of them — they could be shared with others and spread around on the Internet. I started floating the idea to Michael that I could use him in West Virginia should he be so inclined. He lived in New York City and the idea of relocating to help the Alliance intrigued him.

Michael arrived on The Land on 27 July, just in time for an NA board of directors' meeting that I conducted on 1 August, 2015 — the meeting where he was added as a fourth director (me as President/Treasurer, Jan Cartwright as Secretary, and John McLaughlin as Vice President). Jan had been a director with Gliebe and I retained her for board continuity. John was added the day I became Chairman, 24 October, 2014, because I'd known him as a long-time member, and trusted him to be loyal. Both appointments, John and Michael, turned into disappointments later.

DeCourcy tried to attend the closed board meeting and I told her to leave since she was not on the board. This angered her, but I didn't care. She needed to butt out. We did not need her so-called "expertise." More about her corporate "expertise" later. The toadette was already claiming to people that she was Secretary of the Cosmotheist Community Church (CCC), which was a lie. I, as Trustee of the CCC, had named Meredith Kellar to be Secretary. This really irked Ms. DeCrazy.

I was living in Tennessee, visiting West Virginia once or twice a month, so could not fully evaluate how Michael was doing in his new position as "Chief of Staff" — the title I gave to him to make it clear to DeCourcy that he, not she, was my primary contact there. I communicated with him regularly by phone and email, but could soon tell that DeCourcy was interfering. She started badmouthing Michael to Lana as lazy and worthless, and I'm sure she made him feel that way. He was like a fish out of water, coming from a lifetime in New York City to a remote West Virginia mountainside. Mike was proficient with the Internet, but he didn't know how to do anything that is necessary for remote country living. A big-city boy, Mike had no driver's license, had never put gasoline in a vehicle, nor had he ever even used a garden hose — so he was understandably dependent on DeCourcy.

At one point, all of a sudden, DeCourcy's assessment of Michael became more positive. She generally preferred being in charge, and up to that point I'd figured that her badmouthing of Michael was done in hopes that I'd fire him like I'd done with Dilloway. The slick toadette probably changed her tune about Michael, figuring she could continue to control him — and that if I got rid of him, the next person I brought in as Chief of Staff might not be as docile, might put her in her place. She began praising Michael and reporting how well they worked together. Something was up. By September I could tell whenever I talked with Michael on the phone that DeCourcy was on an extension phone. Unacceptable! I could also tell by the rambling, manic, wordy writing style that my emails to Michael were being answered by her. Beyond ridiculous!

I don't know exactly when or how precisely she turned good guy Michael Oljaca into her ally against me, but the alleged "battery" incident of 30 September 2015, with him as her "witness," was premeditated and mutinous, though I did not realize Michael's disloyalty until later. It should be said that all four of the puppets that DeCourcy succeeded in turning against me were lonely single men who were easily manipulated by a seductive female, experienced in using her womanly wiles and injured innocence routine to get them to do what she wanted them to do. Her twisted method of using outrageous lies against me to win men to her side became clear to me about a week after the contrived "assault." That's when at least three, probably four Alliance members received long letters badmouthing me to no end. To my Accuser's disappointment three members turned these letters over to me, giving up her game. They did not fall for her BS. The fourth member who I think received one of these long emails was John McLaughlin. He did not tell me he had received it, but never acted quite the same toward me afterwards. It was nearly three months later when I became aware conclusively that he had become another of my accuser's lonely puppets against me, and another two months until I removed both Michael Oljaca and John McLaughlin from their NA directorships and positions.

The war was on. DeCourcy's working with the NARRG co-plaintiffs in their civil suit against us, her criminal complaints against me and my arrests as a result; her poison pen letters to NA members, illegal *ex parte* letters to the judges; filing false reports to courts, state agencies and law enforcement; her collaboration with the SPLC, and her quarter-million-word anti-Williams blog were formidable obstacles to overcome, but I was confident it would all crash like the flimsy house of cards, built on lies, that it was. Smashing that house of cards is a purpose of this book, since the courts did not turn the tables on her as they should have, nor did they give me legal relief from her.

The reader can see my trial testimony, describing the alleged "battery" incident at p. 045, but also there is a much shorter, one-page statement I gave to Trooper Brock on 31 October 2015, p. 024, when I had to move toadette's junk from the Alliance's red barn that she had declared "was given to" her "as her own." The so-called "battery" was just me holding my right arm out to halt the charging, screaming DeCrazy. Her chin was touched by the crook between my thumb and forefinger for a couple of seconds. That was no battery. There had been no battery whatsoever, but the scheming "victim" managed to convince the court that there had been. This was during the height of the #MeToo mania, which was a factor.

How in the world could I have been taken in so by this "poor, persecuted, abused victim"?

As I write this book, DeCourcy has been a fugitive for two years. I said earlier that my private investigator (PI) acquaintance tried to trace her location once she went on the lam. She was untraceable. Thanks to the Internet there are plenty of effective "people finder" Web sites these days. A PI has more sophisticated tools available to him for locating a fugitive than do the people-finder sites, but mine reported that my accuser uses many aliases, at least two Social Security numbers, and is "deliberately elusive." If one attempts to find Garland DeCourcy under that name or under her birth name Garland Corse, or any of her three married names, through people-finder services, the results come back "zero" (0) — as if she never existed. There is little doubt that fraudster DeCourcy has contacted each of these locator services with a demand for them to remove any information about her, or else!

DeCourcy had been traceable through those sites back in 2015-2016 when I tried to find information about her that would be useful in my defense against her "battery" complaint. That's how I had found her former landlords that she had sued.

Even though I received no satisfaction with my appeals, the fact that I made my accuser run away and go into hiding, and likely to have changed her name again in fear that she will be held accountable for her crimes, gives me a small measure of satisfaction. West Virginia's unethical court system aside, Garlic DeCrazy's frenzied participation in at least three failed coup attempts to wrest control of the National Alliance from me and its lawful board is what counts in the final analysis. Nobody ever said being National Alliance Chairman would be easy.

DeCourcy's infamous anti-Williams blog was created by her in the beginning of 2016. See here: https://willwilliamssplcpartnerandsnitch. wordpress.com/. After my seeing in 2020 all the evidence of her being in hiding, I suspected that she would remove her blog even though she never mentioned her own name on it. The toadette would use her co-plotters' real names while writing about "the real NA board Directors" as she called them, and refers to herself as "that woman" when mentioning the alleged assault of her by me. From DeCourcy's almost unreadable blog posts Lana and I, as well as our friends, "learned" a lot of outrageous things about ourselves, showing how far the fantasies of a sick person can go. The reader may still be able to go there and judge for himself her mental state. She writes that she was William Pierce's relative and that she visited "Bill" and his wife on several occasions. Her crazy fantasies go on and on, like her easily refuted claim that she was the Alliance's "first female state organizer." Her blog totals several hundred thousand words, and that's not counting her other numerous associated letters and court filings. It looks like the obsessed toadette never slept. Here is a vainglorious example of DeCourcy's opinion of herself, pretending someone else wrote it:

This woman is very noble & virtuous.

Who writes like that about herself?

This seven-page article of hers about my guilty verdict in Pocahontas County Magistrate Court, which included this choice quote and her projected story of my "obsession" with her, was submitted as defense evidence by me to the circuit court and the West Virginia Supreme Court of Appeals (WVSCA). (E1b) Since I first printed it out in the beginning of 2016, De-Courcy increased the size of that article by at least 100%. My accuser's true motive — the coup attempt — is clearly seen in that article, along with obvious signs of her mental disorder and of her malignant obsession with me. Had any of the Pocahontas County court officers, including my own defense attorney, or the WVSCA justices, cared to look at just a fraction of the abundant evidence of her lying and craziness, justice might possibly have been served. They all failed in their duties, unless their duty was to convict and label me a "woman beater."

I was wondering, while my appeal to the WVSCA was being processed, why DeCourcy would leave her incriminating blog online to be viewed. Could it be because her valid "donate" button is still there? I suspect that's the reason. Who would donate anything to the nutball fugitive besides the SPLC? The two aforementioned former landlords of DeCourcy in Virginia who I located and interviewed both referred to her independently as a "crazy woman." They both said that she is known in Virginia as "crazy Garland" — no last name is necessary. Why could the various court officers of the 11th Judicial District of WV, whose job it is to recognize reasonable doubt about a criminal complaint, not come to the same conclusion about my accuser in the face of such overwhelming evidence during *four years* of interaction with her? I say it is because the fix was in. They did not want to hear anything about her lying or her pattern of behavior. The entire focus was on her claim that I battered her on 30 September, 2015 and nothing else.

DeCourcy's greediness and twisted ambitions were the actual motivation for her criminal complaints against me. She clearly wanted to be in charge of the National Alliance and its assets. By the age of 50 (born in 1964) she had not achieved anything of real merit besides bringing her three children into the world. Her oldest son was, and probably still is, in prison in Texas, and she likely had lost custody of her younger two children by the time she came to West Virginia. When she first arrived on The Land, she told me that she would need to go to Virginia to see her two by then teenaged children about once a month. However, to my knowledge, during the entire six months of her employment, she did not go to Virginia even once and her children certainly never visited their derelict mom in West Virginia.

In her harebrained plot to take charge of the Alliance, DeCourcy needed a team of Williams-haters as well as cooperation from law enforcement and the courts. Her first puppet was her landlord/roommate Bob DeMarais, the second Mike Oljaca, and the third John McLaughlin (JMc).

JMc was a long term friend of mine, an Illinois farmer I'd first met in 1991. He would call me often wanting to know what was up and was very helpful financially in the beginning, pledging $500 per month for the first two and a half years of my taking over as Chairman. He helped me to move the two large libraries I purchased from Erich Gliebe. Like DeMarais, JMc, in his 60s and naive, had never been married so was vulnerable to DeCourcy's female connivances. He listened to her legalese double-talk and actually told me he thought she was "knowledgeable." He turned from being a trusted friend, whose previous claim to fame was breaking the arrogant Puerto Rican Jew Geraldo Rivera's nose in a fist fight, to becoming putty in her hands. John McLaughlin was essential to her devious coup scheme since I'd appointed him to be Vice President of the National Alliance board back in October 2014. He would be her puppet, and she would be (ahem!) the brains.

Like I said previously, it was during the first week or two in October 2015 when JMc began to fall under DeCourcy's detestable influence. When the other Alliance members who she had been contacting during that period — badmouthing me, telling them how I "had to go," etc. — let me know, forwarding the poison-pen emails she had sent to them, John did not notify me of what she was doing. I am certain she sent those emails to him too. He kept up the pretense that he was loyal to me for another couple of months until I discovered conclusively his treachery as a co-conspirator against the Alliance. It was a clear breach of his fiduciary duty to be working *against* the Alliance while serving as a director and officer of it.

I am positive now that the 30 September "battery" incident had been preplanned with Michael Oljaca (her second puppet/co-conspirator and my "toad number four"), but that DeCourcy had not thought it all the way through. That's why she didn't say a word about any assault to Fred Streed that morning right after I had allegedly "attempted a homicide" of her. Fred, with his wife Marta, had come from their home in Oregon where Fred is from, and they stayed on the property for about a week. During that week we closed on the previously mentioned sale of their cabin to me and Lana. The Streeds stayed in the gatehouse which had been their residence for years prior to and after Dr. Pierce's death, until being run off by my foolish predecessor Erich Gliebe. They had planned to retire there and live in the cabin Fred built for them on the four acres he purchased from Pierce. Fred's plainspoken, credible recollection of the events and of those associated with the alleged "battery" of 30 September can be read in his sworn affidavit at p. 015.

Also, unfortunately for DeCourcy, Lana happened to call our West Virginia office within 30 minutes after the alleged 30 September "assault," and had a perfectly normal discussion with my accuser about work, about me, and about Oljaca for at least 20 minutes. One would expect that "the victim of an attempted homicide" wouldn't be able to speak normally, make several jokes and laugh that soon after being "beaten up" by a large man. With several mentions of her "batterer" — me — during the conversation, the "victim" would have been expected to share her recent shocking experience with Lana. Nevertheless, to quote Lana's testimony at the trial, she "didn't notice any difference whatsoever in [DeCourcy's] mood, in [DeCourcy's] voice, compared to [our] regular conversations." Toadette DeCourcy's testimony at trial, describing the alleged incident can be read at p. 039. It is something to behold.

I called Lana's telephone conversation unfortunate for DeCourcy. It would have been had a West Virginia law enforcement investigator or prosecutor's investigator ever actually scrutinized my accuser's claim, her veracity, or even interviewed me just once.

Lana was a defense witness at trial and her email to DeCourcy of 5 October 2015, E1b, with the description of the alleged incident as exculpatory evidence, was submitted to both the Circuit Court and the WVSCA. As I said above, any evidence in my favor was conveniently ignored by Pocahontas court officers, including my defense attorney Laura Finch, time and again. The reader, when presented with the same evidence, may conclude that this entire judicial process was a farce and should never have seen the inside of a courtroom.

When I arrived home in Tennessee the night of 30 September, 2015, I told Lana about the altercation I'd had with the toadette that morning and had decided that she had to be let go, and that I did not see how I could continue working with her. Lana tried to find some excuses for DeCourcy such as "she used to be a good worker," or "maybe it was her time of the month," or whatever, in an attempt to help her. On Lana's insistence I gave her my permission to notify "Gael Dempsey" that I'd had enough of her craziness and insubordination, but would give her one more chance. I could not fire DeCrazy immediately since there was the active $2 million civil suit with the NARRG co-plaintiffs and we had been subpoenaed to provide them with numerous documents in a harassing discovery process. Oljaca wasn't able to gather the documents for discovery by himself. I had to figure out during October how to get rid of the toadette, which wasn't going to be easy since she was living with fellow conspirator DeMarais and he had a right of way through our gate to get to his home. They would have access to Alliance property while I was in Tennessee 200 miles away — an untenable situation, again!

After the alleged incident, I never said one word to my accuser for nearly three years — not one! — until my trial for "battery," when she heard me speak. Lana communicated with her about necessary work by email only. After receiving Lana's email on 5 October 2015 DeCourcy was trying hard to show us what a diligent worker she was and how much we needed her. But at the same time, all during October, she was scheming her convoluted plot to oust me as Alliance Chairman.

Like I mentioned, she had some contact information for fewer than a half dozen National Alliance members, and she contacted them all. That included our Media Director Kevin Strom and his fiancée Meredith Kellar. She called them twice on 30 September with wildly contradictory stories about the alleged incident. Unfortunately, while informing me about De-Courcy's attempt to "flip" him against me in October, Kevin neglected to tell me in time about her two contradictory calls of 30 September. John Mc-Laughlin and Michael Oljaca were the two who were influenced the most by my accuser's lies, promising them that they would take over leadership of the Alliance once I was gone. All they had to do was go along with her scheme.

After satisfying the harassing discovery demand required by NARRG's subpoena, and while learning what DeCrazy had been doing behind my back, there was no way I could tolerate having such a treacherous enemy on The Land any longer. I had no idea at the time the extent to which both DeMarais and Oljaca, and John McLaughlin, had become my determined enemies. Right after meeting the deadline for discovery, Oljaca left for New York City due to a supposed family emergency. He did not notify me of his unscheduled departure and left his set of the keys to all buildings with his "new boss," DeCourcy, instead of with me — the person who had hired him and had been paying his salary.

National Alliance supporter Chris Larsen had once met DeCourcy on The Land, so was one of the lucky few who had received one of her long unhinged letters on 7 October 2015. (E3a) Larsen forwarded the crazy document to me, but then, thinking he could reason with her, talked to her by phone as an intermediary, a go-between, since I refused to talk to her at that point. Chris was trying to convince the so-called "victim" that after the "attempted homicide" accusation it would not be possible for her to keep working with me and the Alliance. He relayed to her that I was willing to pay her a reasonable severance. Larsen called us to give what he thought was good news: DeCourcy had agreed to move away if I paid her $3,000. Lana and I were pleased that Larsen had managed a successful mediation, but it didn't last long. A couple of days later Larsen called my accuser again, but this time, Chris told me and Lana, she had demanded $50,000 to leave. Lana told the court about this episode in her testimony at my trial but the judge apparently did not believe her. Judge Dent believed only what crazy DeCourcy said or wrote. That included the above-mentioned, *more than*

100 pages in three illegal, private *ex parte* communications, since sealed by Dent behind my back — and over my objections to Finch that the *ex parte* communications were exculpatory and necessary exhibits for my defense.

DeCourcy had been an independent contractor, and I prepared a Termination of Contract document, E1b, by which she would receive $3,000 in three steps if she returned all keys and left our property without causing any problem. Along with the contract Lana sent two $500 money orders by certified mail as the first payment. The fired toadette signed for our certified letter on 29 October and cashed the two tracked money orders the next day. As was explained to me on 31 October by West Virginia State Trooper Damon Brock, her cashing those money orders meant acceptance of the contract's conditions whether she had signed and dated it or not.

Despite cashing the money orders DeCourcy had no intention of following those conditions. Lana sent my accuser emails with the information that, for her convenience, I had reserved a 26-foot U-Haul truck and a large storage unit for moving her property out of the NA's barn where it had been stored. Securing the truck and storage was not easy since there was a shortage at that time, but I managed it. In a friendly, reasonable manner DeCourcy was advised to move all her significant belongings from the Alliance's red barn by herself, and that if she chose not to do that I would use the truck and move her stuff myself to the reserved storage unit. As was usual, the toadette never responded to either our emails or to the certified letter with the Termination of Contract that she signed for. It became clear that moving her out would not take place without another contentious incident requiring law enforcement supervision, as with Dilloway's removal five months earlier.

I was going to have to move DeCourcy's belongings to the storage unit myself. As I said, I had no idea that Oljaca and McLaughlin were working against me at that point. Oljaca was still in New York City and when I asked JMc, who lived in Illinois, to help me with the move, he gave some excuse. Since I needed significant help to load and unload the large U-Haul truck, but was very short on time, I put together a team of four including myself, Lana, a son of my Tennessee friend, Ray, and the National Alliance Media Director's fiancée Meredith Kellar who was living in Pennsylvania.

The four of us arrived at the Marlinton Motor Inn in the afternoon of 30 October, so we'd be rested for the following day's Halloween adventure moving the hostile woman's junk. Prior to traveling to West Virginia for that purpose I called the Pocahontas County Magistrate Court, explaining my situation with the woman, asking for a law enforcement escort to help us take care of everything peacefully. Both magistrates, Cynthia Broce-Kelley and Carrie Wilfong, spoke with me cordially. I sensed a measure of support from the county officials for the revolting predicament I'd found myself in with Garlic DeCrazy.

Earlier that month my attorney friend Tim Kalamaros had searched Virginia court records and provided to me the very interesting one-page document cover sheet for the 2014 172-page *pro se* request by DeCourcy for protection from three Virginia judges and a guardian. (p. 014) I provided the Magistrate Court with the copy of that document. Though this showed the pattern of DeCourcy's filing of outrageous requests for protection, it was never considered at all by any court officer, not even my defense attorneys. An ethical and engaged defense attorney would have been all over just this one bit of evidence, and used it to impugn my accuser, not to mention using all the other evidence that showed her repeated abuse of the judicial process.

On 31 October, 2015, I arranged for State Trooper Brock and Sheriff's Deputy Kelly to meet us at the U-Haul truck rental establishment in Buckeye after we had an early breakfast. Buckeye is seven miles from The Land. They met with us all right, but said they couldn't provide escort because it was a "civil matter." So off we went with the U-Haul truck and my pickup, ready for the confrontation with Garlic DeCrazy.

I backed the 26-foot U-Haul up to the big barn door, then walked the 60 feet or so to DeMarais's house that is adjacent, across a creek bed, and knocked on his downstairs door a couple of times. There was no answer, though I could hear them stirring inside. This was my final effort to have DeCourcy remove her junk from our property, having provided a truck to do so and a place to secure it afterward.

After intentionally ignoring this opportunity, my accuser would later claim that I had committed "larceny" by "stealing" "tens of thousands of dollars worth" of her property.

After giving the troublemaker her last chance, I pulled out my bolt cutters and cut my lock off of the National Alliance barn door. The four of us began carefully loading everything that looked like it was DeCourcy's, and, just to be sure, more that wasn't, into the truck. Meanwhile the cowering toadette called the cops on DeMarais's phone, complaining of "breaking and entering," "grand theft," and whatever else she could think of. Officers Brock and Kelly then arrived on the scene — because now it was no longer considered a civil matter, but criminal. It should have been a criminal matter all along with what she was trying to pull. I had arrived with a "No Trespass Notice" for the fired toadette. I had procured it at the Sheriff's office late the previous afternoon as an additional measure to establish that she had been terminated, had no standing in our organization, and no right to be on the property. Brock advised me that, to be safe, I should affix it to DeCourcy's drivers' side window rather than to DeMarais's house door. I did that while Brock was still on the scene.

When they arrived the officers soon went in DeMarais's house and interviewed DeCourcy, got her to make a statement that Brock transcribed and she signed, saying she agreed with what he had written. That is when my accuser told him of my supposed 30 September "battery" of her a month earlier. So Brock took down the *very first* written statement from her about that alleged month-old "battery." (p. 022) There is revealing contradictory testimony by DeCourcy and Brock about these statements to him in the transcript of my trial. The fraudster lied under oath that Brock prepared that statement out of her presence, then coerced her to sign it without giving her an opportunity to read it. (p. 051) Brock denied that, and he did not lie. (p. 057) He had no reason to lie. He followed police procedure. Yet Judge Dent accepted DeCourcy's lie over Senior West Virginia State Trooper Brock's truthful testimony.

After meeting with DeCourcy, Brock came back outside and took a short statement from me, written up by him, signed by me, about the alleged "battery" that I had just learned about from him for the first time. (p. 024) I knew her claim was just more nonsense and my short statement reflects that. I was never once interviewed by either law enforcement or the two prosecutors' offices subsequent to that. Not once, even though I had requested to be interviewed by them.

Brock also had me write out another statement in my own hand, this one to address the "breaking and entering" and "grand theft" nonsense. That statement was three pages long; I never saw that again, though I had requested a copy of it numerous times from Brock and from the Sheriff who later took over the "investigation" of the "battery." Surely it would have been in the investigative file. Both of my defense attorneys requested a copy of this statement to prepare for my defense — or at least they told me they had — but it was never provided. I explained to Brock that DeCourcy had been terminated, showed him the Termination of Contract that I'd sent to her, plus the postal receipt showing she had signed for the certified letter on 29 October, and tracking evidence showing she had cashed the two $500 money orders the next day, 30 October, that were enclosed with the letter and Termination of Contract. He saw that I clearly had told her in writing that if she did not move her junk from Alliance property by the end of October then I would move it for her. That's when Brock informed me that her cashing the $1,000 in two money orders is considered acceptance of the agreement whether she signed it or not.

There was no arrest of me or any in my crew, and we continued to pack the truck until it was completely full, then put covered bins of her remaining junk in my pickup truck to finish up. The cops left, and as soon as they were out of our gate, DeCourcy and DeMarais came out of his house for the first time, careful to stay a few feet away on his property. DeMarais took pictures of us, ostensibly for the SPLC, while DeCourcy screamed at me like a crazed lunatic. "Put my stuff back!" "This is grand theft!" and the most revealing threat: "I can call Jim Ring. I can call Heidi Beirich!" Law enforcement wouldn't help her, so she would get Jim Ring to do so — he being the ringleader of NARRG's $2 million lawsuit against the Alliance, and who would tell of the "grand theft" on the anti-Williams NARRG blog. Of course her SPLC pal Heidi Beirich would help her like she had helped Dilloway. Anything to destroy the Alliance and have me incarcerated.

By the time we had emptied our barn of everything that could have been hers, and more, onto the trucks, put a new lock on the barn door and the No Trespass Notice on her car, it was already late afternoon and we had a 20-mile trip to the rented storage unit near Lewisburg, West Virginia. As it turned out I needed to rent a second storage unit because the hoarder had too much junk for one. It was already dark when we finished unloading and putting locks on her units. The keys to those two locks were left on the seat of DeMarais's truck by me with a note the following day. That night we turned in the U-Haul truck. I had already paid for that, and then I also paid $120 in advance, enough for the full month of November, for the two storage units to Mr. McCutcheon, owner of AAA Storage, who was present during the unloading. It had been a very long Halloween Day, but our mission had been accomplished. We didn't know it, but more, much more, was to come.

Mr. McCutcheon called me a few days later, alarmed by what he thought was a document from the Pocahontas Court, but actually was from De-Courcy pretending to be a Court Officer, complaining about the "theft of her property" that was being stored in his facility. (E3b) The "wannabe lawyer" described herself in this document in the third person as my "victim." I assured Mr. McCutcheon that storage of the "victim's" junk in units #12 and #8 was legitimate and that law enforcement had been on site as her property was being loaded on the U-Haul for removal. We joked about a "woman scorned," since the unsigned letter from DeCourcy sounded to him like it had something to do with a nasty divorce, or something. I suppose that Mr. McCutcheon allowed the toadette to change the locks on the units, fearing I still had access to her junk. I did not.

Knowing DeCourcy by then, there is little doubt that she attempted to file her complaint about my "larceny" of her stuff, though, if so, I was never informed of any such claim and inquiries I made to law enforcement and the courts yielded nothing of any claim by her for that. In numerous online postings of my accuser she described how I and my team had "stolen tens of thousands of dollars worth" of her property. Actually, as I said above, even when I believed some items in the red barn belonged to the Alliance, they were given to DeCrazy just to be safe. Of course, Brock and

Kelly who followed policy and did not arrest me for the alleged "larceny" as DeCourcy had demanded, were later badmouthed in her writings for not going along with her commands. In fact every Pocahontas County Court and law enforcement officer who displeased her, even clerks and the bailiff, were smeared by the sociopath in the worst possible words. This woman, as the reader will eventually conclude, does not take "no" for an answer.

I have some understanding for this woman's crazy behavior, having researched symptoms of her self-admitted Asperger's disorder. But it was a mystery to me how old and wise Bob DeMarais who had earned a PhD in business management, and who I considered to be relatively normal, would collude and spend thousands of dollars to finance the daffy coup attempt by such an obviously mentally unhealthy woman. He might not like my writing about him in this book, but all I am writing was already discussed on a couple of public Internet forums (Stormfront and VNN). DeMarais and Dilloway had used their given names on those forums, but DeCourcy, as usual, would create tens of fake accounts to write the nastiest lies about me and about anyone who helped me. One fake name she often used for example was "Lucent Noble" on https://vnnforum.com/showthread.php?t=235917&page=129, where she was actively promoting her off-the-wall "truth telling" blog with that handy "donate" button. She likely thought that her insane "diarrhea of the mouth," directed at me and the NA, would get somebody's attention and financial support, if only from her NARRG and SPLC allies. Remember, the real "hate group," the SPLC, has a half billion dollar tax-exempt war chest with which to destroy the National Alliance and others it targets, so might easily support her campaign through an untraceable dummy account.

DeCourcy and her newest "puppet" — number four, Randolph Dilloway — became Internet tag-team allies against their shared enemy: yours truly. Sad Sack demonstrated his own obsessive "diarrhea of the mouth" against me for months on the disreputable anti-NA VNN Forum. The toadette tried hard on forums and on her own "hate Willy" blog to hide that she was Lucent Noble, and, during my circuit court trial, lied with a straight face, under oath, that she was just one of many who might occasionally prepare some article drafts for the blog. However her not-so-bright new partner, Dilloway, blew Lucent Noble's cover on VNN with this:

> Just took a look over at Lucent Noble's website and it looks like she is fixing the problem. Haven't talked to her since May 3rd, 201[5], when Will lost his mind and attacked me for the second time. The problem could be that she is new to website design and fucked up some of my comments.

Besides some of the fake names that "crazy Garland" created to comment on her own blog, Dilloway, as usual, was proudly placing his comments on that blog with his real name. He had been promoting DeCourcy and DeMarais on the VNN Forum until even its anti-National Alliance owner Alex Linder, who years earlier had been an Alliance member but who hated my guts, posted:

> I'm banning Dilloway. No more lying. Get along with people here or leave.

Though Dilloway is apparently still "permabanned" from Linder's VNN, his numerous pathetic posts are all still there. Let me comment on just one short quote from Randolph:

> A shout out to Willie: My mother is not interested in any whiny letters from you bitching and moaning that I ruined your life.

Readers can see for themselves my "whiny letter" to Dilloway's mother that son Randy characterized to VNN suckers as "threatening." (E2h) That letter included the title to the 4x4 Nissan truck, as well as the part quoted earlier from DeCourcy's 3 May, 2015 email to Lana, in which the crazy woman smeared poor Randy in the worst possible words. (E2d) I figured Mrs. Dilloway might warn her son to stay clear of the woman who had shown such visceral hatred for him.

In a secure 17-year marriage to Lana who knows me well, and as National Alliance Chairman, Dilloway's public lies about what a horrible person I am don't bother me at all — I am used to such attacks by detractors. They "come with the territory," as they say. By my sending the truck title to Dilloway through his mom, I was doing the right thing and had hoped Sad Sack would then put his negative experience with me and the Alliance behind him and move on with his new life, having "left the movement" with help from the SPLC.

Betrayal by a Long-time Friend and Comrade

Now comes toad number five, my former friend John McLaughlin, who I had trusted enough to appoint as a director and Vice President of the Alliance's board the day I was appointed Chairman. I never thought that he could have become so corrupted by anyone, but I underestimated just how sinister and Svengali-like DeCourcy's determined manipulation of him could be. John certainly sounded like a fool when he told me, before I removed him from his offices, "She's knowledgeable."

In hindsight I traced JMc's gradual, step-by-step betrayal back to early October 2015, after the alleged 30 September "battery." My accuser had called our Media Director Kevin Strom almost immediately upon receiving Lana's email of 5 October 2015, then she sent out an unhinged email with the subject line "statements/report" to Chris Larsen on 7 October. Probably the same email was Cc'd to JMc. To repeat, Larsen and the others DeCourcy had contacted, forwarded her long email smears to me, as they should, but JMc did not. The crazy attachments to that "statements/report" email can be seen as E3a. Here's an unedited snippet from the body of that bizarre email:

> [R]eport is our statements... Board has many things in it that can be used to protect the corporations...corp is things the help via VA corp commission w boards & some mental health info... With VA another word/term used for someone deemed mentally incompetent & assigned Fiduciary, is Supervised Direct Payment (SDP). then name immediately given to FBI to place on lists.

The only difference in this quote and what's in her original gibberish are the ellipsis points (…) to denote a space between the short lines in the original, for brevity here. DeCourcy's psychospeak sounds to me and to most reasonable people like the writer is either delirious, drunk, or downright crazy. What do you think? John McLaughlin, who DeCrazy said "held two university degrees" in her attempt to promote him as "the real NA President," considered the writer of this nonsense to be "knowledgeable."

The main attachment to that crazy email was a so-called "AFFIDAVIT" in which DeCourcy described the alleged "battery" in increasingly fantastic terms, and making up new stories of my supposed mental illness and violence out of thin air. The point of her spending untold hours to create the "statements/report" email was to prove to the handful of Alliance members she could reach that I am not the legitimate National Alliance Chairman and should not be even allowed to be a member due to my supposed mental illness. I eventually learned that a symptom of Asperger's can be the sufferer of the disorder projecting her own shortcomings onto others. My unhinged accuser had been demonstrating this symptom on a regular basis.

Another Asperger's symptom DeCourcy showed was being delusional. To remind the reader, she declared in writing that "the red barn was given her as her own." By whom? That was crazy, but not the worst example.

Another of her "statements/reports" was titled "Boards." In it my hallucinating accuser DeCrazy created her own version of an organizational chart of directors/officers for our three organizations: the National Alliance, National Vanguard Books, and the Cosmotheist Community Church. She listed herself as "Cosmotheist Community Church Secretary" in that chart, and "appointed" her allies to all executive and board positions.

There were so many examples of my accuser acting delusional. For example, she insisted in numerous documents and letters and even in sworn testimony, under oath at trial, that "MacLaughlin and Oljaca are the true NA Board." Could she have actually believed that when there is such an abundance of evidence to the contrary? Could she convince others of it?

Poor John McLaughlin did not, it seems, notice the contradictions and abnormalities in DeCourcy's writing and line of patter. Or did he have ambitions to become National Alliance Chairman as she told him he would?

That was doubtful, as he would never be able to manage the job (unless she was close by, perhaps, to guide him with all of her supposed "knowledge"). Again, I trusted John since he seemed to be an honest and an idealistic member. He had been so generous and helpful whenever I would call on him. He called me often, always wanting to know "what was going on," and I would share what I thought he needed to know as NA Vice President. For some reason, and for what it is worth, he told me several times that I reminded him of the actor Tom Berenger, I think from his role in the movie *Platoon*. We had a reasonably good relationship.

Once corrupted by DeCourcy, however, John would foolishly sign a seemingly endless number of documents and official letters that had obviously been written by her and must have been hardly, if at all, reviewed by him. Some official-looking letters and documents that she wrote were "electronically signed" by John and by Michael Oljaca. I suspect neither had read them at all. Signing legal papers in other's names — and claiming to be an officer of a corporation when you are not — is fraud. When the document is an affidavit, as she claimed for some of them, it's an especially egregious crime. Michael admitted he had not seen such documents; John never admitted such. John rarely wrote anything. From the stream-of-consciousness writing style, it's obvious that DeCourcy wrote practically everything that ever had John McLaughlin's signature at the bottom. The only document that he wrote and signed was his short, semi-literate recommendation for sentencing of me to the Magistrate Court on 20 April, 2016. (p. 035) He had been coached by her even in that, but botched it.

Even for people who have some knowledge of the law and of the cases in which she and I were both the litigants, it is nearly impossible to read and follow DeCrazy's long, repetitive "diarrhea of the mouth" scribblings. John was a life-long farmer with a 560-acre farm. His skill set did not include writing or really much outside of what it took to run a good-sized farm. He had been around the White nationalist movement in one way or another since the 1980s, and was an Alliance member in the early 1990s when we first met up in West Virginia. His lack of experience and his naivete when dealing with such a devious, twisted character as DeCourcy led to some terribly unwise decisions by him that eventually, literally, cost him his life. More about that later.

After moving the hoarder DeCrazy's junk to the storage room, I knew that someone I could trust had to be found to reside on the property all the time, even after Ray and I changed the locks to all of the buildings. Ray and Lana went back to Tennessee that Halloween night, and I stayed on the Land for a few days until relieved by Meredith Kellar, who I came back to relieve again on 12 November. JMc, who, unbeknownst to me, had already been working against me by then, relieved me on about 16 November, accompanied by his friend Jacob Watson. Though I had instructed John to have absolutely no contact with DeCourcy while he was holding down the fort, I now have little doubt that he did the exact opposite, allowing the toadette to bend his ear and finish her process of corrupting him. The reader can imagine the difficulty of managing the Alliance's property during this hectic month of November 2015, with me in Tennessee and my determined enemies literally inside our property's gate. John soon told me he had to go back to Illinois earlier than planned. I couldn't return to West Virginia on such short notice, so, having no one else, Lana traveled to WV to relieve him.

When Lana arrived on The Land on 19 November, she called me soon after arriving, telling me that she was feeling ill-at-ease based on the way John looked at her during the few minutes they had talked before he left for Illinois. After John's sneaky betrayal was conclusively confirmed in January, Lana recalled that uneasy feeling she had had, and it made sense to her: It was his malevolence, and what she remembered as an impudent gloat in his eyes, as if he had "discovered" that he would soon become the new National Alliance Chairman. Silly John.

A few days later, Lana was relieved, this time by Meredith again. I travelled to West Virginia a couple of days later and did some work with Meredith, but soon had to return home again. Michael Oljaca was finally able to return to West Virginia from New York City right after spending Thanksgiving Day with his family there. While Michael had been in New York, I had regular conversations with him by both email and telephone. I was careful to explain to him that DeCourcy had turned into a bitter enemy of the Alliance and of me, that she was tricky and extremely dangerous. In the beginning, the first third of November, he was trying to defend DeCourcy to me, repeating like a robot, "We are a good team. We work well together." I asked him directly if he and Garland were in a sexual relationship. After a long pause Michael answered, "No, but I find her attractive." Uh huh! A few days later I had another talk with Michael about work and he volunteered without my even asking, "I must confess, 'Gael' and I were sleeping together." Lana was on our extension phone when he told me that. What a revolting predicament!

It is notable that poor Michael was 20 years younger than his manipulative and much more experienced lover, "Gael." Michael was a good young man, an idealistic Alliance member who I believed I could convince that he had been lied to and manipulated by DeCourcy. He told me his loyalty was to the Alliance and to me as Chairman and that he would do as I told him to do. He was told that DeCourcy had been served with a No Trespass Notice. She was permitted only to travel through our gate, across DeMarais's right of way and directly to his home — but was allowed nowhere else on our property. As with John McLaughlin, my instructions to Oljaca when he arrived back to our property to relieve Meredith, was that he was to have absolutely no interaction with either DeMarais or DeCourcy. I told Michael not to communicate with DeCourcy "even if she appeared at the gatehouse door with nothing on but a towel" and he assured me that he wouldn't. But docile Michael Oljaca was to be another pawn in my accuser's coup scheme — one she was willing to sleep with to "bring him around."

It took about three weeks until it became clear to me that Oljaca had been less than honest, assuring me that he was on my side and had not exchanged words or interacted with DeCourcy. We would see how things actually were with Michael soon enough.

My First and Second Arrests

As I wrote in the Introduction, what I am going to concentrate on in this narrative is my wrongful conviction, what led to it, and, actually, the entire Pocahontas Magistrate and Circuit Courts' years-long experience with "unpopular" me. So much of my role in this protracted legal adventure has been documented and can be read in my two extensive Briefs in the appendices to this book. So, beginning with this chapter, I will just briefly describe events that led to court actions, and what is in the appeal briefs and the appendices, including trial transcripts, and eventually in the four complaints against three court officers that will be available at the accompanying pocahontasshowtrial.com Web site for further reading. Those complaints express grievances by me that were not allowed to be admitted during my trial and make for interesting reading from my point of view. The *pro se* briefs also express my dissatisfaction and objections to the conduct of the officers of West Virginia's 11th Judicial District better than if an appellate attorney had prepared them, so are also interesting, especially to a student of the law and/or ethics. I wrote as a man defending himself, saying things no attorney could ever say. I've only clarified scrivener's errors that were in my original briefs for my reader's convenience.

There are additional specific details in my four complaints against three Pocahontas County court officers, especially against Greenbrier County Prosecuting Attorney Patrick I. Via, the special prosecutor who was brought in to prosecute my Circuit Court appeal. There was not space enough in appeal briefs to expand on Via's "prosecutorial misconduct" so his bias against me is explored more at length in my complaint against him to the Office of Disciplinary Counsel.

If I am mentioning a document that can only be seen in my extended Appendix of Record (AoR), E1b, submitted with my appeal, the reader should see the Table of Contents at the beginning of the AoR PDF file to find the correct page number. In the beginning of PDFs for my complaints, the reader can find the full list of documents that the JIC and ODC were provided with. Most of those documents can be seen in the AoR, so only exhibits that cannot be found there are presented in the complaints folders.

So, lets move on to my legal "horror movie."

To remind the reader, in 2014, a few months prior to DeCourcy's fleeing Virginia for West Virginia, she filed a 172-page complaint requesting temporary restraining orders (TROs) *against three Virginia judges* and a guardian. At the end of November, 2015, I received a copy of the "temporary safety order" that had been filed by DeCourcy in Pocahontas County. As is usual with her, it contained numerous pages describing the alleged "battery" that supposedly had happened two months earlier, portraying me as a dangerous, violent monster. My accuser, a fired former employee, was requesting protection from me, her former employer, and demanded that I must be ordered to stay 1,000 feet from the National Alliance property for two years — property that I was charged with managing as Chairman of National Alliance, Inc., and President and Treasurer of the NA's board of directors. There is nothing "temporary" about a two-year order!

She was granted this ridiculous, unquestioned TRO without a hearing or any law enforcement having interviewed me beyond the short statement I'd given to State Trooper Brock on 31 October. The investigation had been taken away from him and turned over to the Pocahontas Sheriff for some reason, and no one from his office ever bothered to interview me to this day — so there never has been a proper investigation of the alleged "battery."

I had no experience whatsoever with TRO requests, unlike my accuser. I expected that, with due process, a TRO would be granted or denied only *after* an investigation and a hearing of facts. But that was not the case. A hearing was scheduled for 17 December, 2015, but, unknown to me, the order was considered to be in effect even before the hearing.

I arrived on our property on 15 December, 2015, planning on attending my hearing on the morning of the 17th, "loaded for bear" against the bogus charge of battery. I also needed to do some work there, and catch up with Michael about what was expected of him. He had been doing good work for our Media Director Kevin Strom, remotely, during this period by putting up articles for him at our online magazine *National Vanguard*. When I arrived on the 15th, and during the morning and early afternoon of the 16th, Mike was standoffish. He was playing his role of a loyal employee and ally, but had trouble looking me in the eye.

My accuser was happy to see naive me coming onto our property, which was less than 60 feet from where she resided with DeMarais. The trap was set. DeCourcy certainly knew that her TRO request was in effect, even though I didn't. She was patient and slick. She waited for the right time to spring her trap. The toadette had to make sure that on the morning of 17 December I would be in jail and she would get her two-year TRO request granted by default. She knew that the standard cash bond amount was $1,000 and that it would be highly unlikely for me to have that much cash on me if arrested. My accuser was aware that I did not have anybody in Pocahontas County who could help me with the $1,000 cash, especially if she called law enforcement late in the afternoon of 16 December. Lana could have brought the required bond on a four-hour drive from Tennessee had my accuser called law enforcement (LE) when I arrived on the 15th or early on the 16th. So DeCourcy waited until late afternoon on the 16th, figuring I'd be hauled off to jail, and unavailable for my hearing the next morning. Her criminal complaint about the "battery" was actually filed on 2 December 2015, *more than two months* after the day I held out my arm and it barely touched her chin when she charged at me, screaming provocatively. Oljaca was with her on 2 December and gave the sheriff's deputy "investigator" his written statement as well. Both written statements can be seen at p. 025-027.

Michael Oljaca dared to pretend to me on 15 and 16 December that everything on The Land was under control and that he had kept his word to me that he would not communicate with DeCourcy or DeMarais while I was back in Tennessee. Needless to say when I arrived on the 15th I had no idea that a criminal complaint had been filed against me on 2 December.

To repeat, the first time I heard about "an assault" was on 31 October, 2015, from Trooper Brock. DeCourcy gave her first written statement about what she called the "attempted homicide" on her for the first time over a month after it supposedly happened. The reader can see her ridiculous answers in her written statement to Brock of 31 October. (p. 023) DeCourcy had spoken to law enforcement about the "incident" before, but refused to cooperate since, she said, she was "scared that Mr. Williams would get even" and "kill us." Her answer to "Why do you want to file a complaint now?" was, "'Cause I am still afraid of him. Afraid for my life." Sure you are. Why don't you just leave?

Despite having been "brutally beaten up" by me — allegedly — and having serious injuries all over her body, according to her court testimony and in other documents, DeCourcy *never once visited any doctor* regarding her "injuries" and only took photos — photos that were selfies taken from different angles of very slight pink spots (like flea bites, or more likely, pinch marks) on her neck.

I am sure that many if not most Pocahontas law enforcement and court officers saw that they were dealing with a serious fibber who has mental problems. However, they either were "just doing their jobs," or preferred to avoid DeCourcy's badmouthing of them, or just maybe they thought they finally had an "unpopular figure," the National Alliance Chairman, in their clutches. Who knows?

My first arrest happened mid-afternoon on 16 December, 2015. I had been working on the computer in the National Alliance office building and then made a quick trip over to our warehouse, less than 200 yards from the office. No one was in the office building and I took Oljaca with me to get the two cases of books that a bookseller had ordered, and for which they had already paid ($960). I needed to ship them those two cases of books. Michael and I were headed back to the office building a few minutes later when I saw some commotion down by our entrance gate, so took a detour toward the gate to see what was going on. It was a couple of sheriff's vehicles with at least four deputies. It was an ambush, pre-planned by DeCourcy, who had called 911 from DeMarais's house, which is less than 60 feet from the warehouse, when she saw that I was out of the building. I was arrested and taken nearly 80 miles away to the Tygart Valley Regional Jail, which is actually a modern prison, when I couldn't pay the $1,000 cash bond. My accuser's plan to have me jailed had worked to perfection.

DeCourcy not only called law enforcement on the days of my two arrests, but she did exactly what she was threatening to do on 31 October: "I can call Jim Ring. I can call Heidi Beirich." I feel sure that my first arrest was preplanned with Miss Heidi of the SPLC. And I am positive that immediately after this first arrest, my accuser called Beirich to report that I'd been arrested and jailed. Beirich then called the Pocahontas County sheriff to confirm my arrest and shortly thereafter, called Lana at our home in Tennessee, to tell her I'd been arrested. As Lana recalls, Miss Heidi's voice was abnormally sweet. She had likely planned trying to convince Lana to "run from" me — just as she had earlier tried to get Kevin's fiancée to "run from" him. Lana told Beirich, "I know who you are. Never call here again!" I learned this from Lana during my "one phone call" from the Pocahontas jail, while the Sheriff and the deputies were standing nearby, observing. I asked the Sheriff if he had called the SPLC and he said, "No, they called me." The Chief Deputy blurted out, "This is harassment!" while I was still on the phone with Lana. The SPLC put up their article the same day, 16 December, titled "William White Williams, Chairman of the Neo-Nazi National Alliance, Arrested for Battery": https://www.splcenter.org/hate-watch/2015/12/16/william-white-williams-chairman-neo-nazi-national-alliance-arrested-battery. Two days later, 18 December, appeared another, much more extensive article with my mugshot, titled "Chaos and Cops at the Compound," with the sub-title "Neo-Nazi National Alliance Chairman William White Williams arrested in alleged battery of female employee." https://www.splcenter.org/hatewatch/2015/12/18/chaos-and-cops-compound. Toadette DeCourcy was quite pleased with herself, as was Miss Heidi, who must have been sure that this was the death blow to the NA that the SPLC hate group had been working toward for years.

My vindictive accuser also kept her promise to call Jim Ring. She probably did this early on, in November. The NARRG losers, who supposedly despised the SPLC, were gloating in articles on their pathetic blog about me, sourced directly from SPLC smears or from their new ally, DeCourcy.

Right after speaking with me, and right before I was hauled off to the regional jail, Lana scrambled and got hold of Paul Detch, the Lewisburg attorney mentioned earlier, who had been paid by me to try and have Dilloway arrested for grand theft and to put pressure on the SPLC for receiving and publishing stolen documents. Detch appeared on my behalf the next morning at my scheduled hearing and secured a continuance for the hearing until 21 December. He also paid the $1,000 cash bond so I could be released from jail. DeCrazy was beside herself that morning, 17 December, when Detch introduced himself to her as my attorney in the hallway outside the courtroom. He told me she wagged her finger in his face and blurted out, "How dare you interfere in my personal affairs!" Detch described the encounter to me as seeing "pure evil" in her eyes — like he'd only seen in one other person, a multiple murderer he'd met several years before. So, my accuser's scheme was temporarily foiled; she didn't get her default ruling. Lana had gotten me lawyered up and granted a continuance.

It took me until dark, around six hours, to hitchhike the 80 or so miles from the Tygart Valley Jail back to my truck that had been parked outside the gate. (The two cases of books had been stolen from my truck. I had to reimburse the bookseller the $960 from my personal funds.) It was the 17th of December, and a cold rain poured down all day. At 68 years old I had no glasses and no money ($100 cash from my wallet had been confiscated by my jailers and replaced with some useless plastic card). I had no hat, no coat, and was wearing tennis shoes. An entire chapter would be needed to fully cover the incredible ordeal I went through that day. Those interested in that can find details about this and other legal "hells" Miss DeCrazy created for me with the cooperation of the courts. It's in my previously unpublished correspondence with the above-named Jaynell Graham, writer of the *Pocahontas Times* report of my first arrest. (p. 010)

I want to briefly point out that a citizen of Pocahontas County, even an entirely innocent one like me, can be treated like cattle — no investigation, no hearing, thrown in a distant jail, and then cast out in the middle of nowhere regardless of the citizen's age, the season, or the weather. A vindictive female in this #MeToo era can make an accusation, pinch her neck, take selfies, recruit some friends to be her "witnesses," file a TRO request, and it can lead to real, and very arbitrary, injustice, with zero due process before the injustice takes place.

If Ms. Graham cared about the truth, she would have published another article after receiving the truthful details of my legal struggle with De-Courcy & Co. in my February 2016 correspondence with her. The *Pocahontas Times* did not honor my right of reply to correct inaccuracies. Graham, or more likely her paper's publisher, was not interested in reporting anything, however true, from an "unpopular figure," a dreaded "Neo-Nazi." Ms. Graham admitted being "acquainted with [DeMarais] for many years." DeMarais, as my accuser's co-conspirator, likely introduced his roommate DeCourcy and her "strangulation" story to his old friend Jaynell and advised her to take notice of the SPLC smears of me and the National Alliance. Ms. Graham did not care about my concern that her *Times* article had tainted my jury pool, and gave the weak and bizarre excuse that most of her article's readers were probably from other counties. Recall that Jaynell Graham was the person who, soon after her "strangulation" article, said to Laura Finch, "That Will Williams is dangerous." Later my probation officer, Robert Tooze, told me that 90% of Pocahontas County residents consider the National Alliance as "Nazi." No wonder, when the county's newspaper of record is as biased as is Ms. Graham. I changed two jury trials to bench trials, arguably my biggest mistake, as I realized later.

Lana and I traveled to West Virginia for that rescheduled 21 December TRO request hearing, staying at the Marlinton Motor Inn rather than risking another arrest by staying on our NA property. After all her drama and lying, shaking and sobbing, DeCourcy's request for protection from me was denied by the impartial Magistrate Cynthia Broce-Kelley who could see through my Accuser's phony claim, if others could not. I should not have been jailed. Broce-Kelley would rightly rule in my favor again, in yet another matter between DeCourcy and me that came up later.

In case of the possible denial of her bogus request, that same morning, 17 December, DeCourcy had already sweet-talked her boyfriend Michael Oljaca into requesting *another* bogus TRO against me. The paperwork granting that unquestioned TRO — again, automatic, no hearing, no interview with the accused — was nonchalantly "served" to me on the desk between me and Paul Detch, without a word and unnoticed among all of our other papers while we were waiting for Magistrate Broce-Kelley to call her court to order. We had no idea that another TRO had been granted against me as a result of Oljaca's bogus claim. And *again*, I was ordered to stay 1,000 feet from Alliance property for *two years*. Magistrate Broce-Kelley and the County Prosecutor Simmons, both also unaware of DeCourcy's latest TRO ploy, told me and Detch that we could go out to the National Alliance property and get the keys to our gatehouse from Oljaca who had been squatting there illegally. Magistrate Broce-Kelley had ordered Oljaca orally in open court to return my keys. We thought the ridiculous matter had been resolved. It would have been nice if I had a transcript of that magistrate court session so toadie number four could be cited for contempt of a direct court order, but unfortunately there was no recording.

Lana and I, my attorney Detch, and Ray, the son of my friend who we had brought with us from Tennessee, then went out to our property about eight miles from the courthouse. Oljaca wasn't there as he had assured the magistrate that he would be.

Detch, with Lana, walked the 200 yards or so from the gatehouse over to DeMarais's house and asked him if Oljaca was there so we could get the keys. I am reasonably sure that both Oljaca and DeCourcy were there with DeMarais, but DeMarais pretended not to know where they were. Both Oljaca and DeMarais had been DeCourcy's "witnesses" at the TRO hearing that morning — more like cozened co-conspirators — so all three had likely traveled to and from the courthouse in Marlinton in the same car.

Side note: When Lana and I entered the main floor of the courthouse on the morning of 21 December, the first person we met was DeMarais who had given us his sweetest "How are you?" smile like we were best friends. This confirmed what a two-faced snake DeMarais is.

So Oljaca was hiding from us in defiance of Broce-Kelley's order. When he failed to return our keys we went ahead and drilled out the front and back door locks to our gatehouse, and installed new locks. I fashioned a makeshift placard from available materials and taped it to the front door, making it clear to traitor Oljaca that his services were no longer needed by the National Alliance. He had officially been fired by me. At this point Mr. Detch, who had arrived in his own car, thinking we had the situation under control, left and returned to his law office in Lewisburg.

What happened then was surreal. DeCourcy made DeMarais call 911 once again to report that I was in violation of her *new* TRO — the one I had no knowledge of — and demanded that I be arrested again. Two Pocahontas County Sheriff's Deputies soon arrived and approached the gatehouse porch with orders from "upstairs" to arrest me. I couldn't believe my ears, but looked over at the access road 60 or 70 feet away to observe DeCourcy, DeMarais, and Oljaca standing outside of DeMarais's truck with cameras in hand to record my arrest (my second in five days) for unwittingly violating this second TRO — this one nominally from my accuser's lover/puppet. I cooperated with the deputies who were just doing as they had been instructed. One of them, Deputy Shinaberry, blurted out, "This is stupid!"

The other deputy was no more pleased to arrest me than was Shinaberry. He was considerate enough to ask me to step behind his squad car to hand-cuff me, so the coup-plotters, snapping their goddamned cameras, could not get a photo of me being cuffed. A good photo of me being arrested again would no doubt have been sent to Heidi Beirich for yet another lovely SPLC hit piece, like "National Alliance Chairman/Pocahontas Strangler Arrested Twice in One Week." Photos of my arrests were published on De-Crazy's endless anti-Williams blog as "proof" of alleged criminality.

That day Lana and I had $1,000 in cash with us, thinking we were prepared just in case I was somehow arrested again — however the cash bond had been doubled to $2,000 for this arrest. Magistrate Wilfong was considerate enough to bend the rules a bit and allow Lana to write a personal check for the additional $1,000 so I wouldn't be hauled off the the regional jail again. I was released that time on bond.

I was not the only one who was arrested on The Land on 21 December. DeCrazy kept calling law enforcement that day for who knows what and was told to cease and desist. Finally Deputy Shinaberry came out and arrested her for defying that order. I only discovered this important fact nearly a year later from reading DeCourcy's first illegal *ex parte* letter to Circuit Court Judge Jennifer Dent. Paul Detch, and later Laura Finch, had withheld this highly relevant fact about my accuser from me for some reason. Here is the quote from my petitioner's brief to the WVSCA:

> On the date of Defendant's second arrest within five days at the hands of Accuser and her co-conspirators, on 21 December, 2015, Accuser was arrested that same day by Pocahontas County Sheriff's Deputy B.A. Shinaberry, 16-M38M-00002, for her 'falsely reporting an emergency incident' under § 61-6-20(3) of WV Code, about Defendant's arrest that afternoon. In Deputy Shinaberry's Criminal Complaint of Defendant DeCourcy he states that Accuser "had no business [being involved] in the incident [of Defendant's arrest for violating her boyfriend's TRO], called in by her roommate [DeMarais]." She had orchestrated Defendant's false arrest for "breaking and entering" NA property. Then had been told to cease calling 911 about this, but kept calling anyway, so was arrested.

I wanted Deputy Shinaberry to be a defense witness for me at my Circuit Court appeal but my "defense" counsel Finch ignored my instruction to have him subpoenaed.

Another complaint filed by Deputy Shinaberry that day was for De-Courcy's failure to register her car despite being told to do so about one month earlier. I have no doubt that "crazy Garland" had been bothering law enforcement with her pesky calls on a regular basis. To quote one of the three *ex parte* letters by DeCourcy to Judge Dent:

> WE have also been told to NOT call 911 unless one of us is shot & bleeding. [original in bold]

Law enforcement personnel probably assumed that arresting this nutcase and filing complaints against her would somehow curb her harassment of me and of them. They had no idea who they were dealing with. Unfortunately, both complaints against DeCourcy were soon dismissed after she lawyered up, with DeMarias paying the lawyer for her. I don't know the details, but suppose that it was just easier for the Pocahontas court officers to let this troublemaker off the hook, regarding these as minor offenses. I suppose that it was also just as easy for the WVSCA to ignore the nearly 60 pages of my two briefs, plus the 373-page appendix record that provided indisputable proof of my accuser's being a professional scam artist — not to mention evidence of the Pocahontas court officers' support of her fraud by violating their Ethical Rules, the West Virginia Code, and my Constitutional rights. The justices' unanimous affirmation of the lower circuit court's guilty verdict of me was simply easier for them than doing their job. Easier!

Charges Against Me by My Accuser's Boyfriend

Just in case I won against her first TRO, DeCourcy had Oljaca file his bogus TRO request. An incredible story of me assaulting Mike was needed for that and was conjured up by the toadette and her paramour from thin air. The hearing for Oljaca's TRO request was held on 3 February 2016. As I described it in the email to Ms. Graham, p. 010, Magistrate Wilfong did not deny this request, but reduced it to the very minimum "no contact" order for 90 days, not two years, and not 1,000 feet. I think she did that to preclude DeCourcy from appealing a denial of the TRO as she does with every adverse ruling. Slick DeCourcy, experienced in abuse of the judicial process, always appeals and always asks for a fee waiver.

Flashback: Lana, who had to be outside the courtroom on 21 December when the toadette's first TRO request was denied, told me that DeCourcy was the first one out of the courtroom and her face expressed shock at the "injustice" of the magistrate's ruling. The toadette could not believe that her BS story, her theatrical shaking and sobbing, did not work with Magistrate Broce-Kelley. The scammer who doesn't take no for an answer could not accept such "injustice."

Almost immediately my accuser created a close to 5,000-word description of the hearing, badmouthing me, Detch, and Broce-Kelley, that was attached to her appeal to circuit court. DeCourcy wrote that I, and even my attorney Paul Detch, had both regularly "growled and grunted" during the entire hearing of 21 December, intentionally terrorizing the poor "victim" and her innocent witnesses. Those who want a good laugh are welcome to see this "masterpiece" at E3c. I'm pleased that this document wasn't sealed like other exculpatory documents later were. But having it as evidence was all for naught in Pocahontas County court.

I am not sure why the appeal was scheduled to be in the Greenbrier County Courthouse, but DeCourcy was a no-show for that hearing — on 19 January 2016 — and Judge James J. Rowe dismissed her appeal. More details will follow about Judge Rowe and his clerk at the time, Laura Finch, who would eventually become my defense attorney in Pocahontas County when Paul Detch had had enough of DeCourcy's circus.

On 21 December, 2015, I was arrested for having unwittingly violated Oljaca's TRO request by changing the Alliance's locks on the gatehouse where he had been squatting illegally even long after required to vacate. At my request, the hearing for that criminal case was scheduled on the same day as my sentencing hearing, 25 April 2016. The sentencing was for being found guilty of the misdemeanor battery of Garlic DeCrazy by Magistrate Carrie Wilfong on 28 March 2016. More about Miss Carrie later.

After my conviction on that day, Detch provided me with the four part civil complaint filed against me and our three National Alliance corporate entities by Michel Oljaca. (E4a) That was prepared by Lewisburg attorney Kristopher Faerber, the shady fellow who had been hired by DeCourcy's roommate and co-conspirator, DeMarais, who admitted he paid Faerber $4,000 for this. I was told Faerber didn't even have an office, but had a very smart telephone. The silly harassment suit claimed several bogus and goofball "damages" caused by me against Faerber's squatting plaintiff when I changed the locks on the NA's gatehouse — excuse me, "on his residence" — among which was his "lost of enjoyment of life, wages and employment opportunities" as well as "reasonable enjoyment of future housing." Seriously. Only "crazy Garland" could come up with such incredible "damages." This is the kind of lawfare crap I had to keep defending myself and the National Alliance against.

This BS civil case lasted from the end of March through 3 November 2016 when it was finally dismissed with prejudice. Poor Michael Oljaca had no idea what his middle-aged Svengali paramour was getting him into. On 4 September 2016, out of the blue I suddenly received a desperate email from Michael stating that 2016 has been the worst year of his life and that he regretted filing the civil suit. He added:

> I've had high anxiety and heart palpitations at the thought of returning [to the gatehouse]... my health has been rapidly deteriorating... i [sic] have been unable to sleep or eat since returning back [to NYC]. Since being in the gatehouse I've lost 40 pounds and have not been able to eat well at all. I've been depressed and have barely been able to function living there.

Michael's 4 September email, P028, ended with this:

> If Bob [DeMarais] and Gael [Dempsey, DeCourcy's alias] find out i have written to you, there is no telling what they would want to do to me, i shudder when i think about that... I want to drop this lawsuit.

Though Michael had implored me to keep this email secret, he for some reason shared my affable response to it with "Gael." I'll expound on this later.

The reader can see at E9b how, when the determined special prosecutor, who DeCourcy had in her pocket, was not having much luck with prosecuting the alleged "battery," switched to prosecuting me for "witness tampering" simply because I answered Mike's email. (P029) No kidding.

Let us return to my criminal case (is your head spinning yet with all these cases?) of unwittingly violating Oljaca's TRO. Paul Detch was to be a defense witness in my trial since he had been there when I had allegedly "broke and entered" the NA's gate house. He would testify that both Magistrate Broce-Kelly and County Prosecutor Simmons had told us that morning that we could go out and take possession of the residence. He could not be both my attorney and my defense witness, so he recommended Laura Finch, who had just opened her own private law practice in Marlinton after serving as Judge James Rowe's clerk in Lewisburg. Lana and I met Laura for the first time on 24 April 2016 in her new office across from the Pocahontas County courthouse and liked her at first. She presented as sincerely nice and professional. Having clerked for Judge Rowe she was already familiar with my case.

Our first appearance together on 25 April was at our hearing for my alleged violation of Oljaca's TRO. It was Finch's very first case in Pocahontas County Magistrate Court. On a legal pad between us I quietly wrote down some questions that she might want to ask my crazy, lying accuser who was making an absolute fool of herself as Oljaca's witness. The piece of paper on which I wrote these questions for her to ask was preserved by me, included herein as P034. Finch was excited that my accuser was exhibiting such insane behavior before the magistrate and wrote on the note back to me, "This is going to be fun." Yes, it was fun for Laura Finch, all right — until, that is, after three and a half years of my paying her by then thousands of dollars to defend me against DeCrazy & Co., I became an "unpopular figure" in her eyes and suddenly unworthy of representation.

Even though my Circuit Court hearings, trial, sentencing, etc. in the large courtroom upstairs were open to the public, no hearings in Magistrate Court were open. Lana wanted to be in the relatively tiny magistrate's courtroom to observe, but no one was allowed in but the judge, the litigants, special guests, and any witnesses who were sequestered until called to testify.

For the trial on Oljaca's TRO violation, Lana, as well as Paul Detch, had been waiting in the hall as witnesses. Neither was ever called to testify. This time Magistrate Wilfong, perhaps not inebriated or medicated (I'll explain), saw through witness DeCourcy's "bad actress" performance.

As soon as Wilfong found me not guilty of violating Oljaca's, really De-

Courcy's, TRO, Lana watched and heard DeCourcy yelling at Assistant County Prosecutor Keith McMillion out in the hall, demanding to appeal the "unjust" ruling. McMillion explained to the "wannabe lawyer" that Oljaca was not the defendant: "Look, lady, this matter is closed; there will be no appeal." To repeat: "crazy Garland" doesn't take "no" for an answer. Lana could see by McMillion's response how annoyed he was with DeCourcy. However, just a short time later that day was the sentencing hearing for my guilty verdict for "battery" of her before the same magistrate, Carrie Wilfong, and McMillion's job in that sentencing hearing was to punish me for declining his plea offer.

After my first arrest the afternoon of 16 December, Oljaca called the NA's Media Director Kevin Strom to inform him about it. Kevin said he could hear DeCourcy whispering to Michael, advising him how to answer Kevin's questions — telling him, for example, to say "I am a witness. I have to tell the truth." Poor Michael was absolutely under the spell of his manipulative paramour which would eventually cost him his health and his sanity as revealed in his above-mentioned email to me of 4 September, 2016. Another reminder: DeCourcy had attempted to turn Strom against me in early October 2015 while Oljaca was, again, on the extension phone with her.

Since DeCourcy's boyfriend Oljaca had been revealed as another NA enemy and was squatting illegally in the Alliance's gatehouse, on the morning of 21 December, prior to my second arrest that day, I filed an "unlawful occupation" complaint against Oljaca. Here is the part of my email, p. 010, to the *Pocahontas Times* reporter, Jaynell Graham, explaining the situation:

> My unlawful occupation claim against Oljaca, Corse's boyfriend, was granted [by Wilfong]. He must vacate my house by 23 February. Additionally, Oljaca was also ordered to turn over all of my keys to all of my buildings, my gate, my truck, my two post office boxes, by the same date, 23 February, or he will be arrested like he and Corse had me arrested for violating temporary protection orders. All three conspirators, Corse, Oljaca and Bob DeMarais, who is Corse's landlord — the man you were chatting with in the hallway — have been served with No Trespassing Notices. They can come through my gate and across my property because they have "tenant's rights" to use DeMarais's right of way (at least DeMarais and Corse do. Oljaca is not DeMarais's tenant, yet).

Of course, Oljaca (actually DeCourcy), as usual, appealed his/her "unjust" ruling on Wilfong's unlawful occupation case on some spurious technicality, once again with her shady attorney Faerber. The legal struggle on that lasted several months until Oljaca left for New York City in the summer of 2016. I finally was able to get another Alliance member, David Pringle and his fiancée Laura Lee to come live on the property. They arrived on Easter Day and stayed in the office building until Oljaca could finally be removed from the gatehouse, where they'd later live. David is a big, tough character and didn't take any crap off of DeCourcy or her co-conspirators.

Pringle is no toad, and he did his job of taking care of The Land in my absence. I could again freely come on the property I was charged with managing — without being arrested — once the "no contact" order obtained by Oljaca had expired. You can read how Pringle supposedly "traumatized" poor Michael between Easter of 2016 and the end of summer in Michael's 4 September email. (p. 028)

Things had halfway returned to normal with Pringle there, keeping the coup-plotters in check. He arranged a nice gathering and cookout, commemorating the birthday of Dr. William Pierce on 11 September, 2016. Lana and I and a dozen or so Alliance members attended, as did some local helpers David had recruited to help him with chores, along with their children. On that day, due to Oljaca's long absence, I instructed David to change the locks on the gatehouse once again, and move into the gatehouse with Laura Lee to finally put an end Michael's unlawful occupation.

More Criminal Fraud from Wannabe Lawyer DeCrazy

Garlic DeCrazy had so far used every ruse in her dirty book of judicial tricks — both civil and criminal — to try and take over National Alliance assets, but she was not finished. On 9 February, 2016 she emailed a 10-page letter (E5a) to the National Alliance's corporate attorney Andrew Bury, who I had hired to defend the Alliance against the NARRG co-plaintiff's $2 million suit. On 8 April, 2016, DeCourcy made JMc mail a 3-page letter to NARRG's attorney Dan Harvill. (E5b) The letter to Bury was allegedly "electronically signed" by "the true NA directors," meaning McLaughlin and Oljaca, as well as by the self-styled "Executive Administrative Assistant and Legal Liaison," Ms. Garland DeCourcy. DeCrazy cajoled John McLaughlin to affix his signature to her bizarre, "confidential" letter to NARRG's attorney Dan Harvill.

Anyone reading these unhinged letters, clearly written by the female who had claimed I criminally "battered" her, can see that they should have been introduced by my defense counsel as exonerative exhibits that would impeach DeCourcy's credibility, not to mention that they revealed her motive, her real reason for claiming I had "battered" her: her attempts to use the courts (abusing the judicial process) to unseat me as National Alliance Chairman and take over the organization and its assets. Whenever I told Laura Finch to use these and similar documents by DeCourcy as defense exhibits, she would say, "They are irrelevant."

These letters are *not* irrelevant, and a responsible defense attorney would have been all over them, and it would have "been fun" for him to expose the lying claimant, as Finch had written early on when she witnessed first hand how crazy DeCourcy is. Andy Bury saw that her letter to him was insane and ignored it. However, he did call John McLaughlin once after receiving "his" letter since McLaughlin was still a Director and National Alliance Vice President in February. John McLaughlin could not explain anything in the letter to Andy. Andy told me after that call that John "sounded confused" and had advised him to speak with DeCourcy. Andy Bury never contacted John again, realizing this was all a scam by my accuser. He never had any contact with DeCourcy whatsoever, though she claimed (that is, lied) later, in writing, that she had communicated with him on several occasions. That's what liars do: tell lies, even when the lies they tell can be easily refuted.

Yet more relevant developments transpired during the period between the February letter to Bury and the April letter to NARRG attorney Harvill, but let's get to the Harvill letter briefly. A quote from DeCourcy to Harvill in that letter:

> I feel that there is a lot of over come [sic] with the NARRG standing. I feel if 2 "Directors" join the case this may help greatly. THERE is your standing. It has been our intent all along to add DeCourcy as a Director.

It's hard to believe that my accuser was stupid enough to put that in writing, but she did. Our main defense against the NARRG co-plaintiffs was that they did not have standing and it was on that point that we finally prevailed, with *NARRG vs. NA* being dismissed with prejudice on 29 July, 2016. As a matter of ethics, plaintiff's attorney Harvill forwarded this crazy letter to National Alliance attorney Bury, then Bury forwarded it to me. I respect attorney/client privilege, but can share these "confidential" letters with the reader because the person who wrote them was not a client of either attorney, but a criminal fraudster who colluded with at least three court officers of West Virginia's 11th Judicial District to have me wrongfully convicted and imprisoned as a "woman beater."

As I said in the Introduction, this book is my reckoning, my settling of accounts with them.

The scheming toadette's attempt to use two Virginia corporate attorneys to assist her in her coup attempt didn't bring her success. However, even that setback did not deter her. At the end of July 2016, just one week before everyone already knew that NARRG's bogus case against us in Virginia was to be finally dismissed, poor John McLaughlin, under his "Legal Liaison's" influence and control, was cajoled by her to foolishly file *his own* civil lawsuit in Virginia, *John McLaughlin vs. National Alliance*. His lawsuit was almost word-for-word the same as NARRG's fraudulent claim. Harvill didn't represent McLaughlin but convinced an old friend and former associate

Douglas Bywater to represent John against us. Big mistake!

On 10 March, 2016, after learning the extent of Michael Oljaca's and John McLaughlin's treason against the National Alliance, I had mailed certified letters to both of them, removing them from the National Alliance's board of directors, without explanation, as I am entitled to do under Article IV-D of the National Alliance's bylaws that had been written by the Alliance's Founder, Dr. William Pierce, when he was Chairman and President of the board:

> The President shall appoint and remove Officers of the Board of Directors at his/her pleasure.

As I said, DeCrazy considered herself to be a lawyer, a "corporate law expert" no less, so she felt qualified to declare that official National Alliance corporate documents signed by the corporation's legitimate President didn't hold any validity to her. She kept insisting that I was not the legitimate, duly-appointed President and that her illegally concocted new versions of the NA's Articles of Incorporation and By-Laws were the "true"ones. I am pretty sure that DeCourcy tried to have Michael Oljaca be a co-plaintiff with John McLaughlin, but he had likely had enough of DeCourcy's "nightmare," as he called it by then, and would have declined. He left for New York in the summer of 2016 due to the serious health problems he had suffered, thanks to his strumpet coach "Gael Dempsey" and her depraved scam. Michael would send me his desperate email of 4 September, 2016 in an attempt to free himself from her claws.

Living a life of ceaseless lying is normal for a professional scam artist like DeCourcy, but that life turned out to be too much for two of her puppets — Mike Oljaca and John McLaughlin. Hapless John managed to endure a little longer in my accuser's scam before he had had enough and met a tragic end that was much worse than was poor Michael's.

Now, a few more examples of DeCrazy's limitless nuttiness.

• In January 2016 she had her hapless stooge John McLaughlin sign and submit a fraudulent National Alliance Annual Report (AR) to the Secretary of State of the Commonwealth of Virginia, Corporate Division, that overrode the Annual Report that I had filed as NA President. Although that was a criminal act, we did not file charges and simply reported it and overrode his fraudulent AR. In about a year she put John's home address on her blog and on VNN Forum, encouraging people to send donations directly to him to "save the Alliance."

• In January 2017 DeCrazy went even further. On 17 January she had John sign and mail to me and others silly "Cease and Desist" letters that were obviously written by her. David Pringle received one of these letters as did the fellow who had been helping Pringle cut trees on our property. There were unofficial "no trespassing" notices attached to those letters prohibiting me and Lana, Pringle, and his fiancee from stepping on our Alliance property in West Virginia. John McLaughlin was named in these letters as "Director/Owner/Custodian/Trustee" of the National Alliance, the Cosmotheist Community Church, and National Vanguard Books, Inc., His home address and home phone number were on the letterhead, represented his personal home as being the "official NA headquarters." (E5c) These "official looking" letters were mailed ten months after McLaughlin had already been duly removed as a National Alliance director and officer by me, in accordance with our by-laws.

• More than that — on 30 January DeCrazy, pretending to be McLaughlin, sent an official request (E5d) to the NA's corporate Registered Agent (RA) in Virginia, InCorp, demanding:

> Fully remove the prior contact person William White Williams II, who is no longer authorized per our 2015 Board meeting and subsequent expiration. Mr. Williams has no rights or authority to act for, nor does he hold any roles or title within the Corporation that grant him such... Please send me the information so I may establish my online account with INCORP to conduct business. Please delete the account associated with the prior person who is no longer authorized to conduct such matters for the Corporation.

• DeCrazy even went so far as to have a *lien lis pendens* filed against the Alliance in Pocahontas County, by a non-existent law firm no less, which later held up the sale of some unneeded Alliance acreage to a neighbor until we could get it lifted (which cost us an additional $10,000 more or less in legal expenses).

It's always good to have an attentive, professional defense attorney who will go to the wall for his client and demonstrate initiative. After plaintiff McLaughlin filed his claim against us in July 2016, Mr. Bury found grounds to countersue Mr. McLaughlin for breach of his fiduciary duty while still our Vice President. This counterclaim, *NA vs. McLaughlin*, was perfected and filed in the same Hanover, Virginia, court where McLaughlin had filed his lawsuit against us. Thankfully, knowing we had excellent grounds for the counterclaim and that the Alliance could not afford to keep paying for his firms's legal services on an hourly basis, Andy took on this counterclaim on a contingency fee basis. Poor John apparently could not imagine such a turn of the tables by the Alliance — not when he had such a "knowledgeable" "Legal Liaison" as Garlic DeCrazy in his corner, handling his lawsuit against us. Unlike his "Executive Administrative Assistant and Legal Liaison," McLaughlin was not judgement-proof. He had a $4,000,000 estate including a 560-acre farm.

I'll tie the elements mentioned above and put them in context with what happened next by quoting verbatim an excerpt from my contemporaneous Chairman's commentary in the March 2017 National Alliance members' BULLETIN:

Commentary by Chairman William White Williams:

Our monthly BULLETINs have informed our members of ongoing legal issues for more than two years now. We finally prevailed in the $2 million Virginia civil suit I inherited, brought by the six disgruntled former Alliance members known as NARRG. Then we prevailed in another civil suit brought against the Alliance in West Virginia by crazy Garland Corse's boyfriend, Michael Oljaca. Another civil suit was brought against our Alliance in Virginia by Corse's employer, John McLaughlin, just one week before the NARRG lawsuit was dismissed. As reported in the February BULLETIN we filed an $850,000 counterclaim to the McLaughlin lawsuit. McLaughlin's attorney, hired by the NARRG attorney, withdrew from the bogus case in February and the then desperate McLaughlin requested an extension of time to answer our counterclaim.

We learned that John McLaughlin died of a heart attack just a couple of days after asking the court for the extension. I will probably be blamed for John McLaughlin's unfortunate death, but it is crazy Garland Corse, his Executive Administrative Assistant and Legal Liaison, who put him in the stressful position he found himself during those last days of his life, not I. His claim ends with his untimely death, but the Alliance's well-grounded counterclaim is still valid against the decedent's estate. Hopefully we can settle that matter amicably and quickly. John's estate is now liable for his unwise decision to sue the National Alliance.

As for crazy Garland Corse there are still two matters before the court in West Virginia: her appeal of the court's order that she either return property she stole from me or in the alternative pay me $2,200, and my appeal of the misdemeanor conviction of an alleged assault of her in September 2015. John McLaughlin somehow was allowed to be a witness to that alleged assault even though he was three states away in Illinois at the time. He can not be a perjured witness for her again at my appeal, nor will her former boyfriend who also lied for her as a "witness" to the alleged assault. Those two, working with the NARRG losers comprised her phony National Alliance board of directors that she has kept insisting owned the organization.

What will the insufferable, meddling maniac do now? I just discovered on 28 March that she had sent an "official" letter to the National Alliance corporation's Registered Agent (RA) in Virginia at the end of January, "electronically signed" by John McLaughlin, on NA letterhead with his Illinois address, instructing our RA to remove me as their contact since I was no longer with the National Alliance, and replace me as contact with John, the new Chairman. I had paid our annual RA fee in January, not John McLaughlin, but I was removed and our password to the RA Web site changed. We have straightened out the fraudulent change by sending our RA a copy of McLaughlin's death certificate and a copy of our 2017 Annual Report (AR) made to the Commonwealth of Virginia's State Corporation Commission.

Corse committed another, more serious fraud a year ago when she overrode the Alliance's 2016 AR by filing a bogus 2016 NA AR with the VA SCC, removing me and our legitimate board of directors, replacing us with McLaughlin and her boyfriend, Michael Oljaca. The Jew has a word for such amazingly brash insolence: *chutzpah*. In my commentary in the January BULLETIN I related how McLaughlin's "Executive Administrative Assistant" and "Legal Liaison" called the mill that was purchasing some timber from us and told the mill owner that he was purchasing stolen timber, that it really belonged to her boss, "National Alliance Chairman John McLaughlin." We got that problem resolved, but were delayed by winter weather and by how long it took the West Virginia Department of Forestry to process our permit to sell some of our trees.

Pictured below is the load being topped off that we delivered to the same mill on 28 March. No one believes John McLaughlin is or ever was "Chairman, Owner/Trustee" of the National Alliance except Garland Corse. The Wicked Witch of West Virginia and I will meet again in Circuit Court on 1 June for my appeal of the assault conviction from Magistrate's court and for her appeal of the same lower Court's order to return items stolen from me. I can hardly wait. Before it is all over I expect this woman will be charged criminally for her outrageous abuses of the judicial processes in West Virginia's 11th Judicial District, not to mention her similar gaming of Virginia's courts.

The reader can take from my legal update above to Alliance members that I was confident that I would prevail against these trumped up criminal charges as well as in the three civil cases filed against me or the Alliance or both. There will be more about the criminal claim against me of "battery." We did prevail in the three civil cases against the NA — NARRG's, Oljaca's, and McLaughlin's — but above I mentioned another civil case: the one I filed against DeCourcy in which I prevailed in Magistrate Court but in which she "[appealed] the court's order that she either return property she stole from me or in the alternative pay me $2,200." DeCourcy's theft of the Alliance's computer and expensive telephone system should have been a criminal matter but Laura Finch instead filed a very brief civil complaint about which Magistrate Cynthia Broce-Kelley simply ordered DeCourcy to either return the items she took or pay me the value of the items, estimated at around $2,200 based on receipts for those items that I provided at trial.

Again, Magistrate Broce-Kelley, who knows how to get to the truth of a matter, was not affected by my accuser's courtroom antics and denied all five of her ridiculous motions in this civil action I'd brought against her for theft; she very nearly charged DeCourcy with contempt of court for repeatedly interrupting and talking over her, telling DeCourcy, "Put that in your blog!" She then ruled in my favor. Of course DeCourcy appealed the adverse ruling like she always does. The appeal went to Pocahontas Circuit Court to be heard by Judge Dent, the same judge who would later hear the appeal of my guilty verdict for the misdemeanor "battery" of DeCourcy. In the summer of 2017 my counsel Finch confessed to me that she had "forgotten" to file a timely response in this civil case that the Court had ordered filed by 2 June, 2017. This blunder by Finch gave litigious DeCrazy, and her attorney Faerber, grounds to file a writ as plaintiff with the WVSCA.

Imagine that, plaintiff DeCourcy's co-defendants were Judge Dent and Will Williams! Ms. DeCrazy has a history of suing judges. Soon after DeCourcy's writ in that West Virginia Supreme Court case was denied, Judge Dent dismissed Magistrate Broce-Kelley's ruling that had rightly ordered DeCourcy to return items stolen by her from me and the Alliance. The reason Judge Dent revoked that sound Magistrate's ruling — without objections from counsel Finch, who had easily prevailed before Magistrate Kelley "with facts in support of [Williams'] claim which would entitle him to relief" — was bizarre and absolutely inexplicable.

When time came for DeCourcy's appeal of Broce-Kelley's order to be heard before Dent, Finch told me that it was not necessary for me to come up from Tennessee for that civil matter because "there is no way the judge will reverse that order." So I did not attend. Finch did attend in my absence and, by then, as I deduced later, she was working against me. Finch contacted me just before entering the courtroom, telling me that I could attend the proceedings from Tennessee "telephonically," if I wished. So I was on the phone, but wasn't allowed to speak and couldn't tell what was going on as Faerber made his case with his usual patter of legalese double-talk. Finch's microphone was conveniently turned off so anything she may have said was not heard by me at all. This peculiar set-up had to be preplanned by the Pocahontas County court officer "club," dealing with an out-of-state absentee defendant, and realizing just how far DeCrazy would carry things should she not get her way. Dent's bias against me was confirmed by this absolutely appalling reversal of Magistrate Broce-Kelley's sound ruling. My recourse was to later deduct the $2,200 DeCourcy had been ordered to pay me from Laura Finch's bill for "legal services."

Finch glibly told me afterwards, "I think the judge just wanted to get rid of that case." Jennifer Dent could just as easily have "gotten rid of the case" by affirming Magistrate Broce-Kelly's judicious court order telling thief DeCourcy, "Give the man his property!"

Another expensive item DeCourcy stole was a nice copier/printer/scanner and fax machine that I had inherited from my mother's estate and donated to the Alliance. Its theft was discovered after filing the claim in Magistrate Court so its value was not included, though Finch could and should have amended the claim had she done her job. We had introduced in the magistrate trial the crazy fax that DeCourcy had sent to the court that has my mother's name and phone number automatically embedded at the top, easily proving that it was mine, not the thief's. (p. 030) I encourage the reader to look at that outrageous letter to Pocahontas County Magistrate Court, especially its last paragraphs wherein DeCrazy gave the long list of organizations, including the U.S. Senate Judiciary Committee, she claimed to have contacted with her complaints. Here is a quote, from the thief DeCourcy using my mother's fax machine:

> The stated reasons were clear, and in the best interest of Justice any matter in which I am a party needs to be heard by Magistrates from another County, than the 2 in Pocahontas County.

Ms. DeCrazy considers herself to be the center of the universe and the courts' job is to please her in that role. My unhinged accuser's successful ploy to disqualify and replace the Pocahontas County Prosecuting Attorney with Special Prosecutor Via from adjoining Greenbrier County will be explained further in later chapters. Apparently DeCrazy had somehow managed to get the entire 11th Judicial District (except Magistrate Broce-Kelley) in her pocket. Amazing!

Let's return now to DeCrazy's puppet, toad number five, JMc, his death, and our Counterclaim.

As I write this now it has been three and a half years since John's tragic death. The Alliance's counterclaim was against him, then was against his estate, and later was changed to be against his co-administrator brothers, Michael and Robert, who also happen to be sole heirs of that estate. The case still drags on in both Virginia and Illinois. In Illinois the brothers' attorney argued that we did not file our counterclaim in a timely manner so it should be time-barred. They prevailed with a weak argument; that adverse verdict was upheld in circuit court on appeal, and we appealed that to the Illinois Supreme Court of Appeals (ISCA) where oral arguments were heard on 23 September, 2020. In Illinois we were fortunate to have retained a competent and persistent attorney, Steven D. Thomas, to fight for us through the trial process and the appeal to the ISCA. As seems to be usual for state supreme courts in the U.S., the ISCA affirmed the Piatt County trial court's ruling, ignoring the proven fact that Michael McLaughlin, the co-sole beneficiary as well as co-executor of the estate, had a serious conflict of interest and a motive to lie under oath, which he was proven to have done during the trial. Steve, being the fighter and truly exceptional advocate that he is, and not accepting the ISCA's wrongheaded affirmation of the trial court's ruling, at the end of October filed a petition for rehearing of our case before the ISCA. That petition was denied (more like ignored), but Steve is still pursuing relief as *Show Trial* is being finished. The result of Steve's efforts will appear on the Web site.

Actually, the ISCA's affirming ruling doesn't really matter, because the counterclaim will be heard in the Virginia court, not in Illinois, and is being enhanced to include conspiracy and possibly fraud, in addition to John McLaughlin's breach of fiduciary duty for assisting NARRG's $2 million lawsuit against the National Alliance while serving as an Alliance director.

I would not be surprised if DeCourcy may have approached one or both of John's brothers to "advise" them. Might they be as gullible as their deceased brother? I doubt that she could worm her way into their lives as thoroughly as she did John's, however, once they realize she essentially caused John's death by involving him in her crazy coup attempt. One recent action by the McLaughlin boys makes me wonder, though: They got their new Virginia defense attorney to file a motion earlier this year to have Andy Bury disqualified as our counsel, claiming he had worked for John, not me and the Alliance. Their attorney actually tried to use crazy DeCourcy's 2016 letter to Andy, signed by John McLaughlin, as proof that John had some sort of attorney/client relationship, thus a conflict of interest in representing the Alliance in its counterclaim against John's now co-defendant brothers. Could that wacky motion to disqualify Andy Bury possibly have sprung from the demented mind of my accuser, DeCourcy? It sounds like something she would do. Regardless, the motion was quickly denied by the judge in a hearing I attended, and the Bury firm is loaded for bear now that we can set a trial date in Virginia.

These ridiculous multi-front legal struggles have never ceased since I accepted the chairmanship of the National Alliance in October, 2014, six years ago. What fun!

The Magistrate Court "Battery" Case

Let us return now to Pocahontas County, West Virginia, and my "battery" case. Mr. Paul Detch had already been my attorney and won the first round when DeCourcy's TRO was denied by Magistrate Broce-Kelley. He told me afterwards that he had not expected a denial — just some reduction of the distance and period of time requested. We didn't prevail in that case as a result of any compelling defense argument by Detch. Any reasonable, impartial judge would see right through my accuser's open lies and courtroom antics. Considering herself better-versed in the law than "lowly" Pocahontas magistrates, DeCrazy tried to talk circles around them with her "shithouse" legal knowledge, throwing in Latin terms for effect. Unlike other Pocahontas County court officers, however, Magistrate Broce-Kelley didn't fall for DeCourcy's bombast and injured innocence routine. She ruled in our favor on each of the two cases before her. The second case was my civil complaint about DeCourcy's grand theft, mentioned earlier.

Since Detch had already felt the sting of my accuser's emotional wrath when he first met her on 17 December, 2015, then witnessed her theatrical shaking, sobbing and obviously lying early on in the trial, he was naturally optimistic about our upcoming "battery" case — I would say overly optimistic. His whole strategy was to tell me, "Don't say a word. Let DeCourcy run her mouth and she will reveal that she is crazy." I am sure Paul did not even look at any of the evidence that I had provided to him. He didn't even point out to the court the obvious contradictions in what should have been my primary defense evidence: the written statements by DeCourcy and her "witness" Oljaca of the alleged incident. (p. 025-027) He and I did not have the customary discussion of my case you would expect of a lawyer and client. Detch was always busy playing the role of the country lawyer, telling me his country lawyer anecdotes. Seeing how little concern he had about my case due to my accuser's craziness — and he used the word himself — I foolishly accepted his idea that my case would be an easy win. I did not even include my wife Lana as a defense witness in the first trial in magistrate court, though she had spoken with my accuser soon after the alleged incident, nor did I ask Fred Streed, an even better witness, to travel to the court from Oregon. Lana and I thought the magistrate would side with normal people — us — rather than with obviously crazy DeCourcy.

Close to the trial date Lana spoke with Magistrate Wilfong over the phone and asked if we could somehow introduce the sworn affidavit Fred Streed had provided for me. Fred based his affidavit on his conversations with me, DeCourcy, and her witness Oljaca which took place immediately after the 30 September, 2015 incident. Wilfong answered that it could not be admitted as evidence, but that she would look at it. Lana immediately faxed the affidavit to her, but it did not help me. It should have raised sufficient reasonable doubt that DeCourcy was telling the truth, since Fred pointed out her lies. See p. 015.

I had been disadvantaged in the magistrate trial for "battery" since I had no witnesses, while my accuser had three: her co-conspirators Oljaca, DeMarais, and McLaughlin. Besides practically no preparation for defending my case, Mr. Detch failed to even object to John McLaughlin being my alleged victim's "witness" to the "battery" — even though he was in Illinois during the alleged incident and could not have witnessed anything. McLaughlin was DeCourcy's employer by this time after I had removed him from the NA board. DeMarais was her landlord/roommate and benefactor, paying most of her expenses, and he also had been nowhere near the so-called "battery" and could not have witnessed it. Oljaca, her boyfriend, witnessed a heated argument between me and my accuser, but there was no physical contact between us beyond my holding my arm up to halt her rushing at me. He was coached by DeCourcy as to what he "witnessed," but not so well that he would have passed the "smell test" of an impartial adjudicator, say, TV's Judge Judy: "Um is not an answer!"

A highlight of the hearing in which the magistrate ruled in my favor on Oljaca's unlawful occupation case was when Wilfong asked McLaughlin directly who was responsible for managing the National Alliance and its Mill Point property. He stammered and bumbled for a few seconds but couldn't give her an answer — not honestly, anyway. So I raised my hand, was recognized, and offered, "Your honor, I am Chairman of the National Alliance. I pay all bills; utilities, property and income taxes, legal expenses, staff salaries, and any necessary purchases." She turned back to John and asked, "So, Mr. Williams manages the National Alliance and the Mill Point property, correct?" John quietly answered, "Yes." He hadn't been coached by DeCourcy on how to answer that unanticipated question. Being under oath to tell the truth, John didn't want to lie to the direct question from the judge.

Though DeMarais and DeCourcy later openly lied in their public writings about how aggressively Detch had been cross-examining my accuser's witnesses, Detch in fact barely asked any really probative questions of them, and when the time came for his closing statement, it was: "Two words, your honor, raging paranoia." Even Laura Finch, who replaced Detch as my defense counsel, said "What? That's no defense!"

Assistant Pocahontas County Prosecutor Keith McMillion's closing statement was, "The photos tell the whole story, your honor," and he recommended six months in jail as my punishment. Again, I was never interviewed about the "battery" by law enforcement, by McMillion's office, nor by the Special Prosecutor's office when my case went to appeal in circuit court, though I had requested to be interviewed at each level. So there was no proper investigation, ever. The selfie photos McMillion said "told the whole story" were ridiculously invalid exhibits, and the three witnesses against me were biased, feeble, and two of the three "witnessed" nothing — they were not there!

Before the trial, McMillion and Detch got together, away from me and without my knowledge, and worked out a plea offer to me. When Detch approached me with it I said, "No, I will not accept a plea offer. Let's go to trial." I believe that for declining that first plea I was punished with an unprecedented six-month jail sentence by Wilfong for a highly questionable "first offense." McMillion requested it and Wilfong didn't hesitate to grant it.

Unfortunately for me, there is no transcript for the Magistrate Court trial. But DeCrazy was repeating the same similarly preposterous story elsewhere, in writing, of being brutally beaten up by me, just like she claimed in magistrate court and later in my circuit court appeal trial. (p. 039) Two judges and two prosecutors in West Virginia's 11th Judicial District played dumb and pretended to believe that my accuser's selfies of two spots unworthy of being called flea bites on the "victim's" neck were credible evidence of a brutal attack and "attempted homicide" — as did all five justices of the WVSCA later.

My biggest mistake may have been that I opted for a bench trial in magistrate court. That meant I had automatically waived the jury option for my appeal to the circuit court. Besides the bad publicity after the *Pocahontas Times* article, as I wrote above, I still sensed at least some unspoken support from both Pocahontas magistrates. Several law enforcement officers and court clerks had expressed support and Bailiff Dreama Sharp even told me: "Everybody can see that you and your wife are normal, and that DeCourcy is batshit crazy." I believed that both Pocahontas County magistrates felt the same way. Only after the crazed behavior of Magistrate Wilfong on the bench did I realize that even a tainted jury would very likely have seen that my accuser was "full of beans" much better than did the emotionally biased Wilfong. It's too bad I didn't have temperate Magistrate Broce-Kelley for my "battery" trial instead of Wilfong.

Carrie Wilfong ignored the facts in my case and was instead influenced by DeCourcy's antics of sobbing and shaking and playing the innocent victim. I had already been found guilty by her, but her sentencing of me was surreal. She confessed openly in court that she had been a victim of abuse herself, wagged her finger in my face across her desk and said, "There will be no battering of females in my county!" She then sentenced me to six months in jail. Amazing!

Looking back, in this #MeToo era when an accusation by a female often becomes a wrongful conviction, I felt real concerns because several court officers I encountered along the way in West Virginia, including the three Pocahontas judges, my own defense attorney, the Assistant Attorney General and a couple of the WVSCA justices were all females. I can only question with certainty Carrie Wilfong's bizarre courtroom behavior and willingness to convict and incarcerate me, especially with what I learned about her later. But I suspect that the general feminization of the courts and of the legal profession, and a bias against me for my "unpopular" racial politics with the other female court officers involved in my case can't be discounted. I feel that if my Pocahontas County Circuit Court judge had been a more fair-minded male the outcome would have been different. Who knows?

In my case the male court officers weren't much better adherents to due process and the rule of law than were the females. All of the court officers with the exception of Cynthia Broce-Kelley seemed scared of my accuser's complaints to the West Virginia JIC, the West Virginia ODC, and other agencies that they might have had to answer to. To repeat: In the above-mentioned incredible letter from DeCourcy to the Pocahontas Magistrate Court she cited numerous organizations, including the "U.S. Senate Judiciary Committee" that she claimed to be in touch with about my alleged misdemeanor "battery." (p. 030) Which court officers would care to be badmouthed by my accuser up to such a high level? Magistrate Cynthia Broce-Kelly was the only female court officer during my legal struggle that showed true impartiality during all the #MeToo hoopla that was in the news at same time, including especially that nasty confirmation hearing for Judge Kavanaugh before the Senate Judiciary Committee, where he was accused of being a "rape gang leader" by a lying female. I can't write this account without saying that Broce-Kelley was not only highly professional, but unlike the others, fearless of crazy DeCourcy.

At my magistrate court sentencing, DeCourcy demanded attention be given to her unhinged 13-page, single-spaced Victim Impact Statement (VIS), E3d. Wilfong may have glanced at that wildly overblown, very long statement before, and she pretended to read it to herself during the sentencing hearing, but neither I nor my defense counsel were allowed to question the "factual inaccuracies" therein as an accused person is entitled by law. We did not even have a copy of her VIS prior to the hearing. The obsession and insanity of "victim" DeCourcy was evident throughout, but that didn't raise reasonable doubt in Wilfong's mind about my accuser's veracity, nor did it temper her intention to punish and make an example of me right after pretending to read part of the long VIS. In my own research later, as I came to represent myself, I learned that according to chapter §61-11A-3(e) of the West Virginia Code the defendant in a criminal case *must be provided with a copy of the VIS at least ten days prior to his sentencing hearing*, and be given an opportunity to object. I was provided with the VIS only *after* my sentencing. Defense attorney Paul Detch didn't object, as usual, and likely was not even familiar with Wilfong's violation of §61-11A-3(e).

Lana managed to fax DeCrazy's article headlined "GUILTY" with the additional heading "Will Williams: Fraud, Conman Thief, Violent Criminal, Narcissistic Psychopath, & SPLC Snitch!" to Wilfong that she had posted to her blog just a few hours after my conviction. (E1b) That "masterpiece" by DeCrazy was so full of lies that Lana naively thought Wilfong would see the extent the "victim" had lied and take that into consideration. Just prior to my sentencing, DeCourcy got a direct question from Wilfong, who had Lana's seven-page fax in hand, "Did you write this?" My accuser confessed: "Yes, that's my blog; yes, I wrote all of that." Yet Wilfong didn't bother reading it out loud beyond that defamatory headline on the first page. Then she sentenced me to six months in jail. Though she told my accuser that she can't post stuff like that, she ordered *me* to delete my and even some of my friends' Internet posts that mentioned the poor "victim." That was an order with which it was impossible for me to comply because I could not remove posts made on discussion boards not controlled by me. That mendacious blog article was introduced as a defense exhibit at my circuit court appeal, but was given even less consideration by Judge Jennifer (Dent) than it was by Judge Carrie (Wilfong).

After the shocking guilty verdict from Wilfong we expected the worst from her at sentencing, so Lana carried $4,000 in cash, expecting bond to be doubled again. Unlike after my sentencing in the circuit court, I was at least given the chance to pay $2,000 bond and file a petition to appeal, which we did right away. Just minutes after I was sentenced to six months in prison, both of my defense attorneys, Detch and Finch, told me that Carrie Wilfong should have recused herself because of her emotional display of bias due to her own admitted history of abuse. However, *neither* of them, specifically my attorney on that case, Paul Detch, informed me that I had a right to request a retrial in the Magistrate Court of Pocahontas County. That retrial would have been heard by Magistrate Broce-Kelley, and likely would have resulted in a favorable outcome.

When Detch exited the courtroom, Lana heard his first words about how unprecedented the sentence by Wilfong was, though I don't recall his objecting as my defense counsel to Assistant County Prosecutor McMillion's same recommendation.

To say both of my defense attorneys were ineffective in their defense is an understatement. My strategy all along was *Falsus in uno Falsus in Omnibus*. That is the common-sense Latin phrase meaning "false in one thing, false in everything" — a legal principle relating to witnesses who lie. Both of my attorneys apparently were never taught that legal maxim in law school, or for some reason pretended not to understand its relevance when dealing with a lying claiming witness. Regardless, a witness who testifies falsely about one matter is not credible to testify about any matter. I explained this to Finch a number of times to no avail. I was so "fortunate" to have Detch to defend me before Wilfong, and then even more "fortunate" to have Finch defending me on appeal before Dent. Not! Laura Finch actually told me she thought DeCourcy was probably glad to have Jennifer Dent hear my appeal "because she has a vagina." Lovely! Score one for the "weaker sex."

Meet the "Pocahontas Court Club"

So far my reader has some idea about Mr. Detch and Ms. Finch as members of the "Pocahontas Court Club." It's time to introduce the others. Laura Finch was Judge James J. Rowe's clerk at the time of the 19 January, 2016 hearing, when Rowe dismissed DeCourcy's appeal of her TRO request denial. As Judge Rowe's Clerk, Finch likely looked through DeCourcy's typically long-winded multi-page petition for appeal. (E3c) I had been told that my accuser was already known by then in West Virginia's 11th Judicial District as "crazy Garland," just as she had come to be known previously in Virginia, for her legal shenanigans. By the way, Judge James Rowe was the one who filed his complaint against Magistrate Carrie Wilfong on 30 October, 2015. More about that complaint will follow.

I found an interesting 2016 newspaper article that tied together several of the Pocahontas County court officers that were involved in my judicial experience: Judge Rowe; his clerk at the time, Laura Finch; Paul Detch; Judge Jennifer Dent, who replaced Judge Rowe who retired; and Special Prosecutor Patrick Via. (E3e) https://www.wvgazettemail.com/news/politics/greenbrier-judge-election-retirement-raise-eyebrows/article_255e-8a2b-8fc2-522e-9e4f-b24c4ae1a789.html

It is understandable that those mentioned in the article must work together in the same courthouses within West Virginia's 11th Judicial District — that is their common workplace. However, further investigation revealed an almost incestuous relationship, at least among those mentioned above when it came to the (lack of) protection of my rights as a defendant. A recounting of my Pocahontas Circuit Court appeal will show what I can now say was an obvious conspiracy against me, at least by the judge in my case, Jennifer Dent, Special Prosecutor Patrick Via, who had been brought in to take over my prosecution from the "disqualified" County Prosecutor, and my own defense attorney Laura Finch. They are the most prominent members of The Club, at least in my dealings with it.

As soon as I was convicted by the second Pocahontas Court for a battery that had never occurred, I knew that I would appeal that second wrongful conviction. Lana and I tried hard to find an appellate attorney. Practically none of the several attorneys we contacted was interested in representing a misdemeanor battery case. I don't want to mention his name, but the only one from a contiguous county to Pocahontas that did not decline immediately did have one phone conversation with me, and with Lana on an extension phone. When I was mentioning Pocahontas County court officers' names, he would respond by saying: "I know Laura [Finch]. I know Patrick [Via]. I know Jennifer [Dent]." Such familiarity with the above-named court officers leads me to believe that not just the Pocahontas County courts, but the greater 11th Judicial District of West Virginia is one big lawyers' club. That attorney didn't inspire confidence that he was not in the same closely knit club that had wrongfully convicted me.

Judge Dent not only showed her bias against me in her rulings, but probably should have recused herself early on, because her ability to be fair and impartial was compromised by her previous, long time professional relationship with a member of The Club, specifically Patrick Via, under whom she had worked for at least four years and who was representing the State of West Virginia against me in her courtroom. Here is the quote from my petitioner's brief, describing one of her suspected violations of six rules of the West Virginia Code of Judicial Conduct:

> Rule 2.11. Disqualification. Possible conflict of interest because Judge Dent served as Assistant Prosecutor to Prosecutor Patrick Via in Greenbrier County until she was elected to be an 11th Judicial District Judge in May 2016, while Defendant's

case was already ongoing. Via was appointed to be Special Prosecutor of Defendant on 12/16/16. Surely, if needed, a more impartial Special Prosecutor, less connected to Judge Dent could have been found.

Laura Finch, as a member of the same tight club, had never mentioned such an important conflict to me. Her email response to Lana, who accidentally discovered the conflict of interest in March 2019 — after my sentencing and incarceration — when she noticed that Judge Jennifer Dent was still listed as Assistant Prosecutor under Greenbrier County Prosecuting Attorney Patrick Via at https://greenbriercounty.net/departments/prosecuting-attorney/, can be seen at E9a. Finch tried to explain to us that such a situation was "okay," but it's not. Maybe it is "okay" only in the 11th Judicial District? Maybe such a conflict is "okay" across the entire state of West Virginia since my guilty verdict was unanimously affirmed without considering the issue of the conflict of interest between the judge and her former boss that I had raised. By the way, several attorneys I spoke with told me that a judge's violations of the Code of Judicial Conduct, much less violations of my Constitutionally-protected defendant's rights, were serious issues that gave me grounds for success before the WVSCA. That had raised my hopes — even if the justices were told I was "unpopular figure."

Circuit Court Appeal of the "Battery" Case

As I wrote above, Ms. Finch was fine when she first began her representation of me. I mentioned that she easily won my case of Oljaca's TRO violation before Magistrate Carrie Wilfong. At first she told me we would prevail in the battery case because of three elements:

1. There was no proper investigation.

2. The only evidence, the undated, un-time-stamped selfie photos, were invalid.

3. My accuser's "witnesses" were unreliable.

What happened to Finch's defense strategy from the time she said that with such confidence, to the time she denounced me in writing as an "unpopular figure," not worthy of her representation? Finch had also known early on what an obvious liar DeCourcy is and that she had previously demonstrated a pattern of abusing the judicial process.

Later, Finch stopped telling me that there was no proper investigation of the alleged battery and began stating that a prosecutor only needs to interview the accused if he does not have enough evidence. The only "evidence" were those eight inconclusive photos that she had earlier agreed were invalid. However, at my trial Finch intentionally failed to object to the inconclusive photos, the state's only evidence, even after DeCrazy had openly lied under oath, describing some nonexistent swelling, scratches and bruising that are not in any of the state's photo "evidence."

I did not realize until much later, but Ms. Finch's attitude began changing after my accuser sent the three illegal *ex parte* letters to Judge Jennifer Dent in an effort to influence her against me — the first two in October 2016, the third one at the end of November. Likely due to an error by counsel Finch, I was provided by her with copies of my accuser's first two letters to the judge, but was only allowed to peruse the third long communication briefly and hurriedly once, in Finch's office, minutes before DeCourcy's magistrate civil trial on 7 December, 2016. That exculpatory *ex parte* letter is still under seal to this day, as are those first two.

I would like to have the reader see those two insane *ex parte* letters that I still have in my possession. However, since they were soon sealed by Judge Dent, behind my back, thanks to the betrayal of my attorney Finch, I must only describe what is in them. My reader can see how DeCrazy writes very similarly, making many of the same accusations against me, in her Victim Impact Statement (VIS), E1b, as well as in her other long, unreadable letters presented as exhibits on the Web site devoted to this book. For the reader's convenience, page one of the VIS, for example, can be seen at p. 031.

I will quote just the first sentences, unedited, of the first paragraph of the first *ex parte* letter:

> This is an urgent matter for my and others safety and protections of our lives. I have been told I have to give you this information for you to help me and protect my life and that of other victims/witnesses. I am fearful, and this letter needs to be held, and protected in confidence. This can NOT at this time be shared with Williams or his attorney's, or as you will see the Pocahontas county prosecutor office, or the Magistrate Court. Already William W. Williams is getting information out of the Magistrates court through Magistrate Wilfong, and Broce-Kelley unprofessionalism, and violating our privacy and endangering us.

Isn't it nice that DeCourcy orders the judge what to do and not do in these illegal letters? In this first 14-page *ex parte* letter the sociopathic toadette badmouthed every single officer of the Pocahontas Court who had failed to do what she demanded of them. Even Magistrate Wilfong, who gave her the big victory by convicting, then sentencing me to six months in jail, felt the sting of DeCrazy's poison pen for not pleasing her enough. Much dirt was dished out about both Pocahontas County Prosecutor Eugene Simmons and his Assistant Prosecutor Keith McMillion. For example, Simmons was smeared by DeCourcy as "corrupt, lazy and senile," who "most days naps or wanders around the courthouse not knowing where he is." DeCrazy claimed that she has "an audio by 2 officials" who provided those quotes to her. She even wrote that Prosecutor Eugene Simmons told her in a direct quote: "Well, why don't you just shoot and kill those bastards [me and my alleged 'criminal gang'] and this would be done with... I would." That is among numerous other incredible quotes and claims she makes. DeCourcy demanded a special prosecutor be appointed to prosecute my appeal. After seeing those nasty accusations in DeCrazy's letters Mr. Simmons' office filed its Request for Appointment of Special Prosecutor, E1b, due to "a conflict pursuant to Rule 1.1 and Rule 1.3 of the Rules of Professional Conduct," meaning "a key witness having an irrevocable opinion that said office and law enforcement officers of the County are not adequately addressing her concerns." Imagine that: the County Prosecutor who would be charged with prosecuting me, or not!, on appeal, stepped aside (disqualified himself and his office) over DeCrazy's badmouthing of him to the sitting judge in my case in her illegal *ex parte* letters.

Bringing a special prosecutor from another county usually costs the county a lot of money, but Mr. Simmons's office would by then have agreed to do anything to cease having to deal with the state's claiming witness, my accuser, "crazy Garland."

Even after my conviction in magistrate court they could easily have stopped "the circus" by interviewing me, seeing the claim was bogus, and dropping the case. But they didn't. I suppose they were all right with seeing me harassed for years by this crazy woman, and with their complicity. Both Simmons and McMillion attended my final sentencing hearing in circuit court. Sitting beside Via at the prosecutor's table was a man I'd never seen. Finch explained to me that he was an investigator. So why was this investigator at my sentencing? He certainly never investigated the claim, or he would have interviewed me. DeCourcy's lies and contradictions during her testimony as the state's claiming witness were so obvious, and her "flea bite" selfie evidence was so pathetic. Once again, I can't emphasize enough that during the three and a half-year duration of my "battery" ordeal I was not interviewed even once by law enforcement investigators nor by any investigators from either of the two prosecutors' offices. Not once!

I can only speculate, but it seems likely that after seeing DeCourcy's toxic criticism of Dent's Club colleagues in those first private *ex parte* epistles to her, the judge didn't want to be badmouthed herself in any future complaints, should I be found not guilty. Had Laura Finch examined those letters full of lies about me, it would not have been possible to convict me, so it was somehow decided it would be better to simply seal them. Finch knew that I would vigorously object to the sealing of DeCrazy's illegal, insane letters, so it was done behind my back.

While denying my motion to unseal the three *ex parte* letters from DeCourcy to her at my second sentencing hearing, Judge Dent justified the denial, saying with her best straight face that those letters had not been considered by her. That is not plausible. The first 14-page single-spaced letter was sent by mail on 6 October, 2016; the second, a 63-page email, describing DeCrazy's and her "witnesses'" daily activities — in an attempt to justify why I and my "gang of domestic terrorists" should be imprisoned — was received by Judge Dent on 18 October, 2016. The alleged "victim" repeated this "gang" charge quite a few times in her letters. Any reasonable person would notice some level of mental disorder in my unhinged accuser's *ex parte* letters, without reading beyond the first paragraph of the first page. Yet Jennifer Dent, an elected circuit court judge, after reading these first two communications from my accuser, called a special hearing with "extra security for safety reasons." Whose safety? Not that of the accused. Whose?

Ms. Finch informed me that this special hearing with extra security for safety reasons would be held on 2 November, 2016. I was informed by Finch about that hearing just 3-4 days prior, at a time when I was overloaded with work with previous engagements scheduled in Tennessee. I asked Finch to request a continuance since attendance on such short notice would be burdensome — a reasonable request. As exhibit E9c shows, Finch first wrote to me: "I cannot represent you in your absence in a criminal hearing" and advised me to attend that special hearing. Nevertheless, instead of requesting a continuance, she secured — which was convenient for the court and for everyone's safety — permission for the alleged "dangerous gang leader," defendant Williams, to appear telephonically. No extra security needed. At that time I still trusted that Laura Finch was representing my best interests and was expecting to be able to say a few words in my defense. Lana and I both listened as best we could to that 2 November "special hearing" on our landline telephones. It was very short. The only issue discussed was my accuser's illegal letters to the judge. We both heard Judge Dent ordering DeCourcy to not send her any more *ex parte* letters.

DeCourcy defied Dent's order and sent her third long *ex parte* letter (via email) three weeks later, on 28 November, 2016. As a rule, defying a judge's direct order leads to contempt of court charges or even dismissal of the case. My accuser was not only not punished, but was granted the special prosecutor she had demanded of Dent to prosecute me in her personal *ex parte* letters to her. By then, this woman with obvious mental issues had caused many headaches for the two Pocahontas courts and for state and local law enforcement in just the 18 months or so since she had graced the county with her presence. Nevertheless, the officers of both courts, excluding Magistrate Broce-Kelley, acted as if they were serving Ms.DeCrazy. Was it due to their fear of my accuser or was it because of my "unpopularity"? Probably both. I believe it helped them also that I was an out-of-state defendant, "represented (read: under court control)" by one of their own.

Many documents were filed around the middle of December, 2016, mostly regarding the by then three illegal *ex parte* letters. Most of the documents can be seen in the Appendix of Record for my Appeal, E1b. Besides two orders to seal the three *ex parte* letters, a Request for Appointment of Special Prosecutor, the Order for Disqualification, and the Order for Appointment of Special Prosecutor; there was also the official letter from Judge Dent to my accuser DeCourcy, reminding her that she was present at the 2 November, 2016 status hearing, where she was told in open court that she was forbidden to send any more *ex parte* letters to the judge. (E1b)

According to Dent's court order, the Pocahontas County Prosecuting Attorney's office was "disqualified" — the very strong word used by the court, meaning "to make unfit" or "to deprive of a power" or "to make ineligible because of violations of the rules." None of those definitions for the word "disqualify" apply to Prosecutor Simmons, his assistant, or to their office.

Judge Dent signed the order of appointment of Patrick Via as the special prosecutor for my circuit court appeal on 16 December, 2016, though the conflict between close Club members Dent and Via was incredibly obvious, except (at that time) to the accused. Finch told me more than once that Via didn't have any interest in my case, but would just do his job. He *did not* do his job. He never interviewed me or bothered to investigate the spurious claim of my accuser with whom he worked very closely, despite my numerous requests to Laura Finch that he or someone do so. He likely had the same fear Dent had that DeCourcy would trash-talk him should he displease her. All Via did was offer at least three plea deals to me through Finch, each a little lighter than the previous one — the final offer being for "disturbing the peace" and "disorderly conduct," which were not even valid because the alleged "battery" did not happen in a public area.

Unfortunately, I realized that my own defense attorney was working against me only *after* being convicted. Lana and I thought that surely justice would finally be served in my circuit court appeal. We had witnesses this time — Trooper Brock, and Fred Streed, besides her and myself — not to mention an attorney we thought was better-involved than was Paul Detch.

I mentioned that I purchased an $800 round trip airline ticket for my primary defense witness, Fred Streed, to travel from Oregon on my behalf. Even though having very serious kidney issues, Fred was willing to come to Pocahontas County, but wasn't able to manage the trip at the last minute. More details about his misfortune at the airport can be read in my first brief, p. 087. When we learned the day before my trial that Fred was unable to travel, I asked Finch to get permission from the court for Fred to testify telephonically due to his age and health problems. Most court officers had

Fred's sworn affidavit in hand so knew what he would testify to. However, Finch, by then, had been simply ignoring most of my requests. Again: "The fix was in." She would do what was best for The Club. For example, she *never once* called my key witness Fred Streed though she had his phone number for a couple of years. She also had been ignoring my repeated requests to provide Via with Fred's affidavit until, under pressure, just days prior to my trial on 14 August, 2018, she finally relented and did her job. However, she decided not to provide Via with the essential two-page exhibit to the affidavit, showing DeCourcy to be a pathological liar. A competent, responsible defense counsel would have provided Fred's affidavit to opposing counsel in December, 2016, establishing that his claiming witness is a bald-faced liar capable of making a false claim of "battery" against a man she obviously hates. See Fred's affidavit, here: p. 015.

Via ignored the affidavit anyway. He clearly demonstrated that he was not interested in any evidence that is favorable to me or that impeaches my accuser. I believe this irresponsible inaction was obstruction of justice by elected officials: interference with the process of justice by withholding important information. Via seriously violated Rule 3.8. Special Responsibilities of a Prosecutor: (A):

> A prosecutor shall refrain from prosecuting a charge [he] knows is not supported by probable cause, (G): When a prosecutor knows of new, credible and material evidence creating a reasonable likelihood that a convicted defendant didn't commit an offense of which the defendant was convicted, the prosecutor shall:...(2)(ii) undertake further investigation, or make reasonable efforts to cause an investigation, to determine whether the defendant was convicted of an offense that the defendant didn't commit.

Also, in violation of this rule, Via began bargaining with Finch who I'd asked to get permission for Fred to testify by phone after getting the shocking message from Fred's wife that Fred was unable at the last minute, at 5 am, to board the flight from Oregon. Via said that he would only allow that to Fred if Oljaca was also allowed to testify by phone. I pointed out Via's witness haggling in my testimony at trial. Via didn't like that and rushed to change the subject. (E9b)

I did not fear Oljaca's supposed telephonic testimony at all, it was doubtful he would continue lying for his former Svengali paramour, telephonically or otherwise. However, Finch was not prepared to cross-examine Oljaca at trial the next day and advised against meeting Via's condition. At the time I didn't know the extent of what had happened to Fred at the airport or if he would even be able to testify by phone, so I declined Via's conditional offer. I should have called Via's last minute bluff and contacted Fred by phone to see if he would testify.

Despite Fred's serious misfortune, Lana and I were confident of our own testimonies and still had a valuable witness in Trooper Damon Brock. Also, we believed that Finch would easily expose DeCourcy as the unrestrained liar she is by at least cross-examining her on, let's say, the numerous "factual inaccuracies" in her *ex parte* letters. But of course Finch did not question DeCrazy about her *ex parte* communications to Dent as we had expected she would. She *still* had not informed me that those exculpatory *ex parte* letters had been sealed by Dent, thus could not be used as my defense exhibits. Again, many of the same wild lies about me in those sealed *ex parte* communications can be seen in DeCrazy's Victim Impact Statement — the document Dent wanted to not just seal, but to strike from the record, like it never existed. The reader can view many of her VIS accusations against me that were also in the sealed *ex parte* communications, here: p. 031.

All three *ex parte* letters, especially the first one, were full of easily refuted lies. Upon seeing the first two (for some reason, the Court counts and lists two first letters of 6 and 18 October as "the first *ex parte* communication"), prior to her being corrupted, Finch said that DeCourcy "shot herself in her foot by sending those letters." Nevertheless, soon enough she would try to convince me and Lana that there would be no point in using those letters — "They are irrelevant," she said. Really!?! Looking back, every time I told Finch that she needed to examine my accuser about the content of those exculpatory letters to Judge Dent, she would engage in double-talk, distract me, and attempt to change the subject, never once telling me she *could not* examine DeCrazy about documents that had been sealed by Dent. Back then I could not even imagine such outrageous betrayal from my own defense counsel, so I trusted and fully expected that she would do as I had requested and expose my accuser as a bald-faced liar by using those letters.

The night before the trial, Lana and I were in Finch's office. I said again: "Tomorrow I want you to make DeCourcy read at least the first paragraph of her first *ex parte* letter, where she orders Judge Dent to not share her letters with anybody, where she states that Pocahontas magistrates and law enforcement 'have been working for Williams.'" Finch again pretended not to know that those letters were sealed. After reading that first paragraph she said that she saw nothing abnormal in it. Had Finch submitted the *ex parte* letters as defense exhibits and properly used them to impeach my accuser's truthfulness, it would not have been possible to find me guilty by a fair-minded judge in an honest Pocahontas County court. That's why Finch admitted that she "failed to do" the cross-examining of DeCourcy, in writing, in her later Motion to Unseal that I demanded she file. (E1b)

When finally seeing my case's docket sheet for the first time, which we only requested after I was found guilty, it became clear that counsel Finch had intentionally kept me uninformed regarding the sealing of those letters. I, with Lana as my witness, had been insisting all along that the exculpatory *ex parte* letters be used as defense exhibits to easily impeach my accuser's truthfulness. Finch *never* informed me that these documents had been sealed since 15 December, 2016, nor did she provide me with copies of even *one* of the numerous court documents that mentioned the sealing of them. Actually, Finch had not provided copies of *any* of the court's orders that we had finally discovered in the multi-page docket sheet after my conviction. How many defendants find it necessary to go around their defense attorneys to request the docket sheet of their case history? I'm guessing only those who discover their attorneys betrayed them.

To repeat, I was provided with copies of the first two *ex parte* letters, but was forbidden to be given a copy of the third one. I want to quote part (B) of the Rule 2.9, Ex Parte Communications, of the West Virginia Code of Judicial Conduct:

> If a judge inadvertently receives an unauthorized *ex parte* communication bearing upon the substance of a matter, the judge shall make provision promptly to notify the parties of the substance of the communication and provide the parties with an opportunity to respond.

I believe that Dent seriously violated this rule by not giving me opportunity to respond.

As can be seen in the transcript of my second sentencing hearing, E1b, Dent gave the following reason to deny my Motion to Unseal. She says that the letters were sealed "due to safety concerns because of the nature of the *ex parte* communications." Again whose safety was it that Judge Dent cared so much about? Certainly not mine. I was characterized in DeCourcy's illegal *ex parte* letters to Judge Dent as a dangerous, violent, homicidal gang leader. The "special hearing with extra security" was called by Dent to protect everyone from me. Fact!

The question of unsealing illegal letters was raised at the first sentencing hearing. Dent said:

> Any new counsel would have access to it [the *ex parte* communications], could request that it be obtained through unsealing the court file.

In the next paragraph Finch says "...he [Williams] intends to represent himself." At the second sentencing hearing Dent denied the motion to unseal *ex parte* letters, arguing that I was allowed to discuss the letters for "purpose of litigation" with my counsel. Sealed documents can't be used as trial evidence, so Dent's statement on the record that discussions between me and my defense counsel can be used for the "purpose of litigation" is an absurd statement. Additionally, Dent could not possibly have believed that close to 100 single-spaced pages of the three letters would have been possible for me, an out-of-state defendant, to discuss "for the purpose of litigation" in my counsel's office. So, by saying that she gave me an opportunity to respond at the 2 November status hearing while the Order for the "special hearing with extra security" was filed just three days earlier, on 28 October, shows Judge Dent was playing dumb — just as she was playing dumb earlier, pretending not to notice the outlandish craziness in DeCourcy's *ex parte* letters to her.

Despite Finch's admitting her failure in the Motion to Unseal by writing that I "requested [of her] that she cross examine the complaining witness regarding the voluminous *ex parte* communications, which she failed to do," at my second sentencing hearing of 12 February, 2019, Dent denied the Motion to Unseal, along with two other legitimate motions: the Motion for New Trial and the motion for a hearing regarding accuser's VIS.

As I said, Lana and I still had confidence that there would be a not guilty verdict in the circuit court appeal trial. Lana had to wait outside the courtroom, sequestered, since she was to be a witness, but we invited three friends: Kevin Strom, Meredith Kellar Strom, who lived in Pennsylvania, and Jay Hess who had replaced David Pringle on The Land in the beginning of summer, 2017. We had the naive belief that having witnesses in court might persuade Judge Dent to avoid showing obvious bias and unprofessionalism. After hearing DeCourcy's outrageous testimony, E1b, that only fools or those who play dumb would find believable, during the lunch break, over a meal, all five of us were optimistic for a not guilty verdict. However, having witnesses didn't make any difference to The Club in their Show Trial. I was wondering afterwards how Laura Finch — who knew full well I was innocent, but had intentionally thrown the case after being paid thousands of dollars to defend me — was feeling when Lana could not stop sobbing in the little room we entered after hearing the guilty verdict?

Incidentally, Laura Finch is a highly ambitious attorney. In 2018 — in just two years after leaving as Judge Rowe's clerk to open her own law practice — she ran for the West Virginia Senate, but lost big, reportedly receiving just 29% of the vote. In 2020 she ran to become the Pocahontas County Prosecuting Attorney and prevailed in the primary against sitting Prosecutor Eugene Simmons. I suppose betrayal of her out-of-state "unpopular" client got her ticket punched by others in The Club on the way up the West Virginia judicial ladder. What next — "Judge Finch"? "Attorney General Finch"?

Being wrongly convicted, I could not accept such obvious injustice. Since I'd always been very busy working for the Alliance, Lana had been doing most of the intensive legal research and found the glaring violations of the West Virginia Code of Judicial Conduct, defendant's Constitutional rights and the West Virginia Criminal Code regarding defendant's right to question Victim Impact Statement. All of this legal information can be easily found on the Internet now, without an attorney, by a bright, diligent and determined researcher like Lana, valedictorian of her high school class and graduate of Moscow University. She doesn't mess around with lessers who think they can get away with doing her husband wrong. Lucky me.

This book would not have happened without her organizing it and pushing me to find time to write it.

In the middle of September, 2018 I met with my probation officer, Robert Tooze, in his Lewisburg, West Virginia courthouse office for my interview with him. Since probation officers can also interview defendant's family members, friends, and neighbors, I brought a letter from Lana to my interview with Tooze, p. 032, along with the standard form I had filled out. I had a cordial conversation with Mr. Tooze who apparently could see before even looking at the form that I was not a criminal type. Considering my clean record, stable financial and family situation, honorable military service, education, etc., Tooze recommended to the court that I only receive probation.

As mentioned previously, after being found guilty by Dent we decided to request from the circuit court clerk my case's multi-paged docket sheet (E1b). We'd never seen it until then, the end of September. It revealed that Finch had definitely been working against her innocent client.

Lana started searching for a potential new attorney (for either a new trial or for an appeal) since we'd figured by then that we could no longer trust Finch. Our research showed several possible grounds we had for requesting a new trial. The above-mentioned attorney, the one who didn't decline discussing our case, told us that "a guilty verdict obtained by fraud" is a very serious ground for a new trial. But nothing, as was proven later, mattered in the 11th Judicial District, when considering an "unpopular" male, defending against a false claim by a determined female accuser.

Recall again that the same month I was found guilty of an alleged battery by my liberal female judge, with the help of my liberal female defense lawyer, was the month during which Judge Brett Kavanaugh's contentious confirmation hearing took place before the U.S. Senate Judiciary Committee to decide whether he could be seated on the U.S. Supreme Court. The feminist #MeToo movement was in full voice at the time, given endless media coverage, and the catch phrase in the media and everywhere was *she must be believed*, even though poor Brett's two main accusers were both proven to be, like my own female accuser, shameless liars.

Lana and I didn't speak with Laura Finch for almost two months after my conviction on 14 August, though she still supposedly "represented" me. In the beginning of October, just a week prior to my first scheduled sentencing, Finch finally returned one of our calls for the first time and spoke with Lana. The first thing out of her mouth was to let Lana know how displeased she was that Lana had written a letter to Probation Officer Tooze. Imagine that, Lana had dared to call Dent's verdict "judicial error" in her letter. Lana wasn't going to take any lip off of my pompous "representative," and let Finch know that we were not going to accept the wrongful conviction. Lana asked Finch directly if she knew about the *ex parte* letters being sealed. Caught unexpectedly, Finch, after a pregnant pause, answered "No." Having secured a copy of my case's docket sheet we knew then that my defense counsel was lying through her teeth. Later however, knowing she had lied to us — a lie that we could prove was a lie — Finch wrote in her response to my complaint that she had told Lana that "in error." In my conversation with Finch later that day we agreed that it would be better for everybody if she withdrew her representation going forward. I didn't bad-mouth her or call her a liar; we just agreed that she had to go.

My first sentencing hearing was scheduled for 10 October. There was no evidence or testimony in my favor, except Officer Tooze's recommendation of probation that was ignored by Dent, whose predetermined goal was to punish me or please DeCrazy, or both. Mr. Tooze's report to the court and his recommendation for my sentence can be seen on the Web site along with my accuser's unhinged 13-page Victim Impact Statement (VIS), that was submitted to Tooze, and attached as an addendum to his recommendation report. (E1b)

At that first sentencing hearing, Dent granted me a continuance due to Finch's Motion to Withdraw, as well as learning of my unexpected discovery of the sealing of the exculpatory *ex parte* letters. The citing by Judge Dent and by her former boss, Special Prosecutor Via, contradicting themselves between the first and second sentencing hearings regarding unsealing the illegal letters can be read in my reply brief, p. 139.

Judge Dent contradicted herself within the first 15 minutes, first granting Finch's withdrawal, then — after a brief, secret, *in camera* powwow (in her chambers) with Via and Finch, came back out and reversed herself, denying Finch's Motion to Withdraw. That can be seen in my petitioner's brief, p. 087.

About that artless *in camera* powwow of The Club: it was after Dent had first granted Finch's Motion to Withdraw — the one that she and I had both signed, not the fraudulent one she later filed with the court that I had not signed — and after Finch told Dent that I wanted to represent myself going forward. In a fair court, since I was then representing myself, it should have been *me* in that back room instead of Ms. Finch who had technically "withdrawn" (read: been fired by me). In an aboveboard court the stenographer would be invited to transcribe the secret gathering of The Club. Obviously I was not going to be allowed to meet with The Club. The *in camera* powwow in National Alliance member Jim Mathias's Iowa trial, that you can read about in our exhibits, was *not* secretive, and it was transcribed for the record. (E7c)

Dent's denying defense counsel Finch's Motion to Withdraw, despite our mutual agreement as well as this document switch by Finch was extraordinary, a clear violation of my fundamental Constitutional rights: the right to self represent and the right to have effective counsel. See the transcript of my first sentencing hearing where I testified that the agreement for Finch to withdraw was "mutual" at E1b. Again, on my appeal the WVSCA justices conveniently failed to see or apprehend the well-stated violations of my Constitutional rights and violations of the Rules of Judicial/Professional Conduct by Pocahontas court officers.

So, the second sentencing hearing was held on 12 February, 2019 after being continued several times during the intervening four months due to court delays. The Club knew by then that they had a tiger by the tail with me. As I described in my first brief, Finch was extremely negligent during those four months between my two sentencing hearings. Since Dent had ordered that I still be represented by the woman I had fired, Lana and I had been sending her many emails with legal research results in attempts to make our desired motions: one for a new trial; one for unsealing the *ex parte* letters, and another requesting a hearing to question the VIS — all to be crafted as strongly as possible. Finch *ignored* those important emails, but after several weeks of our pressuring her to do her job, she finally prepared the requested motions, but they were as weak as they could be. Considering Finch's failure to communicate with us and her ignoring our repeated requests for urgency, I had to prepare those three motions myself. After showing her that I would file my own motions without her help, Finch did her job, but pitifully. She may have drawn her motions so weak so they would be more easily denied by the evident Club Chief, Jennifer Dent.

In violation of §61-11A-3(e) of the West Virginia Code, my motion to question my accuser's VIS as well as the two other legitimate motions were, sure enough, denied by Judge Dent. She generously, by law, allowed me to shortly comment about limited parts of DeCrazy's 13-page single-spaced VIS, though, as the transcript shows, she interrupted me continuously when I touched on "uncomfortable" parts, like, for example, DeCourcy's description of Prosecutor Simmons (who was present in the courtroom) as "corrupt, lazy and senile." Even so, I still was able to say a great deal, for that was the first time I was allowed to speak without my inept counsel's leading questions. My entire extemporaneous speech can be read in p. 073. Here is just one small, outlandish excerpt, unedited, mistakes and all, from DeCourcy's VIS for a taste of what I was up against:

> The ONLY JUSTICE and proper protections of me the Victim of many crimes in WV, & others committed by Williams ie cyber crimes, stalking, shootings, murder of pets, thefts, harassment, intimidation, slander, abuse, is the Court MUST issue a Full Permanent Protective Order, that is detailed in scope, well defined, and fully enforceable. Williams and his gang as has fully stated and gone after others for decades, is fully been going after me, my family & with intent to shut me up for good, because of all I know, & can give evidence against them, and out of vile sick sense of violent

revenge, out of obsession, and hate and his own fear.

There she goes again. That's a sample from hundreds of pages of similar drivel. When I was finally able to comment in court for the first time on these "factually inaccurate" accusations, reasonably pointing out to the court that they must be substantiated, Judge Dent who had by then seen Officer Tooze's favorable report that I had clean record, etc., and having recently read Fred Streed's affidavit, again played dumb. Instead of finally giving the obviously wrongly accused and convicted defendant favorable justice, Dent instead expressed concern that I didn't accept any responsibility for the "battery," so must be incarcerated for six months, suspended except for 20 days plus 18 months probation. I described in my petitioner's brief and my complaint that Dent had tried her best, with Finch's assistance, to strike the outrageous VIS. (p. 087, E8a)

Dent knew that DeCourcy's writings clearly showed how nuts she is, and that a fair-minded, unbiased judge would recognize that fact immediately. That's why it was necessary for her to seal or strike my accuser's craziness in case higher authorities, ones she might have to answer to, were to see them. So, just as at my trial, at the final sentencing hearing Judge Dent didn't even pretend to be fair and impartial.

She informed me about my right to appeal the sentence, as she was required to do, but denied my request for a bond to prepare my appeal. Dent heard what I'd declared in open court and even read in the attachment to my personal amendment to Finch's motion for a new trial that I would definitely be appealing her verdict.

Even if Dent had somehow missed my clearly stated intentions to appeal her verdict, appealing the sentence theoretically could result in a ruling by the WVSCA of no incarceration. Dent violated my fundamental right to at least appeal the sentence. I was remanded straight from her courtroom directly to Tygart Valley Regional Jail again. Patrick Via flippantly argued that I was going to be in jail for just 18 days, so would have plenty of time to take care of my Appeal. The Notice of Appeal must be filed within 30 days of filing the circuit court's final order and is extremely hard to prepare, much less in 12 days, especially without an appellate attorney. It would be to the benefit of The Club if I missed the deadlines for filing the Notice of Appeal to the WVSCA. I described in my first brief that it took me weeks after my incarceration to regain my health, and to jump through all the hoops of filing an appeal to the WVSCA. Fortunately, due to good behavior, I only served 8 days instead of 18 of the 20-day active sentence (2 days served from my first arrest/incarceration were credited). Via wanted to sentence me to the maximum one year in jail for battery but was limited to the six-month sentence of the lower Court.

To wrap up this chapter about my circuit court appeal, I should say that

I'd like to put many outrageous parts of DeCourcy's trial testimony as well as more parts of my testimony in the Appendices, but if I did this book would be way too thick. At E1b the reader can see the entire unhinged testimony of "crazy Garland," as well as the clear evidence of the three court officers pretending not to see her open lies and contradictions, told under oath. I believe that the entire trial transcript makes for interesting reading to some readers. As I said, it's kind of circus-like.

The reader can see for himself in the transcripts that during the trial and the two sentencing hearings Dent and Via were dealing with me in tandem, using practically the same words, like a good tag team that stuck to a pre-planned script to reach a preordained result. I've had the feeling that I was dealing not with responsible court officers — ones who are expected to be honest and honorable in seeking the truth of a matter, but instead with an experienced duo of flimflam artists.

My Appeal to the WVSCA

Filing an Appeal to the Supreme Court is an esoteric process that takes a specialist, an appellant attorney with experience. Judge Dent and the rest of The Club were apparently confident that my appeal would never be filed, and if somehow if it were filed, their conviction of me would certainly be affirmed. Again, the fix was already in: a show trial in a kangaroo court!

The definition of a kangaroo court: "a court that ignores recognized standards of law or justice and often may ignore due process and come to a predetermined conclusion. The term may also apply to a court held by a legitimate judicial authority which intentionally disregards the court's legal or ethical obligations."

After having been convicted in two courts in Pocahontas County, West Virginia, and being incarcerated, sentenced to an unprecedented six months in jail for a questionable "first offense" misdemeanor battery (neither aggravated, nor domestic), I appealed my conviction to the West Virginia Supreme Court of Appeals (WVSCA). After interviewing several West Virginia appellate attorneys, none were interested in taking a misdemeanor appeal before the court, but the one above-mentioned fellow did allow that he would "look at my file for $7,500." I then decided that to clear my name I would need to appeal the case *pro se* — without an attorney. Doing so turned out to be quite a legal education and exercise in futility for me and for my wife Lana, who did much of the leg work, researching West Virginia criminal law, the Code of Judicial Conduct, defendant's rights; talking with attorneys, clerks, and preparing voluminous filings and other paperwork. I expected naively that I would finally be exonerated once

I could present my case before fair-minded justices of the highest court, the WVSCA. I was wrong. But I needed to go through the process to see how it worked or, as it turned out, did not work. Now I get the opportunity to report what I learned.

As I started working on my appeal, I knew little about the appellate process. I even foolishly expected that the same special prosecutor, Patrick I.Via, would be representing the state before the WVSCA. Soon after filing my notice of appeal by the 30 day deadline, thanks to Via's long delay to prepare and file the circuit court's order, I received a "Notice of Appearance" informing me that "Patrick Morrisey, Assistant Attorney General, in the Appellate Division of the Office of the Attorney General," represented the State of West Virginia in my case. My case had been assigned to the Assistant Attorney General (AAG) Shannon F. Kiser. As I told above, Kiser was suddenly and inexplicably replaced with Holly M. Flanigan just a few days before the state's response brief was due.

I called Mr. Kiser soon after to introduce myself and ask some questions regarding the possibility of being granted an extension for filing my petitioner's brief. He was very easy to speak with and had me call him Shannon as he probably let regular petitioner's appellate attorneys deal with him. After seeing how nice and professional Mr. Kiser was, I called him a few more times. After reading my first brief, Shannon told me that I'd done a pretty good job. Each time Mr. Kiser was very helpful to me while giving no legal advice. Here is the precise quote from my reply brief:

> Mr. Kiser, though representing the State of West Virginia, came across in phone conversations with Def.[Defendant] as a fair and impartial party who showed patient consideration with a *pro se* Def., seeking justice. While giving no legal advice Mr. Kiser encouraged Def. to ask him general questions about the appellate process and provided helpful guidance. He stated that he always tries to be objective and that if he sees the State made errors he wouldn't cover for them. That's what Def. and anybody else appealing what they see as a wrongful conviction should expect the State to do. Defendant had confidence his appeal to WVSCA would finally lead to proper justice after three and ½ years in Pocahontas courts, hand-cuffed and led to jail three times, and falsely labeled a "woman beater." Def.'s confidence for an impartial appeal dimmed after reading the SR [Summary Response] of Mr. Kiser's "last minute replacement," Ms. Flanigan.

So, the professional and fair-minded Kiser had been replaced at the "last minute." The state of West Virginia's response was due on 10 October 2019. On 9 October 2019 Holly M. Flanigan filed her Notice of Substitution of Counsel and a Motion for Extension of Time. In that motion she clarified that Mr. Kiser "ended his employment with the Office of the Attorney General on Friday, October 4, 2019." It was terrible news for us and, at the same time as this substitution, very suspicious. Lana and I tried to find out what might have happened. Soon enough Mr. Kiser updated his Linkedin account which showed that since October 2019 he had been working as the

Assistant Prosecuting Attorney for Berkeley County in Martinsburg, West Virginia.

I cannot know the true reason for what I regard as a step down in his career, but my suspicion is that Mr. Kiser might have been asked to leave his position as AAG due to his intention to keep his honor by being impartial in my case.

I called Ms. Flanigan soon after receiving her Notice of Appearance and immediately felt the chill of her opposite attitude. She was cold, short, and all business. Months ago, Lana spoke with the WVSCA clerk and shared with her how nice Mr. Kiser was with us. The clerk immediately reacted: "They all are very nice." I suspected that since Flanigan was not "nice" at all, that she may have been substituted to deal with this troublesome "unpopular figure." During my first and only five-minute conversation with my new AAG, I asked her if Mr. Kiser had done some work on my case. Flanigan cut me off: "I am the one working on that." She requested just a two-week extension to prepare her response to my Brief, which she was granted. Lana and I were surprised that Flanigan requested such a short extension after seeing my 37-page Brief and 373-page Appendix — the one that Mr. Kiser had told me was well done.

Flanigan did not need much time to prepare her response, because she did not plan to pay much attention to what I had presented as my evidence. She had two options and picked the simplest one: the Summary Response with its 15-page limit instead of the Respondent's Brief with its 40-page limit. The WVSCA clerk commented on her choice, without knowing it was by Flanigan, that the state probably just doesn't have much to say in objection to my petitioner's brief.

The reader can see this for himself in my first and second briefs, as well as in Holly Flanigan's Summary Response in the Appendices section. To me it looks like Flanigan had just read and selectively quoted my accuser's testimony as being unconditionally truthful, then promoted the circuit court conclusions by repeating them almost word for word.

Not every petitioner decides to respond with a reply brief, but I was sufficiently put off by the state's covering for their own in Flanigan's half-assed Summary Response that I chose to use every single line in my 20-page limit reply brief to counter Flanigan's sloppy response.

While preparing my first, close to 40-page-limit brief with its unusually long list of legal errors, I was extremely short of space to type long quotes from the transcripts and other documents. At the same time, I was told by the WVSCA clerk that it was not necessary. Citing page numbers from the Appendix of Record is enough, she said. There are well over a hundred page number citations in that first brief as well as some quotes (and lots of abbreviations).

Not having much to argue, Flanigan made my supposed "lack of citations" one of her main arguments that was repeated several times while she failed to comment on close to 70% of the Assignment of Errors section, including the essential error, "guilty verdict obtained by fraud."

In my 20-page reply brief there are plenty of long quotes to satisfy Flanigan's critique of my first brief. I clearly indicated for the justices how "[Ms. Flanigan] retells and selectively quotes accuser's testimony as unquestioned truth," despite numerous cited proofs of accuser's lies under oath. I also pointed out Flanigan's "pretending not to see accuser's obvious lies and some level of mental disability," ignoring "accuser's well explained motive to claim a battery that never happened" and the affidavit of my primary witness Fred Streed. I demonstrated that Flanigan ignored the contradiction of my accuser's lies by the sworn testimony of my defense witness, West Virginia Senior State Trooper Damon Brock, who was much more reliable than lying DeCourcy; how Flanigan was "promoting the Court's conclusions without question." Again, I emphasized how Flanigan failed to comment on the numerous errors in the Assignment of Errors section of the petitioner's brief, and that by doing so, by default means that "Respondent agrees with Petitioner's point of view" — that's from Rule 10 of the West Virginia Rules of Appellate Procedure.

Here is an essential quote from my reply brief:

> A very important error: "guilty verdict obtained by fraud," PB1, including the fact that accuser is now a fugitive, was well explained, PB1-PB6, but totally ignored by [Flanigan] in her [Summary Response].

The WVSCA justices, while selectively naming in their Memorandum Decision just a few of the numerous legal errors I had presented with citations, also conveniently forgot to mention the "fraud" error, pretending to miss every mention of that in both of my briefs. As I realized later, none of my arguments mattered a bit to the WVSCA justices. As I said, it's very doubtful any of them ever saw my briefs much less the Appendix of Record.

I also pointed in my second brief that one of the possible reasons to pick the Summary Response option by Ms. Flanigan was her desire to avoid oral argument since according to the Rule 10(e) of West Virginia Rules of Appellate Procedure "[the] party who files a summary response is deemed to have consented to the waiver of oral argument." Holly Flanigan apparently didn't have much with which to counter my arguments either in writing or orally.

While hoping for the impartial decision by WVSCA justices I was pretty sure that there would be no oral argument granted despite my request for that. If a case is scheduled for oral argument, then both sides' briefs for the appeal are usually presented on the Argument Docket page of the WVSCA Web site. I suspected that it would not be desirable for the state of West

Virginia if both my petitioner's and reply briefs, describing so many legal errors and the Pocahontas court officers' alleged conspiracy against me, to be seen by journalists and the public on the WVSCA Web site.

As was expected, I was denied an oral argument before the WVSCA, so all I got to do was submit my briefs and accept a Memorandum Decision by the court. To my big surprise the WVSCA unanimously affirmed the lower court's conviction without much, if any consideration. No person is identified as the preparer of the Memorandum Decision. But the person who prepared it put unsubstantiated, unquestioned footnotes like this one (6):

> As in other portions of his brief, petitioner relies largely upon assertions not contained in the record to form the basis of his argument.

Anyone who actually read my two briefs can see voluminous evidence contained "in the record," including three trial transcripts, defense witness affidavits, my accuser's deranged Victim Impact Statement, and other included documents. However, just like the lower court officers, WVSCA justices conveniently considered DeCourcy's "circus like" testimony with the pathetic selfie evidence substantial enough to "support [my] conviction."

Upon first reading Flanigan's response to my petitioner's brief I joked to my wife: "Garlic DeCrazy herself might as well have written this response." After reading the WVSCA Memorandum Decision I joked to Lana: "Looks again like either Garlic DeCrazy or Holly Flanigan wrote this." Whoever wrote the Memorandum Decision repeated Flanigan's statements practically word-for-word, just like Flanigan had repeated DeCourcy's version of the alleged incident and Dent's conclusions in her Summary Response. Dent, in turn, was most of the time repeating the state's/Via's statements. Let's just look at the one example in Lana's testimony that every officer named above conveniently found "most telling." Recall, Lana called DeCourcy very soon after the so-called "attempted homicide," when my Accuser had not had time yet to get her story straight. She would not have said a word about any "attack" on her unless Lana asked her at the very end of the conversation to tell me that I should call home before I left West Virginia. With a near giggly voice DeCourcy then told Lana:

> We [Will and I] had some argument during morning consulting. He tried to choke me.

Lana told this story on the witness stand after DeCourcy's testimony. She had been sequestered when earlier my accuser described what had happened when we "argued" as a violent, brutal attack on her. Answering Patrick Via's question, Lana repeated again that Garland told her that [Will] only tried to choke her; the operative phrase being *tried* to choke, not choked. Via, Dent, the second Assistant Attorney General Flanigan and five WVSCA justices conveniently concluded that Lana's testimony was "most telling" since "petitioner's wife, Ms. Williams, testified that Ms. DeCourcy told her that petitioner had choked her." That is not what Lana testified that DeCourcy had told her just minutes after "some argument." That quote is from the WVSCA Memorandum Decision. As they did with most testimony that was anywhere near favorable to me, all of the West Virginia Court Officers named above, including the five WVSCA justices, conveniently ignored this detail in my reply brief, quoted verbatim, here (remember, English is not Lana's first language):

> All three above-named court officers [Via, Dent, Flanagan] conveniently ignored that first part of Lana Williams' testimony: "Garland answered the phone and I asked her standard questions, 'how are you, what's up?' And she started telling me what's going on. She told me several news and she was talking about Will, but she didn't say one word that something abnormal just happened." (AR172) That goes to show the Accuser hadn't had time to concoct her so-called "attempted homicide" story that soon after it supposedly happened. On Judge's question: "was she communicating to you that she had been the victim of a violent crime?" Mrs. Williams answered: "At the very end, very shortly... she wouldn't tell me if I wouldn't ask her to tell Will he should call me... We were about to hang up." (AR174) The fact that in about half hour after being "beaten up" by a large man, for 20-25 minutes conversation, Mrs. Williams "didn't notice any difference whatsoever in her mood, in her voice, compared to our regular conversation," (AR173) apparently didn't raise any suspicions about accuser's claims from the court officers. Yet the idea that accuser, who had been lying and contradicting herself during her entire testimony, could easily lie to Mrs. Williams that Def. only "tried to choke" her didn't seem to raise reasonable doubt about Accuser's reliability among them.

Lana's short testimony and her email to DeCourcy can be seen at E1b, her letter to the WVSCA is at E1c, so the reader can decide for himself whether or not all of the above-mentioned court officers were just being lazy and sloppy, or if they were demonstrating their collective bias.

Showing their ignorance of my 20-page reply brief, which contains several clear citations of DeCourcy's "inconsistencies in her statements," besides other evidence that would be favorable to me — if they ever saw the brief in the first place — the five WVSCA justices, or their clerks, simply accepted the repeated conclusions cited in Judge Dent's biased circuit court ruling.

Here is another short quote from my reply brief:

> Judge Dent could not honestly say in her verdict that she found Accuser's testimony unconditionally credible, but only "to the extent it was consistent with her statements." (AR208) However Def. [Defendant] reasonably showed above the obvious inconsistencies and contradictions in "her statements." (RB3-6) By this standard Judge Dent's conclusion suggests that the Accuser, a documented scammer, can make a false claim of a "crime," that is poorly investigated, then just be consistent with this questionable claim in order to prevail, despite having been caught in several lies throughout the trial of her Accused.

> Def. insists that there was judicial and prosecutorial bias in Pocahontas Court and that Ms. Flanigan, representing the higher authority of the State of WV, in her

Summary Response is no less biased. Def. alleges in PB13,17 that at some point before the end of his trial counsel Finch was also working for the Court rather than for her client. Additional argument for this by Def. will be added below. RB15-17.

Here is the WVSCA justices' conclusion in their Memorandum Decision:

> Despite petitioner's repeated requests, we decline to conduct a credibility determination, especially where the circuit court assessed the credibility of these witnesses. Further, we find that petitioner's conviction should not be set aside because, contrary to petitioner's assertions, the record contains sufficient evidence to support his conviction.

How about that, court fans? Any scheming, vindictive woman is free to pinch her neck, take some selfies and put her imaginary batterer into jail despite being caught repeatedly lying under oath. The reader is reminded that Laura Finch, before becoming corrupted, stated that DeCourcy's undated selfies were invalid — but that was before she had decided that her client was too "unpopular" for her to defend against the state of West Virginia and its nutcase claiming witness. That quote above from the Memorandum Decision reveals that the WVSCA considers the lower court's conclusions to be categorically correct.

Reviewing the WVSCA's order list for 22 June 2020, E1e, that includes the order in my case, here: http://www.courtswv.gov/supreme-court/order-lists/spring2020/June-22-2020.pdf, the five justices affirmed practically 100% of the lower courts' criminal rulings unanimously (5:0), no dissenters. I looked at several other order lists and saw the same pattern of unanimous affirmations!

I am left to wonder what is the point exactly of appealing anything to the vaunted WVSCA? West Virginia appellate attorneys charge hundreds of dollars per hour and naive defendants who know with certainty that they were wrongly convicted and seek final legal relief from the highest state court, would agree to go into deep debt, even mortgaging their homes, to hire an expensive appellate specialist, without awareness of how the WVSCA tends to rubber-stamp lower court rulings. Why would any wrongfully convicted defendant go through an expensive appeal process knowing this?

There was a recent scandal with the five WVCSA justices. At least four were impeached and one, former Chief Justice Allen Loughry, was sentenced to two years in federal prison in 2019 for corruption and lying to investigators. U.S. District Judge John T. Copenhaver Jr., when sentencing Loughry, told him, "The public needs protection from further criminal conduct on your part."

I had hoped that it would somehow raise West Virginia's highest court's professionalism after all that scrutiny. I am not inclined to analyze other cases that were unanimously affirmed close to 100% of the time. What's to analyze? A quick review of rulings on their own Web site tells it all. I can only tell of what happened in my case, and believe that the reasonable reader will agree that there was some degree of bias against me by both lower courts as well as this disgraced highest West Virgjnia court.

Several out-of-state attorneys told me that ineffective counsel is a very serious matter and grounds for an appeal. I provided plenty of proof to the WVSCA that my relatively high-paid "defender" was not just ineffective, but was actually working against me. But the highest West Virginia court's willingness to ignore the numerous legal violations I cited gave me a sinking feeling that their vaunted Codes of Judicial/Professional Conduct are not so vaunted after all, and do not apply all the time to them nor to the court officers I encountered in West Virginia's 11th Judicial District. Do they apply their codes selectively rather than follow due process and simple rules of evidence? Surely the highest state court's justices are expected to be impartial, more so than their lower court colleagues.

If the WVSCA had reversed or even vacated my guilty verdict it might logically have given me an opportunity to sue the state of West Virginia for a wrongful conviction, a malicious criminal prosecution, or abuse of process, not that I would have. Vindication would probably have been enough. There should be some satisfaction for the wrongly convicted defendant, if just an apology, or restitution for the thousands of dollars spent by him defending a bogus criminal claim. But after reading the Memorandum Decision in my case and seeing the WVSCA's nearly 100% unanimous affirmations of lower courts' criminal convictions, it's probably not in their best interests for the West Virginia legal community to open the door for counteractions against it by wrongfully convicted defendants. Otherwise their system might actually be kept honest and "protect the public," as Judge Copenhaver put it, rather than simply covering for their own.

To the very end I had been hoping for a higher standard of judicial professionalism and impartiality from West Virginia's highest court. I provided to it close to 80 pages of DeCourcy's two *ex parte* letters that I had in my possession, with the Motion to Supplement Appendix which means asking for permission to submit documents that were not used as the evidence/exhibits in the lower court for some reason. With the same motion I submitted the above-mentioned one-page Virginia court document about DeCourcy's outrageous 172-page complaint against three judges in that state and a guardian, as well as an above-mentioned letter from my wife clarifying the short part of her testimony when the stenographer had difficulty understanding Lana's broken English. My motion was denied, but I was informed by the WVSCA that: "... the Court may take judicial notice[6] of the

---

6 Judicial notice is a long-held legal doctrine that allows a fact to be introduced into evidence if the truth of that fact is so notorious or well known, or so authoritatively attested, that it cannot reasonably be doubted.

documents, if necessary." I contend that it was necessary.

Of course, the Court did not find it "necessary." It was my belief that each court, especially the highest court, on appeal, should search diligently for the truth to find justice, using every means available — but that certainly did not happen with the WVSCA, not in my case at least.

When I first read the WVSCA's disappointing Memorandum Decision I had the feeling that the WVSCA did not even look at my reply brief, but later I did notice in the Memorandum my quote from that brief:

> [Defendant] was expecting [the] State's comments on each of six presented Rules of Cannon [sic] 2.

So at least someone, perhaps one of the justices' clerks, read my second brief which had many more quoted citations than did the first. However, it looks like that someone in the WVSCA, as well as the person representing the state in the Attorney General's office, during the appeal process had been instructed to ignore any evidence favorable to Appellant Williams.

I've mentioned just a few examples proving that the WVSCA failed to do a thorough, professional, and impartial job in considering my appeal. With this book and its associated Web site the reader has an opportunity to review each document that the WVSCA was provided, but apparently didn't feel a need to weigh against the rulings of the circuit court and the opinion of AAG Holly Flanigan.

My Complaints Against Pocahontas County Court Officers

I could have filed a complaint to the West Virginia Judicial Investigative Commission (JIC) against Magistrate Carrie Wilfong, but trusting that truth would out on appeal of my incredible conviction, and being an out-of-state defendant who was very busy, it did not even occur to me or to my attorneys that I could file a complaint. While working later on my appeal to the WVSCA, I discovered the existence of the complaint against Wilfong to the JIC that was filed by her colleague — the above-mentioned Greenbrier County Circuit Court Judge James Rowe, who had retired in 2016, replaced by Judge Dent in an election that year. The confirmation can be seen here: http://www.courtswv.gov/legal-community/JICAnnualReports/2018.pdf, on page 16. I found and read two public WVSCA orders "In the Matter of Carrie Wilfong." Briefly, Wilfong had been accused of being drunk at a magistrates' meeting and even while on the bench — including the period when she heard my case. Reader can see details of Wilfong's suspension, her court-ordered rehabilitation, her reinstatement, a second suspension, and another reinstatement, in my first brief.

I've since discovered this article: https://pocahontastimes.com/wilfong-reinstated-as-magistrate/. For some reason, Carrie Wilfong, at the age of 43, died on 28 January, 2020 — a little more than two weeks after being reinstated for the second time after two suspensions for her documented history of long-term alcoholism and serious drug addiction while serving on the bench.

Being outraged by the unethical behavior of the three primary members of the Pocahontas Club who had been so determined to brand me a woman beater and incarcerate me, I decided to call the attention of higher authorities in West Virginia about the concerted efforts against me in its 11th Judicial District. So, after my appeal to the WVSCA had run its course, becoming mature in November 2019, I began the process, unfamiliar to me, of filing two complaints against Judge Dent — one for the criminal case she heard, the other for the civil one, both ruled in DeCourcy's favor. I mailed both complaints to the JIC on 20 January, 2020. They can be seen as E8a and E8b. They are prepared much like my WVSCA appeal briefs, with numerous citations and an attached essential Appendix, including three trial transcripts. It's doubtful that JIC has received more carefully prepared complaints, with such voluminous proof of violations of the West Virginia Code of Judicial Conduct by a judge, at least by a complainant who had recently filed *pro se* his appeal to the WVSCA. By then, I venture to say, that I may well have become more familiar with Chapter 61 (Crimes and Their Punishment) of the West Virginia Code, its defendants' rights clauses, and the Judicial Code of Conduct, than most practicing attorneys, especially those in Pocahontas County.

Regardless, about a month later, the JIC mailed me its one-page response, informing me that my complaint had been closed due to insufficient evidence provided. Insufficient? Incredible!

Right after sending my two complaints against Club member Dent to the JIC, I prepared two more complaints against the other Pocahontas Clubbers, attorneys Laura Finch and Patrick Via, this time to the West Virginia Office of Disciplinary Counsel (ODC). Each had the same cover letter. These complaints were in a similar style to those against Judge Dent, again with extensive exhibits, including the trial transcripts, and with numerous citations. (E9a and E9b)

Soon after, I received two responses from the ODC office. My complaint against Via was closed due to some kind of prosecutors' immunity, but it was allowed that I could at least object with a written statement that would have my complaint heard before an upcoming meeting of the Investigative Panel of the Lawyer Disciplinary Board.

I've done enough research, and was told by the ODC's clerk that I am free to use anything I want to use with what I wrote. It's not clear as yet, regarding my lawyers' writings, what I can use, due to privilege, so I'll describe the main points of their correspondence with me with my words.

My responses to the letters from the ODC can be seen as p. 036 for Via, and my 18-page Additional Comments (AC) to Finch's response as E9c. To repeat: Finch's six-page response to my complaint against her was extremely weak and sloppy, as any who looks at those well-stated AC will see. Here is a quote from my cover letter to those comments:

> Ms. Finch paid little attention to my formal complaint and accompanying attached documents when responding, ignoring many documented claims made against her in that complaint. As complainant I expect that Ms. Finch, who styles herself a great defense lawyer, would take my complaint against her to the WV ODC seriously and be thorough in her defense against these claims. Instead she comes across as forgetful, unprofessional and weaselly, equivocating with generalities rather than responding with specificity. She ignores thorough citations in my complaint altogether, while patting herself on her back for what a great job she did defending her innocent client.
>
> In the following ADDITIONAL COMMENTS section I will present my counter-responses with details. Also I will point out, in my opinion, specific instances where Ms. Finch has been intentionally dishonest with the Office of the Disciplinary Counsel.

Finch was given by the ODC an additional opportunity to comment on my AC, but didn't bother. I expected she would respond since in my AC I was requiring that she substantiate her numerous accusations against me by citing the provided transcripts. I also expected Finch to comment on filing the forged version of her Motion to Withdraw from my criminal case, which she accidentally helped to prove was fraudulent in her response to my complaint. Having forgotten about filing a different motion with her signature only, after the aforementioned secret powwow with Dent and Via on my first sentencing, Finch foolishly wrote in her response to ODC: "I prepared a Motion to Withdraw, which *we both* signed." (my emphasis) See more details in E9c.

Despite the ODC's directive in their first letter to her to look at several professional rules including Rule 8.4(c), "Engage in conduct involving dishonesty, fraud, deceit or misrepresentation" and Rule 8.4(d), "Engage in conduct that is prejudicial to the administration of justice," which indicated that some accusations in my complaint were considered valid, Finch apparently decided to play dumb. In her only response she avoided commenting on my most serious accusations, including intentionally keeping me uninformed about the sealing of DeCourcy's *ex parte* letters, failing to cross-examine my accuser, failing to object to her foundationless photos, her attempt to convince me to approve Judge Dent's request to strike De-Crazy's VIS, etc. Since I sent my AC on 15 April, 2020 nobody from the ODC office has ever contacted me during the supposed investigation and likely never will.

130

To repeat what I wrote in the Introduction: "I don't expect satisfaction or even an investigation after seeing how the courts look out for their own in West Virginia." Finch's not taking my complaint seriously makes me think that she knew in advance that there will be no punishment, nor even any investigation. By then I had pretty well gathered how lawyering in West Virginia worked.

Nevertheless, as I write this paragraph on this day, 6 November, 2020, I'm pleased to report that the voters of Pocahontas County, West Virginia, have a new County Prosecutor, Terri Workman Helmick, a Republican. She defeated the Democrat candidate, Laura Finch, by a more than two to one margin (2,639 votes to 1,195). Good for them. How will Mrs. Helmick deal with The Club?

My request for the complaint against Via to be heard by the Investigative Panel of the Lawyer Disciplinary Board (IP) was satisfied. It was heard, but as is common for West Virginia court officers, all seven IP members decided unanimously to not proceed with my complaint despite the numerous serious objections in my written statement, submitted upon receiving the first letter mentioning Via's immunity as a prosecutor. (p. 036) Here is a quote from the ODC Web site:

> You may expect that the Lawyer Disciplinary Board will be genuinely concerned with your complaint. It will receive full attention. No complaint is ever "swept under the rug."

Similar things are promised by the JIC. Those agencies glibly encourage citizens to report court officers' misconduct to them. The reader has an opportunity to decide for himself if these governing agencies' promises to never sweep a complaint under its proverbial rug are sincere.

I want to add that though my two complaints against Dent were quickly dismissed and she likely was never provided with copies of them, I do believe that she knew that I filed them. My probation expired on 19 August, 2020 and Mr. Tooze's discharge report was received and filed with Dent's Clerk on 24 August. While Lana and I were told by her clerk that the final orders are usually signed by the judge within a few days, I finally received that order on *13 October, 2020* after numerous calls and sending an official letter to Judge Dent that can be seen at p. 038. There are indications that Dent's foot-dragging in sending me that order in a timely manner is yet another violation of Rule 2.3 of the West Virginia Code of Judicial Conduct: "Bias, Prejudice, and Harassment." Lana and I were flummoxed to see that repeated calls over a seven-week period to Dent's clerk brought no results. Was it retaliation for filing my complaints? We could file another complaint with the JIC, but the result would be the same as before. I tried to find who was the Chief Judge of the 11th Judicial District — who Dent would have to answer to for delaying the signed order that I should have had in hand by the end of August, but surprise, surprise! — Dent has no Chief Judge over her. She is her own Chief Judge since she replaced Judge Rowe in the 2016 election for his seat.

As I write this in mid-November, the wonderful civic-minded folks at the Department of Homeland Security have still not reinstated my concealed handgun permit that they confiscated as a result of the wrongful conviction by Dent — under threat of a year in prison if I did not comply — though DHS received the required certified order from Dent, stating my probation ended on 19 August, as well as the reinstatement fee, from me nearly a month earlier. My alleged "battery" of DeCrazy was neither domestic nor aggravated so my right to carry personal protection should have never been revoked in the first place. But when one is threatened with a year in prison for noncompliance with an order from federal goons, if one is smart, one will comply, or risk prison. I expect to eventually have back "permission" from the government to carry personal protection. It is a dangerous world out there today and one never knows when he'll need to act on a threat.

After doing more research into how the West Virginia judicial authorities, up to and including justices of its highest court, seem free to support and protect one another in that state's legal industry from the wrongly convicted, I am filing a complaint — again, *pro se* — with the Department of Justice (DOJ), because I can. Federal courts encourage citizens to report civil rights violations so I will. Having joined the military while still in high school, I served this country honorably as an unknowing young man, albeit prior to becoming "unpopular." Perhaps some older patriotic DOJ official may just agree that my rights as a defendant were violated by the West Virginia court system. However, I won't be expecting any more satisfaction from the feds than I've received from West Virginia courts. DOJ on it's official Web site emphasizes "racial discrimination" and so-called "hate crimes" against protected "minorities." While White Americans who practice their rapidly diminishing freedom of association or who advocate for the interests of the White majority are demonized as "supremacists" (what a ridiculous label!) by the DOJ and the FBI, and have no First Amendment protection.

The gals at DOJ wouldn't prejudice a defendant's Constitutional rights even if he was a pro-White "unpopular figure," now would they? Why, no more than the President of the United States does when he "disavows all White supremacists" (again, read: any White who advocates for the interests of his own people). Only the "minorities" in the US are welcome to unite, advocate for their interests, and demand respect for their rights. Donald Trump, his top cop at DOJ, Attorney General William Barr, and his FBI head Christopher Wray, all project that "people subscribing to White supremacist-type ideology constitute the greatest threat to America." Now I understand why my defense attorney told those investigating my complaint against her that I am an "unpopular figure." She considers me a "White supremacist." Separatists by definition are *not* supremacists. Who does she think I want to be supreme over? I'll go ahead and file my complaint against her and others in her little West Virginia Club, including the WVSCA, anyway — because I can. This complaint and how DOJ decides to handle it, will be available to view later on our Web site at E10a.

It's a new day in America and a new "justice" system. Will the DOJ under Joe Biden or Ms. Harris be any better than it has been under Trump? No. It will be worse. Who knows how DOJ might handle my complaint? Perhaps these civic-minded protectors of our Constitutional rights will have to proceed with it, whether they want to or not, and maybe it will force the West Virginia judicial authorities to respond. I'll at least have gone on the record as having exhausted all legal remedies to register my grievance with federal authorities about the West Virginia court system. That's it. Case closed. But then there is still this book that sets the record straight from my perspective.

A last minute update: While *Show Trial* was in the final stage of copy editing, I finally received the decision on my complaint against Laura Finch by the Office of Disciplinary Counsel, dated 15 December, 2020. Just as I expected, the West Virginia ODC found no violations of the Rules of Professional Conduct by Ms. Finch — though many were cited by me. So my complaint was dismissed. Case closed. I find it interesting that, after making my observation about the feminization of the judicial system, my complaint against Laura was heard by the five attorneys making up the ODC: Rachel, Andrea, Renee, Jessica, and Joanne.

I am glad that I received this ODC response before *Show Trial* was sent to the printer. Since my complaint is no longer under investigation, I was told by the ODC that everything is now public record, so I am free to put the correspondence I have received from Ms. Finch and from the ODC on the Web site. To repeat, nobody from the ODC ever called or wrote to me to ask any questions during many months of their so-called investigation. I encourage my reader to see exhibits E9a and E9c and decide for himself if the ODC took my complaint against my sellout counselor seriously and if they were professional and impartial. I was mistaken when stating earlier that only in a case with formal charges will complaints become public record. Still, it's formal charges that usually attract "unwanted" public attention to the complaint. In my opinion, in my case the conspiracy against me by the Pocahontas court officers is what the WVSCA, and both the JIC and the ODC, wanted to avoid having the public know. The incredible unprofessionalism in West Virginia's 11th Judicial District backwoods that I experienced and have described doesn't make the higher West Virginia judicial authorities look very good. If it is not my "unpopularity" that is the reason for the obvious bias against me by the WVSCA, the JIC and the ODC, it may well be just the legal community covering for "their own." To me, West Virginia citizens should not waste their time and money on filing complaints with either the JIC or the ODC. Nor should they waste their resources on appealing anything to the WVSCA. That is a personal opinion based on my experience with the fixed, unchallengeable process. Everyone should make his own choice.

Me and the American Justice System

I have said in the past that being in a courtroom is like being in a theater. The actors all play their roles and I've usually enjoyed watching them, sometimes even playing a role myself, as a defendant, or a plaintiff, a witness, or just an observer. Once I played a courtroom artist, working back and forth around the courtroom, drawing all the players' pictures. The president of the SPLC, Richard Cohen, approached me at the 1986 federal trial against the White Patriot Party, stuck his hand across the bar, inviting me to shake it, wanting to know what I was up to. I grabbed that Jew's grubby paw just right, squeezed his knuckles together hard, holding his arm with my left hand and wouldn't let go until he grimaced in desperation. I told him: "I'm just drawing pictures of people. If you'll hold still, I'll draw yours." Thirty years later, Cohen's "Hatewatch Staff" spread a typical SPLC smear of me, titled "Chaos and Cops at the Compound," https://www.splcenter.org/hate-watch/2015/12/18/chaos-and-cops-compound that included this gem:

> Known to hold a death grip on a grudge, Williams has trolled the major racist forums and conducted Internet guerrilla campaigns against his perceived movement enemies, sometimes for decades. He has hired lawyers and private investigators to drag his detractors into court and he has reportedly manipulated more than one law enforcement officer over the years to help him retaliate.

I can't imagine which law enforcement officers those SPLC hatewatchers are referring to, but the only "movement enemy" I can recall fighting for decades was the nefarious smear artist and political saboteur Harold Covington, who had sued me for defamation back in the late 1980s. He dropped his lawsuit soon after I responded, using truth as my defense. I had to sue that SOB for defamation in 1996 after he spread outrageous lies about the National Alliance and me, claiming I was Tim McVeigh's "handler," among other things. I prevailed in that case and this self-styled "Nazi" leader, after decades of running away and hiding, owed me $250,000. I finally settled for considerably less, just before becoming National Alliance Chairman in

2014. That case was a legal education for me, particularly defamation law. In the 90s I started fighting back, using courts against non-movement "enemies" — suing *pro se* the New York Times Co., Inc. and all of the Jews in that paper's masthead for defamation; a Negro sheriff in North Carolina for false arrest of an Alliance member; and the state of North Carolina for selectively kicking our NA tables out of a gun show that was on state-owned property. At some point Alliance's enemies suddenly ceased abusing our organization and trampling on our civil rights, I expect in part out of fear that I would sue them *pro se*, because I could. Courts don't like it when a plaintiff sues *pro se*.

It is impossible to count the number of lies, including actionable libels, that enemies like Sad Sack Dilloway and his toadette partner Garlic DeCrazy have published about me. They both are judgment-proof and confident they would get away with their lies. These two liars' co-conspirator, DeMarais, was not much less guilty of telling outrageous lies about me, some under his oath to be truthful under penalty of prosecution. I have never been inclined to sue these or any other losers for defamation, but now, thanks to this wrongful conviction, I will finally enjoy some satisfaction exposing them and their pals at the disgraced SPLC with *Show Trial*.

Having experience with the justice system, I could be more aggressive with DeCourcy and Dilloway but that requires convincing a prosecutor to go after them criminally which is not possible, especially in Pocahontas County. Those two liars and thieves are both hiding away somewhere in other states, with Dilloway actually claiming to be in some sort of witness protection program. DeCourcy fled the state on 27 October, 2018, absconding to who knows where.

With *Show Trial*, I'm finished with West Virginia attorneys and their "justice" system. I live and work 200 miles away from Pocahontas County, am quite busy with Alliance-building and still dealing with the legal issues concerning McCorkill and McLaughlin. So much time and resources were spent dealing with the 11th Judicial District and its Pocahontas legal Club that refused to acknowledge the egregious abuse of the judicial process by my accuser DeCourcy, that I'm glad to put the five-year ordeal behind me. Mark it up to experience.

I received no legal relief for my efforts, but a hint of "who is who" after the dust has settled can be seen with one click. If one googles "Garland DeCourcy," the first page will give these results: "GARLAND DeCOURCY v. JUDGE DENNIS LEE HUPP, et al."; "State ex rel. DeCourcy v. Honorable Jennifer P. Dent"; and the WVSCA Memorandum Decision on my appeal where my accuser was found to be a "victim." It's shown that "victim" DeCourcy was suing judges in two of these three results. I say that the WVSCA's Memorandum Decision as the third result doesn't make West Virginia's highest court or that state's lower courts look particularly good, and I prove their rottenness with this book.

I consider every experience, even ones as shocking and boundless as the ones I had for years due to toadette DeCrazy and the West Virginia courts, to be valuable to some degree. For example, without my wrongful conviction, it's likely that I never would have written a book. I am now glad that I have, and I hope some of the things in it will be interesting and informative to my readers.

Conclusion

I could probably write three books about the five-year ordeal with my adversaries and the West Virginia judicial system, but that won't happen. I've provided enough proof to the reader in *Show Trial* of my being wrongly convicted and having my rights as defendant and appellant totally disregarded.

I and my wife Lana were harassed and tested for several years by the boundless scheming of my accuser. At the same time we consider what the fraudster DeCourcy, now a fugitive, put us through to be less stressful than the way the so-called justice system of West Virginia mishandled her scams. Court officers should protect the law-abiding and punish the criminal. In my cases, however, the three West Virginia courts, pursuing their own interests, have not only punished an innocent citizen and wrongly designated him a "woman beater" for life, but have encouraged a documented scam artist and criminal who repeatedly lied under oath and abused the judicial process, and have allowed her to continue her scams unchecked.

In telling my story I couldn't help but try to explain why I would be considered an "unpopular figure." Fighting for one's race, if that race is the White race, is not a popular or very "respectable" position to take, even among Whites, in darkening multiracial America. Our cause, race preservation, has writers and fighters and I consider myself to be more the latter, so never expected to be writing a book. This book, being about my ordeal with the courts, can't be entirely separated from that greater cause and is in fact connected. There would be no court fights had I not become National Alliance Chairman. Some readers will agree with me that the rulings against me were preordained and that the trials were merely for show — that I was "railroaded." Others will say I got what I deserved for my strong racial beliefs and for fighting against strong odds for those beliefs. That is all right; I don't do what I do to be liked. I do it on principle, because it is the right position to take and because taking this position is necessary, whatever the consequences.

Lana asked me to tell readers that when we met in 2003 in Russia I fully disclosed to her my racial beliefs and activism in America. At first she seriously disagreed with my beliefs, but I suppose I showed her enough good qualities to offset my radical racial politics, and she married me anyway. The more I explained my racial loyalty and gave historical and current examples of the intentional genocide of Whites, not just in America but in Russia and wherever else Whites have traditionally lived, she gradually became fully supportive of my beliefs. With her broken English Lana avoids debating politics, especially racial politics with Americans who have been sufficiently "brainwashed" by their churches, their schools, and especially by controlled news and entertainment media. She knows new truths now and is confident that I always try to be truthful.

Most White Americans have no idea that their race is slowly being replaced by non-Whites, systematically genocided. Those who hate our race work hard to keep our people in the dark and distracted with what the Romans called "bread and circuses." An example: our National Alliance sells books and CDs at our online bookstore: https://cosmotheistchurch.org/shop/. Ever since the Charlottesville "Unite The Right" demonstration in August, 2017, there has been an orchestrated effort by the NA's enemies to "deplatform" us — deny us the credit card processing services needed to sell online. They do this even though our Alliance had absolutely nothing to do with that Charlottesville event. The leading enemy, whose stated goal is to "destroy" the Alliance, is the Southern Poverty Law Center (SPLC), mentioned in early chapters. PayPal is one of the companies denying us services. Dan Schulman, PayPal's boss, admitted in a 2019 *Wall Street Journal* interview that it was the SPLC that advised him who to blacklist. See here: https://www.breitbart.com/tech/2019/02/25/paypal-ceo-admits-partnership-with-far-left-splc-to-blacklist-conservatives/.

Lately the center is not holding for the SPLC and other Jewish "hate watchdog" groups like the Anti-Defamation League (ADL) when it comes to their goal of "destroying" groups like ours. Their tribe controls much of "Big Tech" and so-called social media, but they do not control it all. Here is just one of many non-NA Web sites that reveal their sinister plans: http://birthofanewearthblog.com/the-jewish-agenda-to-destroy-the-white-race/. These plans are not new, but have been in the works for centuries.

Here are a couple of telling examples from today of how screwed up our people have become:

We have a friend whose younger sister recently married. She and her husband, both White, have decided to adopt a Negro baby from Africa instead of having their own biological child. Young, healthy White people are taught to do this by their churches, in school and through Jewish-controlled mass media. Commercials on television, ads in magazines and on the Internet, show racially mixed couples/families and "maximum interracial participation" as the ideal. It is sick.

Another example is this one of many articles on the Alliance's on-line magazine at nationalvanguard.org. It is a story about a guilt-ridden White woman, Dr. Ali Michael, who teaches in the "Diversity and Inclusion Program" at Princeton University as well as the "Equity Institute for Higher Education" at the University of Southern California. The article tells of her shame in being White, and of her refusal to have children: https://nationalvanguard.org/2015/06/woman-refuses-to-have-children-for-fear-they-will-be-white/. Google 'ashamed to be White' to see lots of similar articles. Search for scores of other disgusting articles at *National Vanguard* under 'racial genocide.' For the Alliance to oppose genocide of the White race is not "hate." After studying what the NA has to offer and seeing that what we report is backed up with verifiable facts, some Whites are finally waking up today to the truths Dr. William Pierce began telling 50 years ago.

At the same time, most White people have no idea about this intentional genocide and don't want to know. They can see what happened to the Whites in South Africa and Rhodesia, but can't see that the same thing is happening in America and Europe, even with having their noses rubbed in it as Blacks burned our cities during the summer of 2020, even after seeing the corruption of the electoral process in the fall elections. Many of those who *are* able to see the catastrophe feel helpless to do anything about it. However, some long-suffering Whites have had enough and have found themselves attracted to the National Alliance, and its program — and its vision for a future for our people.

American courts are not as bad yet as, say, Canadian courts, however we are getting there. I've provided the example where an NA member's dying wish, to leave his estate to the Alliance, was thwarted by the courts in Canada when the SPLC, and other Jewish pressure groups like the Canadian Jewish Congress, asked a judge to nullify that member's will. Such illegal intervention and nullifying a person's last wishes may not be happening in the U.S. just yet, but in *Show Trial* we've mentioned just a few of the trending number of cases of open judicial bias against pro-White groups and individuals in the U.S. court system.

The demise of the shrinking White race, its eventual fate if we do nothing, is being accepted unquestioningly by too many of our people because of a lack of serious, responsible leadership. It won't end well unless this attitude is reversed, and soon.

Quoting the great Athenian general and statesman Pericles (495-429BC):

Just because you do not take an interest in politics does not mean politics won't take an interest in you.

I could give hundreds examples of how White people have become Judaized and overly materialistic, mostly just wanting to be "happy," without thinking about the coming generations, without concern for the future of our unique people, and without taking responsibility. They cannot see their own slow, mass suicide. The facts of it lay all around their feet but they refuse to look down. This book touches on that briefly, but for the most part only addresses my struggle with a corrupt court system over the past few years — run by my own people, my own kinsmen!, not by the organized "minorities" who aim to replace us.

Although raised in the racially segregated South and being racially conscious for the most part, I did not become truly racially *responsible* until my mid-30s when I began seeking out those who were working exclusively for the interests of our race. I found them, and my search eventually led me to William Pierce. He had dedicated his adult life to devising a long-term plan to save our people, beginning with curing the spiritual sickness that has taken us down so far during the 20th century. As mentioned previously, he named his philosophy, or world view, or ideology — what many now claim as their religion — Cosmotheism. It runs through everything that the political organization he founded fifty years ago, the National Alliance, represents to this day. I am so proud to be holding high the Alliance banner that Dr. Pierce, along with those he activated, carried for more than 30 years. I've come to expect to be hated by many, even many of my own people, but have learned to count only our friends and ignore the unawakened, knowing many of them will come around.

Since discovering the facts about the slow, intentional genocide of our once-great race in my 30s, I've not been one to hold my tongue or simply conform and "go along to get along." Being popular or "respectable" in the eyes of the herd is not something I care for or have sought. I rather enjoy being what some consider a boat-rocker, if that's what it takes to arouse our people. Unsuccessful 1950s presidential candidate Adlai Stevenson had it right when he said "My definition of a free society is a society where it is safe to be unpopular."

Being called "unpopular" by a small-minded defense attorney says more about her than about me. I will take that as a compliment, thank you very much!

Appendices

The following *Appendices* section has its own page numbering, corresponding to the numbers referenced (beginning with the prefix "p") in the main text of this book.

Appendix 1: Accuser Garland DeCourcy's photo

Appendix 2: Accuser's hand written note, coaching her "witnesses"

Apr 2015   Met early 90's

Wed. Sep 30, 2015   Will
Acting as authority or boss
He was pretty volatile,
Wouldn't let us take breaks or go home.
Asking us to do crazy stuff.
He got a phone call, went balistic,
then demanded me to make his fucking coffee.
Armed, volatile & threatening.
Wanted to show his dominance.

Ojaca say's "stop this, it is deplorable."
then pushed Will away.
Chocking trying to catch her breath.
"She knows too much" - Will   She has to die

Bob: Twin bruise on her neck [Bruises take time to appear]
May 96 moved to N.A.

2

Appendix 3: National Alliance's flier "They Hate Us"

THEY HATE OUR HERITAGE. They hate our flag. They hate our freedom to bear arms. They hate our monuments. They hate our traditions. *They hate our very existence.* And they are doing everything possible to wipe us out—and erase White people, and our posterity, from the face of the Earth.

They control our mass media—for now. They control our corrupt elected officials through bribes and intimidation—for the moment. They are importing millions of Third Worlders to replace us. They promote racial mixing as part of their genocidal agenda. And, *so far*, they're getting away with it.

But more and more of us refuse to accept extinction and genocide. More and more of us are fighting back. Join us. We're the men and women of the National Alliance. Visit our Web site at **NATALL.COM**—or send \$3 for more information today.

Appendix 4: 1987 letter by Dr. Pierce used by SPLC to destroy Glen Allen's career

February 14, 1987

Mr Gerald J Domitrovic
2469 South Washington
Wichita   KS 67216

Dear Gerry:

   Thanks for your call tonight. I'll call Glen Allen tomorrow and ask him
to call you. Below is a summary of the facts of the situation here.

   The county's chief legal officer seems to be the prosecuting attorney,
Eugene Simmons. Simmons handled the closing on the land purchase for us
in October 1984, just before he was elected county prosecutor. I haven't
spoken to him since then, but I have received no indication of hostility
from him. When questioned about me by a local radio newsman, he responded
in a very reasonable way, saying that I had seemed to be a decent sort,
and that he didn't have any information to comment further. The county
assessor, with whom I always have had cordial relations, conferred with
Simmons before giving me a favorable ruling last month on the exemption
of the church building and 60 acres of our land from county taxes.
Simmons' address is: Prosecuting Attorney, Pocahontas County Courthouse,
900 Tenth Av, Marlinton, WV 24954.

   The sheriff is Jerry Dale. I've never actually spoken with the man, but
have gotten the impression from others in the county that he is
politically ambitious, not very bright, and not very truthful. He may
have some sort of inferiority complex, accounting for his response to
flattery by news reporters. You can get a partial picture of what he has
been doing and saying in relation to us by reading the enclosed article
from the <u>Charleston Gazette</u> of November 2, 1986. He seems to have in his
mind now the notion that he can win favor in the news media, and therefore
in the eyes of the county's voters, by posing as the protector of the
county from us--as the man who is warning everyone about the menace we
represent.

   In addition to the things attributed to Dale by the newspapers, I have
personal knowledge of the following incidents, all of which I regard as
unwarranted invasions of our privacy and/or harrassment:
   1. Beginning in April 1986 or earlier, Dale repeatedly flew over our
church building, parsonage, and other Cosmotheist Community property,
circling in an airplane for as long as 45 minutes with news photographers
and taking photographs to be used in hostile news stories against the
church. The photographs used in the accompanying newspaper article, for
example, have the legend "Photos courtesy of Pocahontas Sheriff's

                                        (continued next page)

partment." If Dale had done this to any major Christian church, the
county would have been sued.
2. In September 1986 Dale told Douglas Pardue, a reporter for the
Roanoke Times & World News, that Julie Pierce, former wife of Bruce
Pierce, had been visiting me at the church. This information, which was
incorrect, was given to Dale by the FBI. I was able to convince Pardue
that the sheriff was wrong, and so the information was not printed.
Correct or not, however, for the sheriff to give such purely personal
information, gained through the power of his office, to the press is
inexcusable. Pardue also told me that Dale had told him that we have an
electric fence around the church, a lie which he apparently told Epstein
as well. The only reasonable motive for such a deliberate lie is to
create the false impression in the minds of the public that the church
is not really a church.
3. In January 1987 Dale told Jack McCracken, a reporter for WVVA-TV in
Bluefield, WV, that we have a chemist and a biochemist living up here
with us, with the implication that they are here for sinister purposes.
This information, which was incorrect, was, like the Julie Pierce story,
based on faulty intelligence Dale obtained from the FBI. Even if it had
been true, however, it would not have been proper for the sheriff to pass
such information to the press.
4. During the week of February 2, 1987, Dale telephoned McCracken and
told him that he had seen me in the county assessor's office in the
courthouse discussing the church's tax status with the assessor. That was
true: Dale walked into the assessor's office while I was there, saw me
talking with the assessor, and turned around and walked out. It seems to
me, however, that it was improper for Dale to pass such information to a
reporter. In the light of the pattern of his other statements to
reporters about us, it seems clear that his call to McCracken was
motivated by a desire to harm us by publicizing my visit to the
assessor's office--a visit which was none of Dale's business, but
which he wouldn't have known about if he weren't the sheriff. This
incident may seem minor compared to the others, but it should be
included in the bill of particulars sent to Simmons, because then the
assessor, Dolan Irvine, probably will learn about it and will resent the
sheriff's action as much as I do.

I don't know what the Federal civil rights laws have to say about
such behavior on the part of a public official, but Glen believes that
Dale has acted illegally and that a successful action can be brought
against him. I would greatly prefer not to become involved in any action
against Pocahontas County, both because Dale's behavior is the exception
rather than the rule and I don't want to antagonize other county
officials, and because I don't want to expose the Cosmotheist Community
to the jeopardy involved in having to give depositions to the county's
defense attorneys. My principal aim is to cause the county to restrain
Dale by having Simmons warn him that he is breaking Federal laws and is
placing the county in jeopardy by his behavior. My impression of Simmons
is that he is much more a politician than a legal scholar, and that it
will be necessary to spell the law out to him very starkly, albeit

(continued next page)

politely and diplomatically. Presumably he will then advise Dale accordingly. Dale really needs to get a clear and unambiguous message that if he continues to violate our rights we will call him to account for it and it will be very costly to him. That is probably the best insurance we can have against an illegal raid by Dale in the future. My concern about the possibility of a raid is increased by the ADL's current drive to get an anti-paramilitary bill through the WV legislature. The principal effect of such a bill will be to weaken restraints against search and seizure.

If you will send me a draft of your letter before you send it to Simmons, I'll check it over for any errors of fact. Thanks.

Sincerely,

William L Pierce

Enclosure

cc: Glen Allen

Appendix 5: 1-page agreement admitting "Criminal Intent" by Dilloway

THIS AGREEMENT BETWEEN EMPLOYER,
WILL WILLIAMS, & RANDOLPH DILLOWAY,
THE EMPLOYEE, ENTERED INTO THIS DAY,
3 MAY, 2015, SEVERES THE EMPLOYMENT
CONTRACT ENTERED INTO BEGINNING
1 JANUARY, 2015.
IN EXCHANGE FOR THE 2000 4X4
NISSAN EMPLOYEE AGREES TO VACATE
THE NATIONAL ALLIANCE PROPERTY IN
MILL POINT, W.V. FOREVER.
AS PER PARAGRAPH 31. OF THE 1/1/15
EMPLOYMENT CONTRACT, EMPLOYEE
ACKNOWLEDGES & AGREES THAT ALL
RIGHTS, TITLES & INTEREST IN ANY
CONFIDENTIAL INFORMATION WILL REMAIN
THE EXCLUSIVE PROPERTY OF THE
EMPLOYEE.
EMPLOYEE, IN VIOLATION OF PARAGRAPH
31, DELETED OR DESTROYED ALL
CONTENT OF EMPLOYER'S LAPTOP, EM-
PLOYEE KNEW FULL WELL HE WAS
DESTROYING PROPRIETARY RECORDS
OF EMPLOYER IN VIOLATION OF THE
EMPLOYMENT AGREEMENT & WITH
CRIMINAL INTENT.
EMPLOYER ________________________ 3 MAY '15
EMPLOYEE ________________________ 3 MAY '15

Appendix 6: *The Pocahontas Times* on Will Williams' first arrest of 12/16/15

National Alliance chairman arrested at Mill Point

December 23, 2015

William White Williams, II, 68, of Mountain City, Tennessee, was arrested December 16 at National Alliance headquarters in Mill Point on a charge of battery, a misdemeanor.

The warrant for his arrest stated that probable cause had been found that Williams committed the offense in Pocahontas County September 30, 2015.

The Criminal Complaint states that Pocahontas County Sheriff's Deputy B. L. Kelly, along with Sheriff [David] Jonese, spoke with Garland E. DeCourcy about the incident December 2, 2015, and recorded the following information:

"Ms. DeCourcy stated that she worked for the National Alliance, located in Mill Point and worked for William White Williams, II. Ms. DeCourcy stated that on September 30, 2015, she entered her office at Mill Point and Williams met her. Ms. DeCourcy stated that Mr. Williams lunged toward her and began choking her, and that Mr. Williams' force knocked her into the corner of the room, away from the door."

According to DeCourcy, Michael Oljaca, who also worked for the National Alliance was present during the incident and pried Williams' hands from her neck and pushed him away.

Oljaca stated that he was standing outside the doorway to DeCourcy's office and saw Williams get up from his chair and lunge toward DeCourcy while making a motion with his left hand to "smack her." Oljaca stated that Williams began choking DeCourcy with his right hand. Oljaca said he pulled Williams off of DeCourcy and had to physically restrain him to prevent him from doing further damage.

A warrant for Williams' arrest was issued December 16, and he was picked up that day.

Williams appeared in Magistrate Carrie Wilfong's court where he pleaded not guilty to the battery charge, and a cash bond was set at $1,000. He was remanded to the Tygart Valley Regional Jail that day, and was released on bond December 17, under the following terms: "To have no direct or indirect physical or verbal contact by email, social media, phone, text or by any third party by methods listed, with Garland DeCourcy and Michael Oljaca…"

No hearing date has been set for this matter.

A January 7, 2014 article on the Southern Poverty Law Center's Hate Watch website identifies Williams as one of two former senior National Alliance members who "announced their intentions to bring what was once America's most influential hate group back to its glory days by relaunching it in another state under their own leadership."

That relaunching plan was to utilize a barn on Williams' remote property in Mountain City, Tennessee.

It was noted that Williams is a retired Army Special Forces Operator.

Appendix 7: Will Williams' email to Jaynell Graham

From: **Will Williams** <whiteXXX@gmail.com>
Date: Thu, Dec 24, 2015 at 12:57 PM
Subject: Pocahontas Times report about me
To: XXXgraham@pocahontastimes.com

Dear Ms Graham....,

I was just reading your coverage of my recent misdemeanor arrest, where you are quoting my accuser throughout.

I'm curious, Ms. DeCourcy tells the sheriff that Williams' -- that's me -- hands, my hands (plural), were pried from her neck. But then my accuser claims, *"while making a motion with his left hand to "smack her." Oljaca stated that Williams began choking DeCourcy with his right hand."*

Now something is not consistent in your reporting, Ms. Graham. How can the two hands of an accused strangler be pried from someone's neck when one of those hands, his left hand, is raised up, ready to smack his victim, while the other, his right, is around her neck? I never heard of a one-handed strangler. But then the accused decides against smacking and choking with one hand to do the "force knock" thing of his victim into a corner. Oh my! All while having his hands all over the place and being pushed and pried by his victim's young lover and defender. What a horrible scene that must have been. Maybe it was her lover who force-knocked everybody into a pile in the corner by his prying and pushing the alleged strangler?

So, anyway, If you do follow ups on misdemeanor crimes your report about, I thought I'd let you know that my accuser's request for protection from me was denied by Magistrate Kelly on Monday.

There's more to the accuser behind her patented "injured innocence" routine, which I'm sure she turned on for Sheriff Jonese and Deputy Kelly on December 2d. There's more out here surrounding this matter than the accuser's words. I gave a full report to law enforcement on October 31st, a full month before she gave hers, giving my sworn recollection. I haven't figured out yet why *my* statement is not being printed in the *Pocahontas Times,* the *Charleston Gazette,* and all those other papers. It was established Monday that my accuser, -- Ms. Garland DeCourcy aka Elizabeth Corse aka Gael Dempsey aka MNU (married name unknown) -- is not a credible witness, nor were her two other witnesses. The judge didn't believe their stories. My accuser's request for an order of protection from me was denied.

The National Alliance, in our 30th year in Pocahontas County, wish you and your family an enjoyable holiday.

Will Williams <www.natall.com>

Appendix 8: 2/2016 email exchange between Williams and Jaynell Graham

From: **Will Williams** <whiteXXX@gmail.com>
Date: Thu, Feb 11, 2016 at 3:54 PM
Subject: Re: Email from Will Williams
To: Jaynell Graham <XXXgraham@pocahontastimes.com>

On Thu, Feb 11, 2016 at 11:45 AM, Jaynell Graham <XXXgraham@pocahontastimes.com> wrote:

> I would be interested in reading the January Newsletter. Thank you for your offer to send it to me.

Thank you for your quick and courteous reply, Jaynell. I apologize for my sarcastic email to you after that 12/24 story about me "strangling" my accuser.

> I attended the hearing, not as editor of the newspaper, but rather as an interested individual who has been an observer of the National Alliance since it first moved its headquarters to the county.
> You probably noticed that I was not taking notes.

I didn't notice, but recall seeing you had what looked like a notepad.

> I spoke with Mr. Demararis because I have been acquainted with him for many years.

Bob's a nice fellow, but you will learn he has become increasingly hostile to the NA, and perhaps why, when you read my commentary in the January BULLETIN.

> The one and only article published in the Times was to let the public know that
> the National Alliance is still in the community.
> Things have been rather quiet down there for several years.

Yes. Good. We're not looking for publicity in the community because it is almost always adverse. I saw an article in the *Times* about a year ago when some poor sap from Greenbrier County spray-painted "Nigger Lover" on that racially-mixed couple's restaurant in Hillsboro. Our Alliance must have been named a half-dozen times in that piece, along with terms like "hate group" and "skinhead." The Resistance Records corporation that catered to that subgroup of young people called skinheads was sold by my predecessor, Erich Gliebe, in 2013. I discourage skinheads from joining the National Alliance these days myself.

I talked to Mr. Gliebe the other day and he told me you used to own/run Graham's Motel. I met you years ago when I would stay there -- was always impressed by your honor system, leaving the keys to rooms Alliance members had reserved.

I'm including two additional BULLETINS, one from the end of 2014 after I was appointed the new Chairman, and the December, 2015, one that tells a little more about recent legal issues.

10

I would imagine that the 900+ views of the online article were from people outside the county, and not potential jurors.

Maybe all those viewers will check back when all this controversy about the National Alliance "strangler" that was arrested twice in five days blows over and I am exonerated of the accusations.

A story you might be interested in is how those arrested in the county, especially in late afternoon when they are unable to put together a cash bond because the banks are closed, are summarily hauled off to Tygart Valley Regional Jail (actually a prison, serving seven counties: http://www.rja.wv.gov/Pages/Facility-Details.aspx?Facility=TVRJ). Those counties can't afford to build their own jail facilities because it will be too expensive for them to meet federal standards. My overnight experience there wouldn't have been so awful except that neither the county nor the prison would deliver me back to Pocahontas County the next morning when my attorney Paul Detch was able to pay the $1,000 for my release.

I had to hitchhike back from that remote facility to my truck in Mill Point, nearly 70 miles, in an all day downpour on the 17th of December; no coat, no hat, not even my glasses. At 68 it was a wonder I didn't catch pneumonia walking in that cold rain for nearly six hours. A sympathetic couple finally picked my pathetic, soaking wet self up somewhere past Elkins and were going to take me about half way to Marlinton, but I offered them $120 to take me all the way to my truck. I didn't have a penny on me because the jailers confiscated all of my money. Luckily the money I was planning to deposit to First Citizens the previous day was still in the envelope in my truck (parked outside my property) and there was enough cash in it to pay the couple what I had promised.

I had been falsely charged and had not had a hearing. My accuser set a trap for me with that automatic temporary restraining order forbidding me to come within 1,000 feet of my own property. I was entirely ignorant that such an arrest could occur on the strength of a false claim like that, without some sort of hearing first. She did the same thing to me on the second arrest, getting her boyfriend Oljace to file another "assault" charge against me the morning of 12/21. I was apparently served in court during the three-hour hearing when Garland Corse was denied her protection order, but it was just another scrap of paper, among many that morning. Magistrate Kelley and Prosecutor Simmons told me and Paul Detch that after court we could go to my property, retrieve my keys from Oljaca and go about my business, because neither Kelly nor Simmons was any more aware of the new temporary restraining order that had just gone into effect than Paul and I were. It was another trap by my accuser, and Bob Demarais was the one who called the Sheriff because there is no cell phone service on the property. I was arrested again. That time Wilfong was called in and out of sympathy allowed my wife to write a check for the then $2,000 cash bond so I wouldn't have to go to prison again.

Tygart Valley was quite an educational experience for me, especially bunking with "Opie" in the prison pod with 114 other inmates. Opie is 6'-6" tall, 158 pounds, and covered with prison tattoos -- one being the image of Satan as big as your fist on his forehead. Nevertheless, enjoyed talking to him and the other prisoners for a few hours, experiencing prison procedure and learning why the other men were in there (mostly for drugs, "domestic violence," or, like me, violating some protective order.) *Times* readers may or may not find that information of interest. I sure did. I had $4,000 cash in my pocket on 3 February, just in case I was arrested again that day for some new charge?

> Oddly enough, very few people here are fully aware....nor do they care...about the
> National Alliance.

It's not so odd, except for this recent controversy Garland Corse has stirred up that some locals
are aware of. It sure has created a buzz around the courthouse. We stay to ourselves for the
most part and deal with our far-flung supporters who follow the teachings of Dr. William
Pierce.
Those BULLETINS went out in today's mail.

Will Williams
On Feb 11, 2016, at 11:25 AM, Will Williams wrote:

Dear Ms. Graham,

I didn't realize that was you in Magistrate Wilfong's court on February 3 until
after you departed.

I'm wondering if there was a report in the *Pocahontas Times* about the hearings
since you sat in on one of them, the first, hearing my unlawful occupation
claim against Respondent Oljaca? **If so, will you please send me a link to that
article or to any other articles** since the first one you wrote on 12/24 about
my alleged "strangulation" of Ms. Corse aka DeCourcy?

The second hearing in which Oljaca was seeking protection from me -- where I
should stay 1,000 feet away from him for two years because he is deathly
afraid that if I'm any closer to him than that he worries I will murder him -- was
granted to him, but I suspect only so he couldn't appeal to Circuit Court like his
girlfriend, Ms. Corse, did when her request for protection from me was denied
by Magistrate Kelly. By the way, you must know that appeal by her of the
adverse decision was dismissed. Those arrests of me were for violating some
temporary restraining order I was not even aware of at the time of arrests,
granted to them because of Oljaca's and Corse's requests for protection from
me. My second arrest on my property was *after* both Magistrate Kelley and
Prosecutor Simmons had told me and my attorney that we could go to the
property to get the keys from Oljaca, which we did, unaware that there was a
second temporary restraining order in effect.

The hearing you missed for Oljaca's protection request is a simple "no contact"
order, no restriction whatsoever on distance in feet. I had offered to stay 50 feet
from him, a fired former employee, but he rejected the offer and decided to
take his chances with a hearing for the 1,000 feet for two years.

I hope that you will have followed up the first report you made on 12/24, that
quoted other news reports derived from my accuser's communications to the
Southern Poverty Law Center and with the law enforcement investigators who
interviewed my accuser but not the accused: me. With two jury trials still

12

docketed in which I am the defendant I fear that the Pocahontas County jury pool might be prejudiced or tainted by the story that is not sympathetic to me. I just checked the original article and notice it has has 931 views since being published. Some facts that the *Times* readers and my potential jurors might want to know:

1. My accuser's request for protection from me (1,000 feet for two years) was denied, then her appeal of that decision was dismissed in District Court.
2. Her boyfriend's request for protection (1,000 feet for two years) was granted, but is a simple "no contact" order, and for just 90 days. I will soon be able to return to my property to conduct my business without interference from these two terminated former employees.
3. My unlawful occupation claim against Oljaca, Corse's boyfriend, was granted. He must vacate my house by 23 February.
4. Additionally, Oljaca was also ordered to turn over all of my keys to all of my buildings, my gate, my truck, my two post office boxes, by the same date, 23 February, or he will be arrested like he and Corse had me arrested for violating temporary protection orders.
5. All three conspirators, Corse, Oljaca and Bob Demarais, who is Corse's landlord -- the man you were chatting with in the hallway -- have been served with No Trespassing Notices. They can come through my gate and across my property because they have "tenant's rights" to use Demarais's right of way (at least Demarais and Corse do. Oljaca is not Demarais' tenant, yet).
6. You may have noted that the half-baked coup attempt by Oljaca and his two witnesses, John McLaughlin and Garland Corse, is failing to rise. McLaughlin testified under oath that I, as Chairman of the Alliance and President of the organization's board of directors, am in charge of the day-to-day operations in West Virginia, despite his and his co-conspirators' ridiculously lame claims that they are somehow in charge.
7. It might interest *Times* readers that Magistrate Wilfong warned Corse that if she gave further legal advice to her boyfriend Oljaca, as his witness, that she would be charged with the crime of practicing law without a license.
8. Magistrate Wilfong also warned Oljaca that if he interrupted her one more time while she was talking to my attorney that she would charge him with Contempt of Court.

Had I known that was you in the courtroom last week I would have given you a copy of our January National Alliance members BULLETIN, four pages of which are devoted to my side of this contrived controversy. Co-Bailiff Dreama Sharp was given a copy. I'm happy to send one to you, too, if you wish. Things are not as they appear in a Petitioner's claim or in the Southern Poverty Law Center's anti-National Alliance hit pieces.

Thank you,

Will Williams
National Alliance Chairman

Appendix 9: Evidence of filing of 172-page complaint against Va. judges by DeCourcy

f   ☯   8⁺   Comments (0)   🖂   🖨

View Case   Cited Cases   Citing Case

DeCOURCY v. HUPP

CIVIL ACTION NO. 5:15CV00060.

GARLAND DeCOURCY, Plaintiff, v. JUDGE DENNIS LEE HUPP, et al., Defendants.

United States District Court, W.D. Virginia, Harrisonburg Division.
October 9, 2015.

Garland DeCourcy, Plaintiff, Pro Se.

ORDER

MICHAEL F. URBANSKI, *District Judge.*

Pro se plaintiff Garland DeCourcy filed a 172-page motion for temporary restraining order and preliminary injunction on November 13, 2014 in miscellaneous case number 5:14mc00047. See ECF No. 2; see also Case No. 5:14mc00047, ECF No. 2. DeCourcy never filed any complaint against defendants, nor proof of service, and failed to respond to the Show Cause Order issued by the United States Magistrate Judge on March 11, 2015. See ECF No. 4; Case No. 5:14mc00047, ECF No. 4.

On September 10, 2015, the court directed the Clerk to close miscellaneous case number 5:14mc00047 and open this matter as civil action number 5:15cv00060, and thereafter referred all motions in this case to the magistrate judge pursuant to 28 U.S.C. § 636(b)(1)(A) and (B). ECF No. 6. The magistrate judge issued a report on September 17, 2015, recommending this case be dismissed for failure to prosecute. ECF No. 7. No objections to the report have been filed and the court finds that it should be adopted in its entirety.[1]

As such, it is hereby ORDERED that the magistrate judge's report and recommendation (ECF No. 7) is ADOPTED and that this matter is DISMISSED without prejudice on account of plaintiff's failure to prosecute.

It is SO ORDERED.

The Clerk is directed to send a copy of this Order to the pro se plaintiff and to counsel of record.

FootNotes

1. The docket reflects that the court's oral order directing the opening of this civil action (ECF No. 5) and order referring this matter to the magistrate judge (ECF No. 6), as well as the magistrate judge's report and recommendation (ECF No. 7), were mailed to the plaintiff but were all returned as undeliverable with no forwarding address for plaintiff. See ECF Nos. 8 & 9. It is the plaintiff's obligation to keep a current address and telephone number on file in the clerk's office. W.D. Va. Civ. R. 11. The court notes that the Show Cause Order mailed to plaintiff at the same address on file back in March 2015 was not returned.

Magistrate Court of Pocahontas County, WV

GARLAND E. DeCOURCY
MILL POINT, WV

Plaintiff

15-M38M-00687

-vs-

Will W. Williams
Laurel Bloomery, TN

Defendant

AFFIDAVIT

I, Fred G. Streed, of Klamath Falls, Oregon, MAKE OATH AND SAY THAT:

1. I, Fred G. Streed, of Klamath Falls, Oregon, was present on the properties belonging to the National Alliance and the Cosmotheist Community Church, located near Mill Point, Pocahontas County, in the state of West Virginia. along with my wife, Marta A. Streed, from September 14th, 2015, through October 3rd, 2015. I worked on the National Alliance staff from August, 1992 until August, 2003, and was president of the board of directors from June, 1996 until August, 2003, and lived on the property during that time. I was also executor of the estate of Dr. William Pierce after he died in 2002. During our 2015 visit we stayed in a house belonging to the National Alliance. While there I had several conversations with Garland Corse, also known as Garland De Courcy, or as "Gael", whom I will hereafter refer to as "Garland." I had known Garland since the early 1990s.

2. Garland had been hired by Will W. Williams of Laurel Bloomery, Tennessee, Chairman of the National Alliance, to work on the National Alliance-Cosmotheist Community Church Property. She was living in a house adjacent to her workplace belonging to Bob Demarais, a man my

03/24/2016 02:42 PM

wife and I had worked with for several years and who we consider to be a friend. There was also a young man employed by Mr. Williams to work with Garland, who went by the name "Michael Oljaca," and who was introduced to me as "Michael Olanich," and whose living quarters were in an office building on the property.

3.   During conversations with Garland it became apparent that she was insisting events happened that I knew to be untrue. As an example Garland insisted that the FBI had "raided" the National Alliance several times, with search warrants, including several times prior to the death of founder and former chairman of the National Alliance, Dr. William L Pierce. I knew this to be untrue because I was there and I would have known about any "raids", there were none. Garland would spend an hour or more detailing convoluted conspiracy theories and I began trying to avoid her while we were there. See "Exhibit A" for more on this.

4. After we had been there for around a week she began to claim Will W. Williams was involved in what I considered her increasingly unlikely conspiracy theories. It was apparent to my wife and me that there was a lot of friction between the people involved there, and I explained to all parties that I did not want to become involved in other people's feuds. Many of the people involved are friends, and I hoped things would improve. On September 30th, 2015, Mr. Williams told me he and Garland had just had a heated conversation . I talked with Mr. Williams right after it happened, he was calm and did not appear angry. I also talked with Garland and Mr. Olanich soon after my conversation with Mr. Williams. She seemed very excited and angry but made no mention of an assault on her. I did not see any bruises on her throat or other signs of a physical altercation.

5. My wife and I left WV a few days after this, on October 3rd, 2015 to return to Oregon. I told Garland and Mr. Olanich to call me on my cell phone if they had any more problems. I thought I could possibly help defuse any situations that developed by talking by phone to those involved. About 3 or 4 days after we left I called and talked with Garland, it seemed that things had calmed down.

16

SUBSCRIBED AND SWORN TO   )

BEFORE ME, on the   )

24th day of March, 2016   )

)

)

_______________________   )   _______________________

NOTARY PUBLIC   )   Fred G. Streed

My Commission expires:

Nov '9' 2019   )

Fred G. Streed

Falsehoods in email from Garland De Courcy to George Wright

I recently had this email from Garland De Courcy to George Wright forwarded to me. The entire email is long so for brevity I will just quote a few passages containing falsehoods concerning my wife and myself, and which I know from first hand experience to be false. Garland's quotes are in italics and quotation marks, my replies are in in normal text.

1.) Garland said: "*When Fred & Marta were here they warned Mike Oljaca & I many times of Williams also. They said with Will it will not work, for everyone to give up, the NA is dead & to let Dr. Ps work be his legacy & stand on it's own, & live on that way. They told us to leave, to get out fast.*"

My reply: This is the opposite of the truth. I had thought the National Alliance was finished as an organization under the chairmanship of Mr. Gliebe. I expressed to Garland and Mike Oljaca that I was excited about Mr. Williams' appointment as Chairman of the National Alliance and that I thought he was an excellent choice for the position.

2.) Garland said: "*WE just couldn't give up yet. And Fred had to protect both of us also.*"

My reply: I did not have to protect them from anyone, nor were they ever in any danger that I was aware of.

3.) Garland said: "*They did NOT want to be in the bulletin seen supporting Williams. He put that picture in there with out their permission.*"

My reply: Mr. Williams asked me if he could put Marta and my pictures in the next bulletin. I said yes, no problem. If we had not wanted our pictures in the bulletin I would have said so.

4.) Garland said: "*We only got a new working hot water heater in Gate house because Fred & Marta stayed there & had to also point out the need to Will so they could shower. He actually tried to get them to pay for it. But then Will make Fred install it.*"

My reply: The water heater in the "Gate house" worked but the lower element was burned out and new elements were no longer made for it. I suggested to Mr. Williams that it should be replaced with a new heater. Mr. Williams and I went to a hardware store in Marlinton, WV, and bought a new replacement. He paid for it. There was never any suggestion or attempt to get me to pay for it. Mr. Williams did not "make me install it." I offered to install it since Chairman Williams had been kind enough to let us stay in the house for free while we were there I thought it was only right to help out by installing the water heater.

5.) Garland said: "*And recall the 2 times Will was fired & kicked out the gate by Dr. P. 1994 when he was beating & restrained his 2nd wife Albina, & my right hand man in my VA unit who was law enforcement was called to come up to WV & get his wife to a hotel & guard it with another while Will was kicked out, as to not bring harm to NA.*"

18

My reply: I was on the National Alliance staff and living on the property when these events supposedly took place. Williams was not fired. His marriage to Albina was not working out. As far as I knew Albina was never threatened or assaulted by Mr. Williams. She just simply left him. He was not "kicked off the property." No one had to "guard" Albina when she left.

GARLAND DIDN'T HAVE A "VA UNIT".

Fred G. Streed

Date 24 March, 2016

OFFICIAL STAMP
ERIKA ORTEGA
NOTARY PUBLIC-OREGON
COMMISSION NO. 944585
MY COMMISSION EXPIRES NOVEMBER 09, 2019

Appendix 11: Two photographs of Accuser's neck as State's evidence

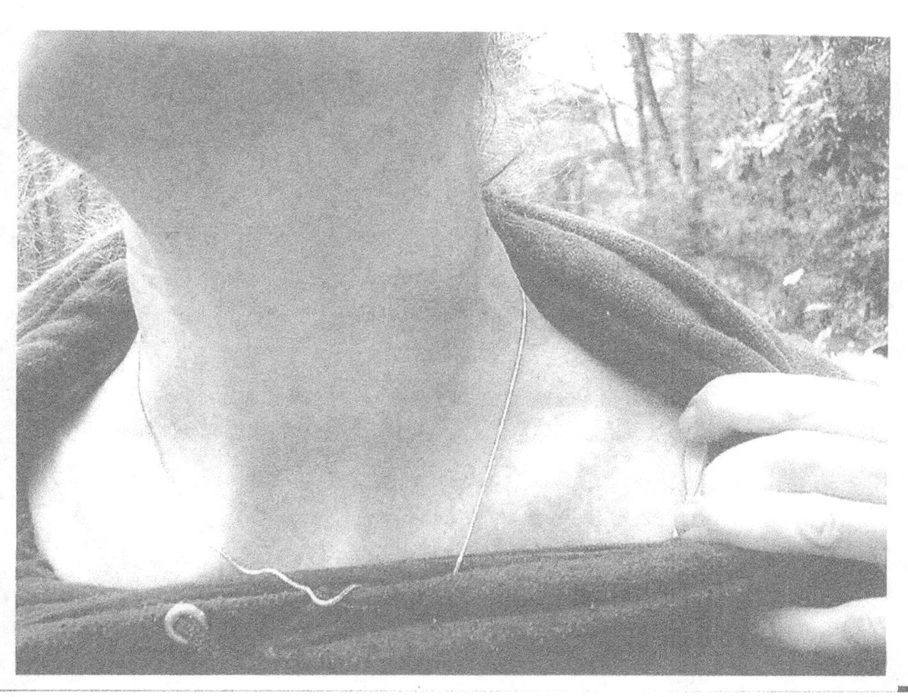

Appendix 12: DeCourcy's statement taken on 10/31/15 by Trooper Brock

GARLAND ELIZABETH CORSE DECOURCY.

STATEMENT TAKEN ON 10-31-2015 @ 1532.
BY TPR. D.M. BROCK

Q. WHAT HAPPENED?

A. ON TUESDAY, SEPTEMBER 29TH 2015 AT APPROXIMAT.
1100 HRS, WILL WILLIAMS JUMPED ACROSS THE
ROOM TOWARDS ME. HE MADE CONTACT WITH MY
THROAT AREA WITH BOTH HANDS. THIS CAUSED
ME TO LOOSE MY BALANCE, AND I FELL BACK
INTO THE CORNER. WILL WILLIAMS FOLLOWS
ME AND STARTED CHOKING ME w/ BOTH HANDS.
MICHAEL OLJACA WITNESSED THIS. MICHAEL
ENTERED THE ROOM, AND FORCEFULLY SEPERATED
WILL FROM ME. DURING THIS TIME, WILL
WAS SAYING " HE NEEDED TO SHUT ME UP, I
KNOW TOO MUCH". AND THAT HE WANTED TO
"FINISH". MICHAEL AND I RAN THROUGH THE
BUILDING, AND GOT AWAY. I WANTED TO CALL
THE POLICE, BUT MICHAEL SAID IT WOULD
TAKE TO LONG, AND HE WOULD KILL US

Q. HAVE YOU SPOKEN TO LAW ENFORCEMENT ABOUT
THIS INCIDENT PRIOR TO TODAY?
A. YES. BUT REFUSED TO COOPERATE.

Q. WHY?
A. WE WERE SCARED THAT MR. WILLIAMS WOULD
GET EVEN. Kill US

Q. WHY DO YOU WANT TO FILE A COMPLAINT NOW?
A. CAUSE IM STILL AFRAID OF HIM.
Afraid For my life

X GMcCoy

Q. DID YOU RECIEVE INJURIES from THE CHOKING
INCIDENT?
A. BRUISING AND SWELLING IN THE NECK AREA.
(usually lasted 3 days, marks

X GMcCoy

WILLIAM WILLIAMS

STATEMENT OBTAINED ON 10/31/2015 AT 1602 HRS.

Q. WHAT HAPPENED?

A. ON 9/30/2015 AT APPROX. 0930 HRS, MYSELF, MICHAEL AND GARLAND WERE SETTING. I WAS BEHIND HER DESK. I WAS COUNSELING THEM. SHE KEPT ARGUING, SO I TOLD HER TO SHUT UP. SHE JUMPED UP FROM HER SEAT, AND POINTED HER FINGER IN MY FACE AND STARTED YELLING. SHE CHARGED ME AND I PUT MY RIGHT HAND OUT TO STOP HER. MY HAND CONTACTED HER CHIN. THEN (SELF DEFENSE) I ~~SHE~~ WALKED OUT OF THE ROOM. I DID NOT LEAVE MARKS ON HER NECK.

X ______________________

Appendix 14: Accuser's and Michael Oljaca's statements of 12/02/15

On Wed Sept 30, 2015 William White Williams, II met me as I entered my work place office where he began abuse, It resulted in him threating me & then lunging towards me hand in Fist to smash me in face or head & then began to choke me. The force of the attack knocked me back into area of corner of Room away from door. Mr Michael Oljaca was present at the door listening & watching & Jumped in & with great effort & force had to push back & pry him of my neck. Williams fought him & continued to come after me shouting he needed to finish it. "She knows to much" "She has to be dealt with".

"I was in pain & scared for my life.

12/2/15
2:40 pm

Garland E De Courcy

Michael Oljaca (Chief of Staff/Employee of National Alliance

Incident of Assault on Sept. 30, 2015

On the morning of Sept. 30, 2015, Ms. Garland DeCourcey (employee) entered the office to report for work. Upon her arrival into the office, our employer, Will Williams, had been waiting in the office when she arrived. He was in a very volatile and bad mood that morning, at least as it had appeared to me.

Mr. Williams began immediately arguing w/ Ms. DeCourcey. The argument had taken place in Ms. DeCourcey's office, w/ Williams sitting at her desk. At this time I was watching from outside the doorway to her office.

The main thrust of Mr. William's argument was that Ms. DeCourcey had received a personal phone call at 11pm the night before. Mr. William's demanded to know why her friend had called so late, and why he was calling the office phone #.

During his interrogation, Williams became quickly irate by Ms. DeCourcey's answers, and at this point Mr. Williams got up from the chair, lunged at Ms. DeCourcey, made a motion w/ his left hand to smack her, then

December 2nd, 2015 / 14:48 hrs   Michael Oljaca

Michael Oljaca

Then Mr. Williams took his right hand and started choking Ms. DeCourcey. As soon as this happened, I quickly jumped in to pull Mr. William's off of her, and physically restrained him so he would not do any further damage.

Michael, Officer
December 2nd, 14:48 hrs
2015

Appendix 15: Williams' email exchange with Michael Oljaca

---------- Forwarded message ----------
From: **Michael Oljaca** <XXXoljaca@gmail.com>
Date: Sun, Sep 4, 2016 at 5:56 AM
Subject: Fwd: Email from WWW
To: Will Williams <whiteXXX@gmail.com>

CONFIDENTIAL: I ask you to PLEASE DO NOT SHARE to anyone or on forums

Will: This is Michael Oljaca, I've reviewed some of the communications you've had with my brother from the past couple of months.

The year 2016 has has certainly been the worst year of my life; chalk full of mistakes and bad decisions on my part. I regret filing a civil suit against NA and other entities. I was out of my element and did not know what i was doing. I am not experienced with lawsuits and had no idea the amount of time they can drag on.

You mention Pringle. Since Pringle has come to the mountain in May, i have feared for my life on a daily basis. He has discharged firearms on a weekly basis and I've had to plan my trips to Bob's house for safety reasons when i know he's not watching. Whenever he happens to see me walk to Bob;s house, he yells more derogatory things at me. Just last week he was yelling outside the gatehouse to "kill myself" over and over. This is just simple harassment to make my life a living hell; I am not sure if you put him up to this or not, but it's a frightening situation to have a man screaming insults outside your home. Not only that he has yelled extremely vulgar epithets towards Bob and Mr Sims outside their homes on the same night..

In any event, I've been scared to death about having to return to WV to the gatehouse with no water or electricity, and with a hostile pringle just around the corner, ready to yell slurs at me.

I have been in New York since Wednesday to take care of things here, but I've told Bob and Gael i would return a little before October 26th, but again I've had high anxiety and heart palpitations at the thought of returning in a couple months time... and i highly doubt i will be ready to do that, my health has been rapidly deteriorating..i have been unable to sleep or eat since returning back.Since being in the gatehouse I've lost 40 pounds and have not been able to eat well at all. I've been depressed and have barely been able to function living there.

One more thing i need to clarify, which is just as important--- I have never had any sexual relationship with Garland ever. If i ever said something to you in the past to give you that impression, it just simply wasn't the case. SHe is not my girlfriend, and i am not her lover by any stretch of the imagination. Never had that type of romantic relationship with her ever. It just isn't and never was so. She was not into me, and nor I into her. I just desperately want to be done with this nightmare that has unfolded.

If Bob and Gael find out i have written to you, there is no telling what they would want to do to me, i shudder when i think about that.

I want to drop this lawsuit, i don't have the stamina or the patience to continue with it.

Michael

28

---------- Forwarded message ---------
From: **Will Williams** <whiteXXX@gmail.com>
Date: Sun, Sep 4, 2016 at 8:53 PM
Subject: Re: Email from WWW
To: Michael Oljaca <XXXoljaca@gmail.com>

Thank you for writing, Michael. I understand your conflict and will work with you to do what is best for you and for the National Alliance. You will go a long way towards helping by dropping those frivolous lawsuits filed by Kris Faeber. Those lawsuits and John's will be no more successful than was NARRG's. They all simply waste precious funds for lawyers that could be going to Alliance-building.

I instructed Pringle to have no communication whatsoever with you or Garland or Bob, but understand his frustration with you, occupying the house he and Lara Lee are supposed to be living in, videotaping and photographing them. It's disappointing to learn that David yelled at David Sims, who is caught in the middle of something simply for being our neighbor who is friendly with long time neighbor Bob and somewhat dependent on him.

It's best for the National Alliance if you'll write a notarized letter, addressed to the Pocahontas County, WV, Circuit Court, officially withdrawing the four civil lawsuits and surrendering all claim to the National Alliance's gatehouse.

The letter should also admit that you are neither a Director on the NA Board of Directors nor Chief of Staff of the NA, as Garland Corse -- not Gael Dempsey -- keeps claiming, here, and elsewhere: https://willwilliamssplcpartnerandsnitch.wordpress.com/2016/07/27/xecutieve-director-of-the-boards-sues-to-save-the-national-alliance-from-williams-illegal-usurpation-crimes-fraud-and-irreparable-damage-a-noble-and-valiant-victory-is-foreseeable-as-the-light/ **and that there was never a NA board meeting authorizing you and Garland to take my two sets of keys from my truck and two cases of books on 16 December, 2015, and to not allow me on the property -- or that "Executive Director" McLaughlin was then appointed to take over the Chairmanship of the National Alliance.** That is an insanely convoluted coup plot hatched by Garland and she has used and abused you and John to try to accomplish it. Bob, too. He claims he gave Faeber the $4,000 retainer to stay the orders to vacate the gatehouse and turn over all stolen keys back to me, then file the four civil suits. She has had all of you on a fools' errand.

You should say that the HP stand alone computer and the telephone system belongs to the NA and not to "Executive Director" McLaughlin or to his "Executive Administrative Assistant" and "Legal Liaison" Garland Corse.

You should also include in this letter that you will not testify against me in the assault case, that your memory is not clear as to what happened during the altercation between me and Garland on 9/30/15 and that Garland coached you as she did John on how to testify for the prosecution.
Do this, Michael, and I'll see that you are absolved from any and all liability in the "feud" between the National Alliance and Garland, Bob and John, et al. You have nothing whatsoever to fear from those three as long as you are in New York.

Our WV attorney, Laura Finch, will help you perfect your letter and deal with Faeber for you, then present it to the Pocahontas Circuit Court.

You should stay away from Pocahontas County, West Virginia, regain your health, relieve unnecessary stress on your family, and go about rebuilding your life.

I apologize to you for any stress I have caused you while fighting off all of these legal challenges and criminal charges.
Sincerely,

Will

Appendix 16: Accuser's unhinged letter to the Pocahontas Magistrate Court

Magistrates Court Pocahontas County, West Virginia

Re 16-M38C-00109   Williams vs. DeCourcy

I have not heard back from nor received any documents with decisions / orders from the Court in reference to several Motions and filings with the Court in which the Court was to notify me in writing. They were filed with the Court Tuesday October 11, 2016.

On Tuesday October 11, 2016 I filed a formal notice of proper contact information and addresses with the Court, as in the past I and others had not been notified by the Court in many matters despite our continued giving it in writing & verbally.

On that date I filed many motions to which the Court has failed to respond, or follow WV Supreme Court rules for procedure. The Court must answer my requests, Motions, and acknowledge my enactments in order either grant them, or for me use those denials and the statements of reason for denial of each as is required to issue a writ of mandamus, and file any appeals on each of those with the Circuit Court.

There has been no Court ordering the Plaintiff for a more declarative statement which is my right as a Respondent to receive. That is necessary due to the grave failings of the initial filing which did not meet the requirements to more forward with the Court. If this is to go to hearing I will need those to be use to build a proper defense with enough time granted to do so as is my right. Discovery and Interrogatories as is standard then need to be served and received to build any defense upon. Then the notifications / serve any Parties which were not joined so they can be legally represented in this matter. Time must be insured to notify many out of State witnesses who are witnesses, and parties, as well as others in privity.

I still have not heard back from the Magistrates Court in the matter of the mailed "Motion and Affidavit Disqualification of Magistrate" plural that the Clerk via telephone told me to write up in October. That was mailed to the Court in October 2016. Has the Court responded to this? Did the Court perhaps send the response to an improper address for me? Or was it ignored as not on the proper from which I have since found as was advised of this by another organization. (October was very difficult for myself and many other victim/witnesses with all the threats, blackmail, and shooting of 100s of rounds near my home, and the murder of my nursing mother cat. In the last few days another victim/witness who is in hiding has notified other victim/witnesses that he was told/warned that Williams is still actively hunting him down to murder him, and looking to hire others to do so, and reiterated Williams' intentions to murder me.). A response from the Court to know how to proceed.

The stated reasons were clear, and in the best interest of Justice any matter in which I am a party needs to be heard by Magistrates from another County, than the 2 in Pocahontas County. The citations were clear, conflict of interest, past violations, lack of impartiality, failure to follow Federal and State procedures, violations of Civil rights, and the fact that there have been reportings to the Judicial Investigation Commission; Office of Disciplinary Counsel; WV Fraud, abuse, corruption Division; WV Attorney Generals Office, WV Governors Office, US Department of Justice, and the WV FBI, other Judicial Watch dog organizations both State, Federal & International; Victims Rights organizations, US Senate Judiciary Committee (who just drafted additions to the Federal Code/Act on the rights of Victims of crime), and others.

Do I need to follow up and file again but with the Circuit Court, The WV Supreme Court, or another Judicial body or office?

Your prompt attention to this notice, request, and query is expected.

Garland DeCourcy
P.O. ___
Hillsboro, WV 24946

Appendix 17: First page of Accuser's Victim Impact Statement

State vs. William W. Williams   CRIMINAL CASE NO. 16-M-AP-01(D)

VICTIM IMPACT STATEMENT

NAME: Garland DeCourcy
ADDRESS: P.O. Box 505 Hillsboro, WV 24946-0505
PHONE: 304-653-4593

Q: Do you wish to appear before the Court to make an oral statement?
A: YES. Already spoke to Probation Officer Tooze on the phone and stated that also.

Q: Do you wish to make a written statement to the Probation Officer in charge of this case?
A: YES.   And I spoke to him on the phone to try to set up an interview, & had questions about my personal safety. I also made him aware that Williams has prior published things prohibited by Courts, & in violation of Orders, Seals, & would likely make anything I send in fully public to further harm me, & incite others to do harm to me, as he has well documented done in the past.

Q: Did you suffer any economic loss as a result of the crime: example: loss of property, damage to your property, etc?

A: YES. Convict/Defendant Williams seized all corporate funds, accounts, assets, income and the Corporate/Entity Boards were unable to pay me. Williams had been removed via Board meetings 8/1/2015 but continued to act illegally. The Board of the Virginia Corporation sued in VA Circuit Court to try to protect the Entities, & Boards, Associates from Williams' crimes, and physical abuse, threats to property and life he and members of his personal criminal gang/domestic terrorists were causing/making.

Williams and his criminal gang associates committed intimidation/obstruction, attempted blackmail, fraud and grand larceny against me Sat 10/31/15. Stealing $ 10s of thousand of dollars of my personal property, and my most personal papers, photo albums, family heirlooms, possessions, evidence against him (in State and Federal crimes/murders/paid murder for hire contracts etc), & priceless family heirlooms. This was his phase 2 of blackmail/intimidation/coercion against me, in which he also did commit more continual crimes & he did personally through fraud sign & enter me into a financial contract in Greenbrier County for 2 storage units he was holding some of my property hostage, while he took others across State lines back to his home in TN. William's also lied to the owner Mr. McCutchen and told him he/Williams was my ex husband and was helping me out, to be able to initiate this illegal contract/fraud. On this criminal act/fraudulent contract Williams gave false contact information for myself to include false address, false phone number so the owner would have no way of contacting me about my possessions or their disposal should Williams fail to pay to this $120 a dollar a month contract Williams through criminal acts fraudulently illegally entered me into. Williams of course never gave me a copy of this contact nor knowledge of where he had taken all my property he had stolen. Email evidence between Williams and others, others who Williams was in contact with relaying information to me, & further evidenced this was blackmail/coercion to in phase 2 try to intimidate/coerce/force me to under duress /fear sign a contact that was fraudulent and only benefited him, caused me harm and liabilities and demanded that I NOT report his crimes, that I not testify against him, that I not work w/ any state or federal law enforcement or courts, or watch dog groups, media, or other organizations, & that I never use his name, or disclose the information he knew I knew & came to know about his many crimes/acts of terror/paid murder for hire contracts/embezzlement/fraud/scams, his fraud upon courts/perjuries/submitting and creating/editing false documents, & withholding documents in courts that were in his possession, & major tax fraud in States & w/ IRS for himself, his wife & many Entities connected to him, & his Federal benefits fraud, his false reporting to WV State Police/Magistrates/Prosecutors/Pocahontas County Sheriffs dept crimes he was reporting that were false upon a prior employee he attempted to murder April 1 2015, & then assaulted/battered several times where I was a witness, & last physical attack & grand larceny was 5/3/15 to which I was a witness to also. That

Appendix 18: Letter to Probation Officer Tooze from Lana Williams

Mrs. Lana Williams

Pt

17 September, 2018

Mr. Robert Tooze
Greenbrier County Probation Departn......
200 N Court St, Lewisburg, WV 24901

Dear Mr. Tooze,

As far as I understand, you are supposed to speak with Will Williams' family members, friends, neighbors. I am his wife and his closest family member. You are welcome to call me, but I decided to write you since my English writing is much better than my English speaking.

I am attaching the picture of Will and me that was taken a couple of years ago. Will and I have been happily married for over 15 years. I consider meeting and marrying Will the biggest luck of my life. Will is an amazingly decent and honest person, great friend and neighbor, perfect husband and a true gentleman who is *not* capable to assault a woman.

I consider Will's guilty verdict a judicial error. In fact, Will and I are the true victims of the accuser Garland DeCourcy who is a professional scam artist with the history of legal system abuse.

Besides smearing Will and me with the dirtiest "out of blue" lies all over the Internet she has done huge work in three failed coup attempts, using civil lawsuits to try and oust Will as Chairman of National Alliance. I am Will's main assistant and can confirm how many times DeCourcy abused legal system in attempt to get in charge of National Alliance assets. So can National Alliance Corporate Attorney in Virginia Andy Bury who successfully defended against the two lawsuits against NA in Virginia. Nothing about the coup attempts was admitted in the battery trials though they clearly show DeCourcy's motives to accuse Will of battery.

I hope Will's clean records and testimonies of his neighbors and friends will help to somehow correct the judicial error.

Will is not only good, law obeying citizen, he was a hero of Vietnam War. He became Army volunteer in high school and got his Special Forces Captain rank as soon as he turned 22 year old.

This letter is 100% my initiative and my words.

Thank you for your time and consideration, Mr. Tooze!

Sincerely,

Svetlana Williams

Appendix 19: "This is going to be fun" note by counsel Finch

DEP. ~~SHINNENBERRY~~ SHINNENBERRY   " THIS IS STUPID!"

DECOURCY WAS TAKING PICTURES
OF ME BEING CUFFED TO PLACE
ON INTERNET.

DEPUTY SHIELDED ME FROM
PHOTOGRAPHY

This is going to be Fun
                    PERSONAL
HOW MUCH/PROPERTY DID YOU
HAVE IN THE HOUSE?   good

DID YOU HAVE ROMANTIC RELATIONSHIP
W/ MS. DECOURCY?
DID YOU TELL WWW THAT YOU DID?

DID BOARD AUTHORIZE YOU TO
TAK W's KEYS, BOOKS, ETC?
WHEN DID BOARD MEETING TAKE PLACE
MINUTES? DID YOU NOTIFY W? JAYNE
                              CARTWRIGHT
                                   ?

Appendix 20: John MacLaughlin's only letter written without his "coach"

April 20, 2016

Dear Magistrate Wilfong:

    Enclosed are my thoughts about a sentence for William Williams in regards to his Criminal and reprobate behavior.

    1.) He must spend at least one year from West Virginia.

    2.) He must spend at least one year from Storm Front, and/or other such social media, and away from the internet.

    3.) He must allow Garland DeCoursey and others to access the buildings where she kept a lot if items that Will Williams stole along with other items he stored in West Virginia and Tennessee.

    4.) He must have a mandatory psychological exam, and to abide by the medical treatment.

Sincerely,

John McLaughlin

Monticello, Illinois 61856

Appendix 21: To West Va. Office of Disciplinary Counsel from Williams

William White Williams

5 March 2020

Office of Disciplinary Counsel
City Center East, Suite 1200C
4700 MacCorkle Avenue SE
Charleston, West Virginia 25304

Dear Ms. Frymyer and the Office of the Disciplinary Counsel,

I received your 28 February, 2020 response to my formal complaint of professional misconduct against Patrick I Via, Esquire, the Special Prosecutor in my appeal of the misdemeanor battery conviction in Pocahontas Circuit Court. I understand that your Office can not deal with my allegations against Mr. Via, essentially because he is immune from complaints by those he prosecutes due to special discretion allowed him while representing the State of West Virginia.

Although you say my complaint against Via is closed, you allow in your response that I can still raise my complaint before an "upcoming meeting of the Investigative Panel of the Lawyer Disciplinary Board." Please let this letter serve as a formal request that my complaint be heard by this Investigative Panel of the Disciplinary Board.

I was aware of limited prosecutorial immunity before filing my complaint. However my research revealed that if my prosecutor was obviously misrepresenting facts, intentionally making false statements, or obstructing justice, that those are serious violations that give me grounds for filing my complaint against him. I was also told by the Clerk of your Office that I may file complaints against both my attorney and the prosecutor on the case. Everyone must answer to someone, even County Prosecuting Attorneys and judges.

You tell me that Mr. Via's conduct, or rather what I see as his misconduct, did not violate Rules of Professional Conduct: as you noted, numbered 1, 2, and 3.

> **1. He was obliged to seek justice, not only to convict.** Yet he refused to look at significant exculpatory defense evidence and was determined to convict me.
> **2. He was obliged only to represent the State,** yes, but he also worked closely with my Accuser -- an individual client -- with total disregard for her many contradictory statements and lies, specifically the exculpatory evidence (more than 100 pages of illegal *ex parte* communications to the judge by her) that were sealed, without my knowledge, or affording me an opportunity to object to the sealing. My Accuser's 13-page Victim Impact Statement (VIS) was disregarded by Mr. Via, by the judge, and by my own defense attorney. I was disallowed from questioning the many factual inaccuracies and libels in that VIS. Thus my complaints against all three Court Officers. In three *ex parte* letters and VIS I am falsely accused of committing numerous crimes, including murder, that the Court conveniently accepted as true.
> **3.** Absolutely no **reasonable doubt** that I battered the State's claiming witness, my

Accuser, was afforded me. None. To put in lawyerly terms, Via, the judge and my defense attorney *concealed evidence that lawyers would reasonably believe have potential or actual evidentiary value*. Again, despite many of Accuser's proven lies and contradictions, under oath, and the obvious lack of sufficient evidence, Via and the Court did not consider any of that to raise reasonable doubt. The *fix was in* to convict me, disadvantaged by my being an out of state defendant. I offer proof of that in my WVSCA appeal and with my four complaints. The Court and Via were not interested in my Accuser's clear, documented motive for making her false claim and for filing her false reports to the Court and to law enforcement. To avoid giving me my day in court Via offered me several plea deals, all of which I declined immediately because no battery ever took place. I refused to "accept responsibility" and guilt for being a "woman beater." He never questioned the false claims, up to nor after my lying Accuser fled the state of WV in October 2018 for fear of facing and being questioned by the Accused -- me -- or of possibly being arrested for filing false reports, perjury, harassment, abuse of process, etc.

In my 12-page complaint I provide several examples of Via's misrepresenting facts, **pages 3-4, 6-7**, and obstructing justice. **pages 8-11**. Also, besides evidence of violating **Rule 8.4 *(c,d,f)*** by Mr. Via, I specifically cited ***Rule 3.8. Special Responsibilities of a Prosecutor*** and provided proof of that Rule's violations, **pages 10-11**. I am surprised that my complaint, showing Patrick Via's concealing of evidence, making false statements and obstructing justice do not constitute violations of the Rules of Professional Conduct.

Again, my criminal conviction for an alleged 2015 misdemeanor battery is under appeal *pro se* to WVSCA, though in both the Petitioner's Brief and Reply Brief I was limited by space to present detailed evidence to *each* of Via's violations. Prosecutorial Misconduct was in the last chapters in my limited Briefs.

Hopefully, my complaint will be presented for consideration at an upcoming meeting of the Investigative Panel. It is shocking to me that Special Prosecutor Via was free to do everything he wanted: show his obvious bias against the Accused; prosecute without probable cause, nor properly investigate Accuser's claim. During the three and one half year ordeal I was never interviewed by either law enforcement or by the prosecutor at the Magistrate level or Circuit Court. Fact! Via and the other court officers, including my own defense attorney, concealed exculpatory evidence and used unverified, unquestioned, undate-stamped selfie photographs as the court's *only* evidence. The three trial transcripts, the ignored affidavit of my primary witness and other exhibits should have raised more that just reasonable doubt that no battery took place as my Accuser claimed back in 2015. Via, in fact *did* represent my Accuser, spending untold hours working closely with her while never once interviewing me. Why should he since he's protected and unaccountable? So far, that is.

Respectfully submitted,

Will Williams

Appendix 22: Letter to Judge Dent from Williams after completing his probation

William White Williams

Phone   '017

26 September, 2020
Ref: Case #16-M-AP-1

Judge Jennifer P. Dent
912 Court Street N
Lewisburg, WV 24901

Dear Judge Dent,

The 18-month probation that you imposed on me ended on 19 August, 2020. Probation Officer Robert Tooze's Discharge Report informing the Court that all conditions had been satisfied as of that date was mailed to your Pocahontas County Circuit Court Clerk (CCC) on 20 August, 2020, and it was filed on 24 August, more than one month ago as I write this letter to you.

Yesterday I called CCC for the fourth time in the past month, checking again on the status of the Final Order that must be signed by you. It will finally put an end to my five-year ordeal with the 11th Judicial District of West Virginia. I was told again that you have not signed it.

Is there some reason I should know about as to why you have not signed the Final Order? Your Clerk, Cindy Beverage, was quite surprised when told by my wife Lana that the Order had still not been signed. When asked how long it normally takes to sign one Cindy replied, "just a few days."

Is there an extended time limit before you must sign this Order? If so, please let me know how long it will be before we can wrap up this case. I've paid my debt to society for the alleged "battery" of my Accuser, Miss DeCourcy, and my understanding is that I am no longer on probation or under the control of the 11th Judicial District of West Virginia. Am I wrong?

I need a certified copy of the Final Order signed by you.

Surely, you wouldn't slow-walk the signing of this Order as retaliation for my filing those two Complaints against you with the Judicial Investigation Commission, would you? That can't possibly be the reason I still do not have the Final Order in hand five weeks after my probation ended. I shouldn't have to wait several more weeks or months to receive a certified copy of the Final Order.

I don't want to file another Complaint, but see no other recourse if I do not receive the necessary Order soon, or an explanation from you as to why I'm not getting it.

Sincerely,

Will Williams

Appendix 23: Accuser on alleged incident at Circuit Court (CC) trial

1 had my banana and yogurt in it. But, anyway, it was when I had

2 started to move my feet that he just, don't you walk away from

3 me. I'm not done with you, you know. You're going to stay,

4 you know. And so then - and I said no. I said you're acting

5 stupid. You're acting crazy. This is nonproductive. I'm

6 trying to get out, so I'm trying to disengage. And he comes

7 across the room. He gets all crazy, which he's done before,

8 where he tried to bash my head --

9   MS. FINCH: Objection. Prior acts.

10   THE WITNESS: Okay. And, anyway --

11   THE COURT: I'm sorry. Stop.

12   Your objection was prior acts. And what was her

13 statement?

14   THE WITNESS: That he had attacked me before.

15   THE COURT: I'll sustain the objection.

16 BY MR. VIA:

17   Q   Talk about the events of the day, ma'am.

18   A   And so --

19   Q   Describe the physical aggression. Answer the

20 question if you would, please. That's the question pending.

21   A   All right. So, anyway, so he came at me.

22 Originally when he started across the room, he had a fist that

23 was going to smash me in the head. And when he came across,

24 he's aiming and he's hitting my neck. I got knocked back into

 1   chairs that are in front of the wall on my side. And so I'm

 2   trapped there. And then he's choking me and screaming about I

 3   know too much, I know too much. All kinds of crazy shit.

 4   And so he pushes me then towards the corner where there

 5   was a sharp filing cabinet. So I'm tripping over that. And

 6   then, up in towards bookcases that are right there at the

 7   corner. So it's a corner, this. And so in all this, he's -

 8   I've got it -- anyway, I'm trying to fight, but I'm stunned.

 9   And I keep on getting -- I can't - I'm off balance because I'm

10   getting shoved into stuff. At one point when I can, I look

11   over at Michael. Michael's in the door. And he is just -- and

12   so then he comes in the room. And he starts screaming, stop

13   this, stop this, stop this. This is deplorable. And he

14   wouldn't stop. So he had to use his body.

15   MS. FINCH: Hearsay, Your Honor.

16   MR. VIA: It's an excited utterance, I think, Judge.

17   THE COURT: I'm sorry?

18   MS. FINCH: I'll withdraw it, Your Honor.

19   THE COURT: Thank you.

20   BY MR. VIA:

21   Q   When that kind of thing happens, we need to stop and

22   pick up where we were. Okay?

23   A   Okay. I can't hear what she said.

24   Q   Well, okay. Now you described - you used the word

1   choking a moment ago.

2   A   Oh, yeah.

3   Q   Now I need to ask a very specific question. Can you

4   describe how choking? Was it an arm, bar, hands?

5   A   Hands.

6   Q   Well, you describe it. Tell me what you meant when

7   you said choking.

8   A   His hands. 'Cause he had his hands on me. And he

9   had his hands around my neck. And then at one point, I was

10   trying to do something with this arm. But the filing cabinet

11   is really sharp. And so, anyways - so I'm getting shoved up

12   against other stuff.

13   And then Michael came in with his body and just rammed

14   Williams to knock him off of me, which first pushed him that

15   way. Okay? And then he yells, fuck you, Michael. Fuck you,

16   Michael. He goes, she needs to be shut up. She needs to be

17   shut up for good. She knows too much. Fuck you, Michael. Get

18   out of the way, because Michael had gotten in front of me. And

19   he was yelling, what the hell are you doing. You know, you're

20   attacking -- so he's blocking. So at that point, the injuries

21   were all being pushed into stuff, sharp things, blunt things,

22   up against the phone and the cabinet, filing cabinet. Blunt

23   compression.

24   Q   Let's stop there for a moment, ma'am. When

```
 1    Mr. Oljaca intervened, as you describe, did that conclude

 2    the --

 3           A     No.  Oh, no.

 4           Q     Well, you haven't heard the rest of my question,

 5    ma'am.

 6           A     Okay.

 7           Q     Did he intervene and stop the physical altercation

 8    at that point?

 9           A     Williams wouldn't stop.  It went on for a long time

10    after this.  I'm - so - because he thought it would.  And he

11    went like this with his body.  And then had to turn around

12    because Williams - he was staring -- he turned.  He's around.

13    He's got Williams here.  He's looking at me.  I'm choking now

14    and I'm trying to catch my breath.  And then Williams keeps

15    coming through and around Michael and keeps on trying to grab

16    my neck.  But I'm still up against the chairs and the filing

17    cabinet.  And so that's where all the scratches happened

18    because he kept screaming that she knows too much, she knows

19    too much, you know.  I need to end it.  This is - Michael, fuck

20    you.  Get out of the way.  Kept on saying stuff to him.

21           And then - but that's how he kept on doing it.  And so at

22    one point, Michael pushed him back up to the -- so, we were

23    here.  This way.  Okay?  And I was just stunned.  And I was

24    kind of frozen in fear.  And now, I wanted to leave.  But now,
```

1 I'm just choking, but I'm watching. And now I have to --

2 they're fighting. And he's hitting - he's on Michael. And I'm

3 just stunned. Then they push back towards me again. This just

4 kept on going on with him. Kept on -- I'm having to hear

5 someone trying to justify to the other person, no, no. Stop

6 defending her. She has to die. She knows too much.

7   Q   Let's stop there --

8   A   I'm horrified.

9   Q   Let's stop there for a moment. So the altercation,

10 as you've described it, went on in that --

11   A   Oh, yeah.

12   Q   Let me finish my question, ma'am. Went on that way

13 for a period of time. But, ultimately, it concluded. Is that

14 correct? You'll need to say yes or no.

15   A   Yes.

16   Q   Okay. Now what did you do when the altercation

17 concluded?

18   A   Well, at one point in one of the breaks towards the

19 end and I got my voice back, I'm bent over and I'm leaning and

20 screaming. And I'm going, call the police. Call the police.

21 Call the police. And then Michael looks at Williams. And it's

22 like -- and he did a growling thing. And the point is, if

23 you --

24   Q   Did you leave the building?

     1   A   Yeah.

     2   Q   Okay. Who went with you when you left the building?

     3   A   Michael and I went out the door and ran through -

     4   it's a pretty big building. Went the full length of the

     5   building, out the back of the building, out into the yard, in

     6   the woods up at the end.

     7   Q   Where was Mr. Williams when you last saw him at --

     8   A   In my office at that point.

     9   Q   So as you described it, you and Mr. Oljaca left that

    10   room, exited the building. And the last you saw Mr. Williams,

    11   he was still in your office. Is that correct?

    12   A   Yeah.

    13   Q   What did you do specifically after you were able to

    14   exit the building?

    15   A   While we were out there, Michael took his pictures.

    16   But there was a lot of discussion there. We wanted to call the

    17   police. But the problem is, it's like a - you're thinking like

    18   mafia, mob gang and a cult.

    19   Q   Well, we're not going to get into the discussion you

    20   and Mr. Oljaca had. That's not going to be admissible here.

    21   Okay? So you indicated some photographs were taken by

    22   Mr. Oljaca. Is that correct?

    23   A   Yeah.

    24   Q   Now subsequent to that, were any other photographs

Appendix 24: Williams' testimony on alleged incident at CC trial (direct)


```
 1        A     Yes.

 2        Q     When she arrived, you were sitting there?

 3        A     Yes.

 4        Q     What was the conversation that ensued?

 5        A     Well, I wanted to talk to them, particularly

 6   Mr. Oljaca.  And I had some questions for him.  And she came in

 7   the room too.  And, you know, I didn't object to that.

 8        Q     So you were speaking with Mr. Oljaca?

 9        A     Yes.  He wasn't outside in the hall as she said.  I

10   was sitting at my desk, and he was sitting here.

11        Q     And this was her office?

12        A     Well, it's my office.  But, yeah, that's where the

13   telephone is and the computer.

14        Q     What was the conversation about?

15        A     I was asking Mr. Oljaca why he hadn't gotten a key

16   to that office.  She was keeping it locked and keeping him out,

17   even though he was put there between us as chief of staff.  And

18   I asked him about that, and she wouldn't let him answer.  She

19   was talking over him.  I told her to just shut up.  And then I

20   wanted to know why, when I e-mailed him, that she writes the

21   return - the reply to my e-mail to him.  And why is she

22   listening in on phone calls between me and him.  That's what

23   the conversations were about.  But he couldn't answer.  She was

24   running her mouth, talking over us.  I told her to shut up.  And
```

1   that's what brought it to a head, I guess.

2   But she was sitting across from me by the window. And at

3   some point, she jumped up and comes at the desk and starts

4   shaking her finger in my face, calling me psycho, and I don't

5   have any friends, and nobody likes me, and, you know. I said,

6   well, okay. But she comes right at me. And I hold my arm out,

7   like this, to stop. I'm behind a desk, mind you. I'm not able

8   to choke her, if I could. And it did touch her chin. So she

9   was touched. But she touched me, my hand with her chin, you

10   could just as easily say.

11   Q   Was the conversation as Ms. Decourcy described about

12   her telephone calls or her investigation on the Internet about

13   what people were saying about you?

14   A   Not really. Part of it, the night before, I was in

15   the office across the hall, which was Mr. Oljaca's office. And

16   I was typing, working on a monthly bulletin. And it was, like,

17   10:30 -- 11 at night. I didn't even know she was in the other

18   office. The phone rang. I picked it up. And it was this

19   fellow, Harrington, who I'd met years and years ago. And

20   nothing sensational. I asked him, well, how did you get this

21   number. He said, oh, on a "E" list. And said, well, okay. I

22   said, she's not here, but give me your number. And I wrote her

23   number down - I mean, his number down. And we ended the

24   conversation.

1   And when I left, I saw the light was on. And I went over

2 there. And I gave her the number. I remember when I wrote it,

3 it was the driver's license manual so Michael could get his

4 driver's license for West Virginia. And I wrote it on the back

5 there and handed it to her and asked her about this "E" list

6 thing. What is this "E" list thing? And she gave me some

7 answer that really wasn't very satisfactory. I said, well,

8 okay. That was about the end of it. She left and went home

9 and I went to bed. I don't remember ever even mentioning any

10 of that the next morning because it wasn't a big deal.

11   Q   So you were seated behind the desk. And how was it

12 that Ms. Decourcy was going to be able to get across the desk

13 to get at you?

14   A   She wouldn't. She was just coming right in my face

15 and screaming. Really, I'd never seen anything like it. When

16 she worked for me, she called me psycho and all this silly

17 nonsense. Michael Oljaca was sitting there. He wasn't out in

18 the hall, like she says. And when we were both standing, he

19 stood too. But there was no choking. There was no beating

20 with my fists or slapping with my hand or any of that, pushing

21 her into the corner, into the filing cabinet and the table or

22 whatever. It just didn't happen. And I left. I went across

23 the room, the hall to Michael's office. And I was working on

24 the bulletin.

```
 1        Q     You left first?

 2        A     I left first, yes.  I ended it.  I wasn't going to

 3   engage with this woman screaming at me.

 4        Q     Did she frantically run away from you?

 5        A     No.  I don't know.  They went out back.  And then

 6   they came in - what she didn't say was, they came back in about

 7   ten minutes later.  And I paid them.

 8        Q     For the month?

 9        A     Yes.

10        Q     What did you do next?

11        A     I met with Fred Streed, who was there with his wife

12   Martha, who was going to be a witness today.  We bought him a

13   plane ticket to fly here, but he couldn't make it.

14        Q     Did you go home after that?

15        A     I had dinner with them at the gatehouse and then

16   drove home.  But I'd been working with Fred for a couple of

17   days.  We fixed the water heater.  We fixed the tractor that

18   had been sitting in the woods for 13 years, got it running.

19   Still running.  He was very helpful.  Fred stayed there for 11

20   years.  He was president of the board of directors.  He was

21   Dr. Pierce's executor.  I mean, he's a very reliable fellow.

22   And his affidavit couldn't be admitted 'cause you can't

23   cross-examine a piece of paper.

24        Q     In the days that followed the 30th of September of
```

Appendix 25: Williams' testimony on alleged incident at CC trial (cross)


```
 1        A    Yes.

 2        Q    Told them to shut up?

 3        A    I've told people to shut up all my life.  Have you?

 4   I mean . . .

 5        Q    Now there was a desk between you and her?

 6        A    Yes.

 7        Q    You felt physically threatened with that desk

 8   between you?

 9        A    No.

10        Q    You think she was going to hurt you?

11        A    Not until she jumped up and got in my face.

12        Q    How'd she get in your face with that desk between

13   you?

14        A    With her finger.

15        Q    Okay.  Did you feel physically threatened by that?

16        A    I'm not afraid of her.  But I was being advanced on

17   by this screaming lunatic.  And I was trying to talk to my

18   employee, my other employee.  I told her to shut up.  Actually,

19   I probably cussed a little bit in there, but no need to say

20   that here.

21        Q    Well, you can say what you said.  What'd you tell

22   her?

23        A    Shut the fuck up.

24        Q    Okay.  So that's the circumstance of this incident.
```

1   That's the kind of language that was being used. Is that

2   right.

3   A   That's probably what I said.

4   Q   Yeah. Now were you afraid she was going to hurt you

5   coming across that desk?

6   A   No, not afraid.

7   Q   How come you told the state trooper that you were

8   acting in self-defense? Defending what?

9   A   I'll tell you what. If you'll sit there, I'll

10 pretend like I'm her and I'll come at you.

11   Q   I'm asking the question, sir. And I asked you why

12 you told the trooper that you did what you did in self-defense,

13 and you're sitting here today saying you felt neither

14 threatened nor afraid she was going to hurt you?

15   A   I never said that.

16   Q   You didn't say what?

17   A   I didn't say I felt like she was going to hurt me.

18   Q   I know. You said you didn't think she was going to.

19 I agree with you. That's what you just said here. What I'm

20 asking is, why is it that you told the state police that you

21 were acting in self-defense?

22   A   She came at me first. I didn't go at her. She was

23 very provocative.

24   Q   She's a lunatic?

Appendix 26: Accuser lying about Trooper Brock preparing her statement


```
 1          Q     You reported this event on the 31st of October.
 2    Correct?
 3          A     Oh.  He asked again for another statement.  Yes.
 4          Q     So is it your testimony that you provided the
 5    written statement several days after the event?
 6          A     Mr. Oljaca and I.  We went in to the Marlinton
 7    barracks.  And we talked to them.  They - we talked --
 8          Q     Is it your testimony that you provided a written
 9    statement several days after the event?
10          A     What word are you saying?  That I provided a?
11          Q     A written statement.
12          A     Oh, did we write anything?  No.  He did.
13          Q     And then on the 31st, you gave a statement.
14    Correct?
15          A     On the 31st, was in the middle of some crimes
16    that -- yeah, that the police reports, the felonies.
17          Q     On the 31st, you gave a statement.  Correct?
18          A     He wrote a statement and asked me to sign it while
19    he was stealing my property.  And he had done the breaking and
20    entering.
21          Q     And I'll object to your testimony as being
22    nonresponsive.
23          A     I'm trying --
24          Q     If you could --
```

```
 1          THE COURT:  Let me interrupt you.

 2          You need to answer the question.  She'll ask a question.

 3  You answer it.

 4  BY MS. FINCH:

 5          Q    I'm going to show you what I'll ask the court

 6  reporter to mark as the defendant's first exhibit.

 7          DEFENDANT'S EXHIBIT NO. 1 MARKED FOR IDENTIFICATION

 8  BY MS. FINCH:

 9          Q    It's being designated as Exhibit 1.  If you could

10  just please take a look at that exhibit.  And without going

11  into its contents, if you could, describe what that is.

12          A    Mr. Via?

13          MR. VIA:  No.  You can't ask me questions.

14          THE COURT:  Ma'am --

15          THE WITNESS:  I need my glasses.  I can't read it.

16          THE COURT:  I'll allow you to step out and get your

17  glasses.

18          THE WITNESS:  I have never seen this.  I don't recall it.

19  BY MS. FINCH:

20          Q    And, again, the question that has been posed is, if

21  you could please, without going into its contents, describe

22  what this document is.

23          A    Describe what this document is?

24          Q    What is this document?  Without going into its
```

1   contents, what is the document?

2   A   I don't know. You handed it to me. I'm going to

3   guess. It's something - it's written by Trooper Brock.

4   Q   Does this document bear your signature on both

5   pages, ma'am?

6   A   Yep.

7   Q   And is that, in fact, your signature?

8   A   Yes, it is.

9   Q   And did you review this document prior to affixing

10 your signature?

11   A   I don't recall ever reading it, but, yeah, I

12 probably did. I don't know. I was shaking and -- anyway,

13 yeah, we had reported to 911. And I was a victim of a crime

14 that day. And he was busy stealing all my property and my

15 evidence. And it's --

16   Q   Again, I'm asking that you identify the document.

17 And my last question was if that document bears your signature.

18   A   Oh, yeah.

19   Q   And so is this, in fact, a statement that you

20 provided to Trooper Brock on the 31st of October?

21   A   I did not - it's not like he transcribed anything I

22 said. It's as if he pre-wrote all this stuff and then came in

23 and was alluding that if I signed this, he was going to make

24 Williams put my stuff back and stop stealing my stuff.

1   Q   Okay. So your testimony to me is that you didn't

2 dictate this document, that this was prepared separately apart

3 from your presence?

4   A   Yeah. He kept on going back and forth outside. He

5 was mostly spending time with Williams and watching them load

6 up a U-Haul truck and their vehicles and cherrypick through my

7 stuff and steal --

8   Q   Your testimony is that this document was prepared by

9 Trooper Brock without your assistance?

10   A   Yeah. I didn't write it.

11   Q   And your testimony is that it doesn't accurately

12 reflect what you reported to Trooper Brock on the 31st of

13 October of 2015?

14   A   I would have to -- I haven't seen this since --

15   Q   Okay. Take as much time as you need.

16   A   -- since then.

17   Q   Take as much time as you need.?

18   A   So I would have to go through things. I don't know

19 if it's exactly what I said exactly.

20   Q   Ma'am, if you could just please take as much time as

21 you need. We'll be talking about this document for a few

22 moments. So, please, take as much time as you need.

23   A   I've become a bit more familiar with it.

24   Q   Have you finished reviewing the document?

1   A   I guess. Yeah.

2   Q   Have you read it in its entirety at this point?

3   A   I believe so.

4   Q   Okay. And so you've agreed that you signed this

5 document. And it appears to contain several inconsistencies

6 from your testimony here today. The first of which is that

7 this document recites that the incident happened on September

8 the 29th. Is there a reason why you misremember the date?

9   A   I didn't misremember the date. I didn't write this.

10 Trooper Brock did.

11   Q   Okay. So you seem like a pretty sophisticated

12 person. And my next question is, why you would sign something

13 that wasn't accurate?

14   A   Because he never said he was doing anything formal.

15 We had called 911 because he cut the gate lock, trespassed --

16   Q   And my question is --

17   A   -- was stealing my property.

18   Q   I'm sorry. If you could please just answer the

19 question, this will go much better. If you could please

20 explain, if you have an explanation, as to why you would sign a

21 document that wasn't an accurate report that you made to law

22 enforcement --

23   A   Because --

24   Q   -- on the 31st of October?

1   A   Because he said he would stop him. He's stealing my

2   property, my personal papers, which that would endanger me.

3   Q   So that was the reason you signed a document --

4   A   Yeah.

5   Q   -- that didn't accurately reflect what happened?

6   A   Yes. They were --

7   Q   So there's no explanation for why he said the

8   incident happened on the 29th of --

9   A   I didn't say --

10   THE COURT: For about the tenth time, it is going to be a

11   question and an answer. A question and an answer. And you

12   will subsequently be given an opportunity for any explanation,

13   I'm sure. But at this point, you answer the question.

14   BY MS. FINCH:

15   Q   This morning, you testified that the incident

16   happened shortly after or around the hour of 9:00. Correct?

17   A   Uh-huh.

18   Q   And in the statement which you signed, it says that

19   the incident happened not on September the 30th at 9:00, but,

20   in fact, on September the 29th at about 11:00. Is there any

21   explanation for that inconsistency?

22   A   Yeah. Trooper Brock wrote this. I didn't. And at

23   this point, I was shaking in fear and had gone into shock.

24   He's stealing all my stuff and evidence of crimes.

Appendix 27: Trooper Brock on preparation of DeCourcy's statement


```
 1   regarding something that's been admitted into evidence as

 2   Defendant's Exhibit 1.  If you could, please take a look at

 3   that document and let me know if you recognize it.

 4        A    Yes.  This is a statement that I have obtained with

 5   Ms. Decourcy.

 6        Q    Do you recall sitting and discussing what would be

 7   contained in that statement?

 8        A    Not particulars.

 9        Q    When you take a statement which is to be a written

10   statement from someone, do you normally write it down yourself?

11        A    A lot of times, I'll - most of the time, I'll try to

12   have whoever that person is write their own statement.  But not

13   many people want to do that.  So when they don't want to

14   cooperate with that or they don't want to write it themselves,

15   I'll write what they say for them.

16        Q    Do you write what they say right in front of them?

17        A    Yes.

18        Q    And have you ever written what someone said apart

19   from them and then come back to them with their statement and

20   asked them to sign it?

21        A    Meaning, do I write a statement without them

22   present?

23        Q    Right.

24        A    No.
```

     Q   And so if the testimony was that Ms. Decourcy had no
idea what that was, and it was her signature, but you had just
written it and asked her to sign it, that would not be correct.
Right?

     A   Right. That is false.

     Q   In fact, when you review that, what is generally
your procedure for asking folks to review their statements?

     A   Well, this one, I have two pages. On the back page,
I've got other questions that I had concerning it. I will ask
the question, get their answer, write everything down for them.
Once I've completed it, I'll tell them to look over it, see if
that's what they told me. If there's anything they want to
change, they can change it. They can add it in themselves or I
will do it for them. However. And I can see on the second
page, that's actually been the case, where this is not my
handwriting on some of the answers. So she has undoubtedly
filled that out as well and then signed the document.

     Q   So to the best of your knowledge, she thoroughly
reviewed that document after you prepared it with her
assistance?

     A   I gave it to her to read it. I don't know that she
read it or not. That's up to her. But she stated that she
understood it, she signed it, and she agreed with it. So I
would assume that means that she did.

Appendix 28: Accuser's lies about "real NA board" and "pay off"


```
 1        Q     And so the incident that you were describing

 2   regarding the removal of your belongings, which you asserted as

 3   grand theft, that happened on the 31st of October.  Right?

 4        A     Yes.

 5        Q     And that's the same day that you gave a statement

 6   about this having been the 29th of September?

 7        A     Well, I didn't give the statement about it being the

 8   29th.  It was pre-written outside while he was hanging out with

 9   Mr. Williams.

10        Q     And so my question was, that day that your items

11   were being removed from the warehouse, that was the same day

12   that you signed the statement that Trooper Brock prepared for

13   you.  Right?

14        A     Right.

15        Q     And so you at least reported the alleged assault on

16   the 31st of October?  Even if, as you've testified, you

17   reported it before, you also did report it on the 31st of

18   October?

19        A     Oh, yes, 'cause he'd already had the photographs in

20   their - the police already had a copy of the photographs.

21        Q     But your testimony is that you were never fired, you

22   were never dismissed, you were never asked to separate from

23   employment?

24        A     No.  Who would've done that?
```

1   Q   Who would have asked you to separate from your

2   employment?

3   A   I was still working for the board and working for

4   them and continued to.

5   Q   Okay. Who did you describe earlier today as having

6   been your supervisor?

7   A   My immediate supervisor?

8   Q   Correct. Who did you describe as being the boss?

9   A   Oh. Well, Williams was trying to take control of

10   what was going on on the property. But we'd already had a

11   board meeting. And things had already been recognized. And he

12   just wanted a payoff. So he wanted - he was going to give

13   someone else the chairmanship, but he wanted a payoff.

14   Q   Who hired you?

15   A   The board did. The corporation.

16   Q   Who? Who hired you? What person hired you? What

17   person told you, yes, come to West Virginia?

18   A   Oh. The first contact? That was Mr. Williams. And

19   then after that, I met some of the board members.

20   Q   Who paid you?

21   A   Pardon?

22   Q   Who paid you?

23   A   Mr. Williams because he had --

24   Q   And who asked you to leave prior to the 31st of

1 October?

2   A   No one.

3   Q   So your testimony is that you were never asked to

4 leave, you were never - your employment was never terminated

5 and you were never asked to separate from employment with the

6 National Alliance?

7   A   No. When are you saying this happened?

8   Q   Prior to the 31st of October when your belongings

9 were removed from the property and when you made this report,

10 were you asked to separate from your employment?

11   A   No.

12   Q   Okay. And so you testified earlier about a contract

13 that was sent to you, wherein you were asked to leave, never

14 come back, leave your home, as you testified.

15   A   Right.

16   Q   What was that?

17   A   We had been getting - people that Williams had been

18 talking to about his plans, we had been getting information

19 from them. And so that he had been threatening me. Like, he

20 had been threatening -- okay.

21   Q   What I asked was what the contract was.

22   A   The contact was what they had been planning. There

23 were several stages. There was stage one, a blackmail. And

24 then there was stage two.

1   Q   What was the contract?

2   A   What do you mean, what was the contract? What do

3 you mean specifically?

4   Q   What type of contract was it?

5   A   It was just something that benefited him personally.

6 That I would not go to the police, that I would not report his

7 crimes. I would never testify against him. I wouldn't go to

8 the media and stuff like that, 'cause we were getting phone

9 calls on people he was talking to about this.

10   Q   But you've explained that you were never terminated.

11 Right?

12   A   No. Not by --

13   Q   You weren't asked to leave, you weren't asked to

14 separate from your employment?

15   A   No. In fact, when he was stealing this stuff, the

16 director of the corporation was on the phone with Brock,

17 telling him to have Williams leave. And then later saying that

18 another director, John McLaughlin, had talked to the police

19 about these things.

20   Q   But these folks, they weren't the person that hired

21 you or --

22   A   They were directors of the corporation and officers.

23   Q   So at what point did you decide that Williams was no

24 longer your boss?

         A   He had published and was telling us all that he
wanted his payoff. He was getting off, out of it. We had
someone who was going to do a payoff. And then the idea was
John. But then at the 8/1/15 board meeting, two board
meetings, he kept going on and on about his plans to murder
people in detail.
         Q   Okay. So the question --
         A   And right beforehand, the guy who was going to take
his position --
         Q   So the question was, at what point did William cease
to be your boss? If you remember. And the answer would be a
period in time or a day, a week in October.
         A   I worked for the corporation's entities. Okay? And
they each had things that needed to be done for them. And then
regular things to take care of, things. He was continuing,
after the assault, to have me work on stuff for a law case, a
corporate lawsuit in Virginia because he personally --
         Q   Williams was?
         A   -- was in contempt. Yes.
         Q   You were working for Williams after the assault?
         A   His attorney and this other guy, they were
submitting to us what they needed because we had documents at
the office that they needed - he wanted to use.
         Q   Were you talking to him on a regular basis after the

1   assault?

2   A   No.   His wife was sending things from his e-mail

3   account. And then Timothy Calomerus was sending constant stuff

4   because he was in contempt --

5   Q   So let me ask you for a third time.

6   (interruption by court reporter due to simultaneous speaking)

7   MS. FINCH: I apologize.

8   BY MS. FINCH:

9   Q   Who replaced Williams as your boss?

10   A   When they had the votes at the October 1st board

11   meeting, 2015, the votes at the National Alliance meeting was

12   first, then the National Alliance on the books. He wanted out.

13   This other guy was supposed to pay him. The same thing. He

14   just wanted out. The same stuff he's published.

15   Anyway, his tenure -- chairman is a one-year - following

16   the Virginia Nonstock Corporation Act and the other things, the

17   articles of corporation, it's a one-year role and you have to

18   be renewed. So at the board meeting, he was not renewed. That

19   then there was a unanimous vote that John McLaughlin was to

20   take on those positions. And so - and that that would end up

21   occurring on October 24th, 2015. In the meantime, he wanted

22   some payoff.

23   DEFENDANT'S EXHIBIT NO. 3 MARKED FOR IDENTIFICATION

24

BY MS. FINCH:

     Q   Okay. So what I'm going to show you is what has

been marked as Defendant's Exhibit No. 3. Without going into

its contents, if you could explain for me please, ma'am, what

this is.

     A   Yeah. This is the thing he sent me, that then we

had sent - we sent out 'cause -- anyway. Yeah.

     THE COURT: You need to respond to the question. Ma'am,

you need to respond to the question. All I got from that is,

this is the thing. What is it?

     THE WITNESS: I don't - this looks like -- I don't have

my copy that he had sent me. And then they'd been used in

exhibits in other cases. So I don't know if this is the exact

same thing that I'd been given before. But, yeah. When we got

this, this is -- yeah.

BY MS. FINCH:

     Q   What is it?

     A   This was his little attempt to get me to sign this,

to try to protect himself.

     Q   What is this document?

     A   If this is the same thing.

     Q   What is this document?

     A   Oh. He was trying to state that I was a contractor.

And that therefore he was trying to state that I was a - like,

 1   a subcontractor and that he had a contract with me and that he

 2   was now going to terminate that contract and therefore dissolve

 3   a contract.

 4   Q   So this is a termination agreement?

 5   A   Oh. It states I'm a contractor. He's trying to --

 6   at this point, he was already committing tax fraud. And so he

 7   - lots of -- the records that were supposed to be given to the

 8   IRS in the court case, he was -- there was a lot of stuff going

 9   on that he --

10   Q   Is this a termination of contract?

11   A   Yes. This is a termination of a contractor

12   contract, which we never had. This was, again, another illegal

13   ploy.

14   Q   And so you testified earlier that there was no

15   attempt at any point to sever your contract, to terminate your

16   employment with the National Alliance, to separate you from

17   employment. Correct?

18   A   No. I was still in full contact with the other -

19   other directors and working for them and working on all the

20   different --

21   Q   Is this a document that was transmitted to you by

22   Mr. Williams?

23   A   Is it in the document that --

24   Q   Is this a document that was transmitted to you by

```
 1  Mr. Williams during the month of October, 2015?

 2       A    It looks similar to something I've gotten.  It's

 3  been since 2015.  And the only time this was - I'd seen my copy

 4  was when they were submitted in other court cases of evidence

 5  of his crimes against me and then the corporate case for fraud.

 6       Q    And this document was transmitted to you, if I'm

 7  correct, prior to you giving the statement on October 31.

 8  Correct?

 9       A    It was mailed to me, yeah.

10       Q    And prior to you giving the statement on the second

11  of December.  Right?

12       A    Yeah.  'Cause we presented my copy thing as evidence

13  of part of the crime, yeah.

14       Q    So, in fact, Mr. Williams had attempted to separate

15  you from employment with the National Alliance.  Is that

16  correct?

17       A    No.  Mr. Williams -- this was given to the other

18  directors.  But Mr. Williams was illegally claiming that I was

19  a contractor, which I wasn't, and that he was terminating a

20  contract.  And what he was doing is the same thing - he had an

21  illegal contract with Eric Gliebe --

22       Q    Okay.

23       A    -- same thing.  He's using things to try to protect

24  himself, but they're false.  And if you sign that, you're
```

 1   committing a crime. So I wasn't going to sign any of this

 2   stuff.

 3   Q   I don't desire to make life difficult for the court

 4   reporter. But for that reason, I need you to answer my

 5   questions in a manner in which they're presented. And so my

 6   question was, Mr. Williams did, in fact, attempt to separate

 7   you from employment prior to your report of October 31.

 8   Correct? And the answer would be yes or no.

 9   A   Oh. No.

10   Q   Okay. Thank you. You had stated that you had been

11   living on the property. And then in another portion of your

12   testimony on direct, you talked about living at Mr. DeMarais's

13   home. Could you clarify that? Were you living on the property

14   or were you living at DeMarais's home?

15   A   Which property? 'Cause there's a whole bunch of

16   different parcels. My employment came with free housing,

17   utilities. And when I moved my things there, I had stuff in

18   storage units at other places.

19   Q   Were you living on the property or were you living

20   at Mr. DeMarais's home?

21   A   Originally, I was living on the property. He had

22   told me that there was ample suitable housing.

23   Q   On the 30th of September, were you living on the

24   property or were you living in Mr. DeMarais's home?

Appendix 29: Weak closing argument of Finch


```
 1          (Excerpt - closing argument of defense counsel)

 2          THE COURT:  Ms. Finch?

 3          MS. FINCH:  Thank you, Your Honor.  Upon the State's

 4   amendment, their obliged to show the Court that Mr. Williams

 5   unlawfully and intentionally made physical contact with force

 6   capable of causing physical pain or injury to Ms. DeCourcy or

 7   unlawfully and intentionally did cause such physical pain or

 8   injury.

 9          And what Mr. Via has described was an incident, as

10   Ms. DeCourcy described in her testimony, of punching, pulling,

11   choking, and holding down.  She explained that she had gotten

12   injuries, bruises after being pushed against filing cabinets

13   and bookshelves.  But the evidence doesn't show that.  She

14   didn't take any photographs of those injuries.  She didn't take

15   any photographs of any bruises that she incurred, as she

16   described, after these red marks dissipated, the bruises that

17   she described.  There was no photographic evidence of that.

18   And so we're not talking about insulting or provoking contact,

19   but rather unlawful and unintentional physical contact with

20   force capable of causing physical pain or injury.

21          Putting the aside issue of credibility, which I think

22   there are great many, these photographs show a pressure mark.

23   And while Ms. DeCourcy did describe physical pain or injury,

24   that's not what the photographs depict.  She explained the
```

1 discrepancy in these two statements given approximately one

2 month and three days apart as being the fault of Trooper Brock,

3 that he just wrote this up and brought it to her and explained

4 that she needed to sign it in order for him to deal with her

5 stolen property.

6 And you heard from Trooper Brock that nothing could be

7 further from the truth. That he sat and took her statement,

8 that he allowed her to make modifications to that statement,

9 which you see clear as day. And then she signed. So, I agree

10 that the date and time might be errors that can be explained

11 just by human error. But I disagree that Ms. DeCourcy saying

12 that Trooper Brock made this statement up and had her sign it

13 isn't relevant. I think it's very relevant to her credibility.

14 And, so, she lied when she told you that she didn't

15 prepare this statement. She lied when she told you who was in

16 the room at the time. She lied when she told you that she was

17 afraid. Because it's clear in her statement, she responded to

18 Trooper Brock that she had refused to cooperate because she was

19 scared that Mr. Williams would get even or kill her. When she

20 was asked by Trooper Brock, why do you want to file a complaint

21 now? Because I'm still afraid of him. So it doesn't stand to

22 reason that someone would refuse to cooperate because they were

23 afraid and you choose to file a complaint because they're

24 afraid.

1   What's very clear here is that Ms. DeCourcy believed

2 herself to continue to work for the National Alliance, that she

3 knew she didn't continue to work for Mr. Williams, and that she

4 was going to throw as many wrenches into this as possible in

5 order to maintain her position. That's one thing that she

6 didn't lie about, that she believed she still works for the

7 National Alliance. But she had lied about what happened here.

8   Mr. Williams lied when he was asked if he had tampered

9 with witnesses. And he was impeached on it. He wrote an

10 e-mail that was very foolish, indeed, and very unadvisable.

11 But I don't think that that undercuts what he otherwise

12 testified, which was that this just simply didn't happen the

13 way Ms. DeCourcy explains it. And I think that when you think

14 about what happened in the days following this incident, it

15 stands to reason that Mr. Williams's account is correct.

16 Because, Ms. DeCourcy told us on the stand that she immediately

17 ran out of the place. She went back in to use the bathroom,

18 which is unexplained if you're in fear for your life. And that

19 she went over to DeMarais's, went on the mountain, and had a

20 planning and strategy session with Mr. Oljaca.

21   What we heard from Ms. Williams is that she had an

22 extended telephone conversation, with Ms. Williams, which is

23 corroborated by the e-mail that Ms. Williams said referred to

24 that telephone conversation. And it's consistent with the fact

1 that Ms. DeCourcy believed that she continued to work for

2 National Alliance. Mr. Williams, in fact, testified he paid

3 Oljaca and Ms. DeCourcy after this incident.

4   I don't disagree that there was clearly a fracas. But it

5 was not, by this photographic evidence, punching, pulling,

6 choking, or holding down. There's no evidence of the injuries

7 that Ms. DeCourcy says that she incurred by being pushed

8 against filing cabinets or bookshelves. And we know she knows

9 how to take photographs of herself. I am encouraging the Court

10 to think about the instances today where Ms. DeCourcy has been

11 dishonest and see that as establishing reasonable doubt that

12 Mr. Williams is guilty of battery. Thank you, Your Honor.

13   (End Excerpt)

14   * * * *

15

16

17

18

19

20

21

22

23

24

Appendix 30: Williams' speech at the second sentencing hearing


```
 1        THE COURT:  Noting no objections to the report - to the
 2   probation portion of the report?
 3        MS. FINCH:  Correct, Your Honor.
 4        THE COURT:  At this time then, I'm going to allow,
 5   Mr. Williams, if you'd like to speak not only to the victim's
 6   impact statement, but also if you would like to speak in
 7   mitigation of sentence at all, any information that you want
 8   the Court to be aware of that may relate to your presentence
 9   report as well, now would be the time you're allowed to do so.
10        THE DEFENDANT:  Okay.  Well, I'm not sure where to start.
11   The ex parte communications, I got them early on, copies of the
12   first one and second one.  And it's obvious that the state's
13   claiming witness was trying to influence the Court by making me
14   out to be a monster.  She accuses me of murder, multiple
15   murders, multiple hiring of hitmen to kill people.  Specifics,
16   kidnapping, rape, embezzlement, arson, fraud.  I mean, the list
17   is just endless.  It's contained in both the ex parte
18   statements and the victim impact statement.  And she swears
19   that they're true.
20        And she sent this victim impact statement to Officer
21   Tooze and then called him and said she wants to be here today
22   to back up her written statement.  And I'm entitled to question
23   what she claims.  I'm not a murderer.  I'm not a rapist.  I'm
24   not a batterer.  I've never been arrested.  He claims I'm a
```

 1 | good character. She says I'm Charles Manson. I wasn't here
 2 | when they sealed the ex parte statements. I did not know they
 3 | were sealed. I was expecting them to be used at my trial.
 4 | I got an order sent to me Thursday, first time I'd seen
 5 | it, sealing the ex parte statements. They weren't used in
 6 | evidence. Yet, they were in evidence. They were sent to you
 7 | to influence you. The prosecutor was attacked in this ex
 8 | parte. Says he's corrupt, senile --
 9 | THE COURT: Mr. Williams, although I'm allowing you to
10 | respond to the victim's impact statement, I think I made clear
11 | on the record the portion of -- the victim's impact statement
12 | asked specific questions. I'm listening to your general
13 | comments. But what I'm trying to do is only consider that
14 | portion of the victim's impact statement as it relates to this,
15 | what's before the Court. What's before the Court is this
16 | battery charge.
17 | THE DEFENDANT: If I could just finish that thought, the
18 | prosecutor requested to withdraw because of allegations made
19 | against him in the ex parte. She wanted a special prosecutor
20 | assigned to it because she didn't think they would prosecute me
21 | again. They asked to withdraw. When I got that docket sheet,
22 | it said they were disqualified. Why were they disqualified
23 | from prosecuting me? She got everything she wanted. She got a
24 | special prosecutor.

1   In the first paragraph of the ex parte, she's more or

2   less telling you not to share it with me or Ms. Finch or the

3   prosecutor's office or the magistrates. Well, that's illegal.

4   She can't tell you what to do. Yet, she got everything she

5   wanted. And it's sealed. I'm going to have to use these post

6   sentencing because this is my defense. Falses in omnibus.

7   Falses in uno. Falses in omnibus.

8   THE COURT: Mr. Williams, I've ruled on the motions

9   regarding the victim impact statement as well as new trial.

10   But what I am giving you now is an opportunity to make any type

11   of direct response to the victim's impact statement as

12   permitted by statute, as well as any statement you wish to make

13   in mitigation of your sentence.

14   THE DEFENDANT: The first question in the victim impact

15   statement is, do you wish to appear before the Court to make an

16   oral statement? Her answer, yes, already spoken to Probation

17   Officer Tooze on the phone. It's stated also.

18   THE COURT: Okay. And I'll note for the record that

19   Ms. DeCourcy does not appear to be in the courtroom for that

20   purpose.

21   THE DEFENDANT: Your Honor, Ms. DeCourcy fled the state

22   soon after I made it clear that I wanted to question the victim

23   impact statement. She's left. And nobody seems to care that

24   she's gone. But I've always been raised that you get to face

 1   your accuser. I haven't said one word to that woman since

 2   September 30th, 2015. Not one word. Yet I'm accused of -- you

 3   said you read the victim impact statement. It's 14 pages,

 4   single spaced, typed.

 5   Again, in her claim of battery, I don't have all those

 6   documents, but she makes me out to be a monster. She does the

 7   same thing in here. It's unsubstantiated. Her witnesses were

 8   her boyfriend, her employer, and her roommate. And I didn't

 9   have witnesses, but I know it didn't happen. And I'll fight it

10   to the end.

11   I mean, do we really want to question if she's asked,

12   what were the economic - did you suffer any loss as a result of

13   the crime, property damage to your property? It's a short

14   answer. Only five lines. But then she goes into paragraph

15   after paragraph. Arson. I committed arson. That doesn't have

16   anything to do --

17   THE COURT: That's my point, Mr. Williams, that the - I

18   think that the answer was the five lines that you make

19   reference to --

20   THE DEFENDANT: That's all we can do. Okay.

21   THE COURT: No. No. What I have stated, I think

22   numerous times on the record, is I have looked at this in

23   response to the questions - what is the response to the

24   questions that are allowed by statute.

1   THE DEFENDANT: Okay. So the economic loss, that's

2 interesting. A convict -- this is her answer. Yes. Convict

3 defendant Williams - I didn't realize I was a convict - seized

4 all corporate funds, accounts, assets, income, corporate entity

5 boards, or unpayable to me. Well, I'm chairman of the

6 corporation. Of course, I'm in control of the funds. I fired

7 her that day for insubordination.

8   She says I was removed from board meetings on August 1st,

9 2015. I conducted the board meeting. She wasn't there. She's

10 not on the board. And she says that I've been removed. It's

11 really insanity.

12   She supported civil suits against me and the Alliance,

13 three different civil suits. One here in West Virginia that

14 her boyfriend filed with Mr. Faerber. And I believe it was

15 Mr. DaMarais that paid for it. That's the roommate. And

16 then -- anyway, it's just so outrageous.

17   It goes to motive, Your Honor. The reason that they

18 could charge me with battery - not the reason, the reason for

19 the charging me was to get me off the property. There was a

20 temporary restraining order without a hearing or anything. And

21 she wanted me off the property. It's my responsibility, this

22 property. I didn't realize it, but there was this temporary

23 restraining order against me because she had filed it. And

24 next thing I know, they're coming in. They're arresting me. I

1   get sent up to the regional jail. And five days later, the

2   same thing happened again. They arrested me again. Put me in

3   jail. Luckily, we got the bond scraped together.

4   So her economic loss is nothing like my economic loss as

5   a result of this. I'll finish that one about economic loss. I

6   mean, it's a lie. They didn't remove me as chairman. As a

7   matter fact, her witness is dead. Her other witness went to

8   New York City. Said he'd never come back. And the other

9   witness is Mr. DaMarais, there, who wasn't present at the

10 alleged strangling or choking or whatever, the charge of

11 battery. My defense, nobody ever interviewed me. There was no

12 investigation. They came out and talked to her December 4th, I

13 believe, Sheriff Jonese and deputy --

14   THE COURT: Mr. Williams, there's already been a bench

15 trial on this. And the conviction, the Court has found you

16 guilty. The purpose of today is sentencing and anything you

17 wish to offer to the Court in mitigation of sentence. But it

18 is not the time to reevaluate whether the conviction is there

19 or not. The conviction is there. Is there anything else you

20 want the Court to consider?

21   THE DEFENDANT: Well, her answer, yes, that I was removed

22 from the board, which is absurd. I'm still chairman of the

23 Alliance. The board of the Virginia corporation sued in

24 Virginia Circuit Court - that's the National Alliance - to try

1 and protect the entities and boards associated from Williams's

2 crimes and physical abuse, threats to property and life. He

3 and members of his personal criminal gang/domestic terrorists

4 were causing --

5   THE COURT: Mr. Williams, so that I can cut this short,

6 the answer to the question that the Court considered was - to

7 the question of, did you suffer any economic loss as a result

8 of the crime? Example, loss of property, damage to your

9 property, et cetera. Her answer was, yes. And apparently, she

10 was unable to be paid. That's the short of it. That's what

11 the Court considered.

12   THE DEFENDANT: I paid her that morning.

13   THE COURT: Okay. Then your responses is, you dispute

14 that she was unable to be paid?

15   THE DEFENDANT: Well, yes.

16   THE COURT: Okay. Next question.

17   THE DEFENDANT: Next question, please list a description

18 and value of your losses. Use additional paper if necessary.

19 Her answer doesn't really describe her losses.

20   THE COURT: So you're saying the answer was unresponsive?

21   THE DEFENDANT: Well, it would take a few minutes to read

22 it here. I'm just looking at the highlights here. Everything,

23 murder, torture, shooting, two people dead. Who are these dead

24 people? What is -- why am -- okay. So those were her property

1 losses. The next one is, has she been paid by an insurance

2 company for loss or damage? If so, please supply name and

3 address. Well, no. She didn't even go to the doctor over this

4 attempted homicide.

5   THE COURT: So the answer is no?

6   THE DEFENDANT: No. That's right. Okay. So my point

7 was, she didn't go to the hospital. There's no medical report.

8 Okay. So has there been a change in your personal life,

9 welfare, lifestyle or family relationships as a result of the

10 crime? Yes. She says, I've continually been - this is what

11 she writes. I have continually been - continually -

12 continually been continually re-victimized, tormented, abused,

13 terrorized, intimidated, harassed, blackmailed, and corruption

14 attempts in violation of my basic human rights. Blah, blah.

15 Like I said, I never had one more word with this woman until

16 today. I thought she would be here. Well, I knew she wasn't

17 going to be here because she's fled.

18   THE COURT: So what the Court's doing is, under the

19 statute, I give you an opportunity to introduce evidence of

20 other information that's related to any of these alleged what

21 you consider to be factual inaccuracies. So your response to

22 that is, I've not spoken to her since. I consider that.

23   THE DEFENDANT: I haven't said a word to her.

24   THE COURT: And I'm letting you know, I'm considering

1 that statement.

2   THE DEFENDANT: Almost four years, Your Honor.

3   THE COURT: Yes, sir.

4   THE DEFENDANT: So there's another full page to that

5 answer. Let's see. There might be several pages. Yeah, page

6 and a half. I hire people to murder, murder, murder, attempted

7 murder, assault, battery, grand larceny. Just, I mean, I could

8 keep repeating this page after page. But it's all

9 unsubstantiated. If you want to call it factual inaccuracies

10 like the code says, that's what I want to question. I want her

11 to substantiate who I murdered. Who did I rape? Who did I

12 kidnap? What did I burn down? She wanted to influence you to

13 make me out to be a monster, where they could get control of

14 the Natural Alliance. These were - her witnesses were her

15 co-conspirators. Three different civil suits filed. That's

16 the motive.

17   There's some highlights here, but it's just the same

18 stuff page after page. What's interesting is to get to the

19 last page. Question, are your answers to these questions true

20 and correct to the best of your knowledge? Simple, yes. Well,

21 they're not. I mean, to her knowledge. She's delusional. I

22 think she has Aspergers Syndrome or something where she focuses

23 on something and - obsessed. And lucky me.

24   She kind of sums it up here on the last page. The only

1 justice and proper protection of me, the victim, of many crimes

2 in West Virginia and others committed by Williams, i.e., cyber

3 crimes, stalking, shooting, murder of pets, thefts, harassment,

4 intimidation, slander, abuse. The Court must, all caps, issue

5 a full, permanent protective order that is detailed in scope,

6 well-defined, and fully enforceable. Williams and his gang has

7 fully stated and gone for others for decades. I have no idea

8 what she's talking about, my gang. I don't have a gang. I'm

9 not a gang leader. I'm a corporate chairman, president of the

10 board. I'm responsible for the corporation.

11   And she and her co-conspirators - there's one of them in

12 the courtroom right there - wanted to take this away from me.

13 They failed. All three civil suits have been dismissed with

14 prejudice. And I have an $850,000 counterclaim against her

15 employer who filed a civil suit against me in Virginia. And

16 it's a real tragedy for her to have talked them in to suing the

17 National Alliance. The previous lawsuit by a group of former

18 Alliance members failed. And when that was getting ready to be

19 dismissed, she got Mr. McLaughlin to file another lawsuit.

20   So when they saw - when the lawyer they hired saw what a

21 mess it was, he withdrew. And Mr. McLaughlin had 21 days to

22 answer my counterclaim. He died three days later. He got a

23 21-day extension to answer the claim. He died of a massive

24 heart attack that really could be traced to her for putting him

 1   in that position as a plaintiff.

 2   THE COURT: I'm not here for -- I understand your

 3   reasoning. Your reasoning is, you want the Court to consider

 4   the fact that you believe there's unclaimed suits. But is

 5   there anything else with regard to your sentencing hearing that

 6   you're wishing for the Court to consider?

 7   THE DEFENDANT: There's one more paragraph here that she

 8   sums things up. Without a well-crafted, properly-worded

 9   permanent protective order by this Court, I have no, all caps,

10   no ability to ever be safe or free to exercise my basic human

11   and civil rights and to register or exercise my duty, right to

12   vote. I've damaged her to the extent that she can't -- by

13   holding my arm out like this, I've damaged her life to the

14   extent that she cannot even vote. And without such an order,

15   my voter registration information, my home location will be

16   public record. And Williams, his gang, and any murderous

17   nuts --

18   THE COURT: Mr. Williams, I understand what she's asking

19   for is a permanent safety order. And you're providing to the

20   Court your thoughts as to why that's not necessary. Is there

21   anything else you want me to consider?

22   THE DEFENDANT: I think that makes the point. Do we just

23   go through the probation officer's recommendation or do we just

24   go straight to sentencing? I don't know. Whatever. Whatever

 1 you're going to do. Whatever it, is what it is.

 2   THE COURT: Ms. Finch, do you have anything that you wish

 3 to say on behalf of your client with regard to sentencing?

 4   MS. FINCH: Yes, please, Your Honor. I would ask that

 5 the Court consider permitting Mr. Williams to remain in

 6 Tennessee with his wife who dearly loves him. They're good

 7 support for one another, I think as is evidenced by the

 8 presentence investigation report. I think that outside the

 9 circumstances that led to Your Honor's verdict, he is not a

10 dangerous person and not a person for whom confinement for the

11 period of time that this charge would allow would serve any

12 purpose. And I would just ask that he be permitted to return

13 to Tennessee to be on some type of probation and be at home

14 with his wife. He's expressed to me that he doesn't intend to

15 frequent Pocahontas County. He finds it to be an inconvenience

16 to come in for court. And I don't believe that he will be

17 causing any problems. So that would be my request to the

18 Court, Your Honor.

19   THE COURT: If granted any alternative sentence, such as

20 probation, this is a misdemeanor case. And probation could not

21 be transferred to the state of Tennessee. So any supervision,

22 if granted, would have to be under this circuit, which would

23 require your client to make himself available to the probation

24 department. And in that respect, I believe would further

1 require a waiver of extradition in the event of a violation.

2 So have you spoken to your client regarding all those things

3 prior to requesting an alternative sentence?

4   MS. FINCH: I've spoken with him regarding the fact that

5 a misdemeanor probation cannot not be transferred out of state.

6 And what I've described to him was that he would need to call

7 in. He would need to stay in contact. I understand he may

8 also need to make himself available from time to time for

9 purposes the probation officers may direct. I haven't talked

10 to him about the waiver of extradition. But if I could have

11 about 60 seconds?

12   THE COURT: Yes, ma'am.

13   MS. FINCH: Thank you. I've had the opportunity to

14 discuss that with him. And I think he is agreeable to those

15 terms.

16   THE COURT: Do you have any other statements on behalf of

17 your client?

18   MS. FINCH: No, Your Honor.

19   THE COURT: Thank you.

20   MS. FINCH: Thank you.

21   THE COURT: Mr. Via, does the prosecuting attorney wish

22 to address the matter of sentencing?

23   MR. VIA: Yes, ma'am. The state's position is that

24 Mr. Williams should be sentenced to six months in the

 1   appropriate regional jail facility. I think that's - if I

 2   understand the rule, that's the maximum this Court can give

 3   because that's what the magistrate court gave. And so there's

 4   six months there that are not available to this Court for the

 5   12 months that is available statutorily.

 6   This was a violent offense. The Court heard the

 7   evidence. It involved a choking. I don't think a legal

 8   strangulation, the way that term is defined by statute. But

 9   nonetheless, a violent choking, a violent incident, a very

10   volatile incident. We've heard a lot today, but not one word

11   on acceptance of anything relative to his responsibility in

12   that incident. And just no acceptance of responsibility at

13   all. But rather what we heard today was combative and was

14   questioning this Court, questioning the victim. All of which

15   was done at trial appropriately.

16   But this Court made the finding beyond a reasonable doubt

17   that the offense of battery was committed. And looking behind

18   the offense at the actual conduct of the battery, it was

19   particularly violent, as this Court heard. And a misdemeanor -

20   an alternative sentence of probation on this offense would

21   significantly, I think, and unduly depreciate the nature of the

22   offense. This is an offense for which six months of

23   incarceration is appropriate. And we would strongly encourage

24   the Court to impose that sentence at this time.

Appendix 31: Petitioner Brief on Appeal to the WVSCA by Williams

ASSIGNMENT OF ERRORS

Defendant William White Williams, a resident of Tennessee, was wrongly convicted of misdemeanor battery in both Magistrate and Circuit Court of Pocahontas County of West Virginia. During both trials there were numerous legal errors: no presumption of innocence; no proper investigation; insufficient due process; lack of any sufficient evidence; unreliable witnesses, and significant reasonable doubt that a battery took place on 30 September, 2015. Both Defense counsels, **Paul Detch** for the Magistrate trial, **Laura Finch** for Circuit Court Appeal, were extremely ineffective; both were removed from representation of Defendant by the Defendant. The guilty verdict was obtained by fraud. The Accuser, Garland DeCourcy, who uses several aliases (her birth name is Garland Elizabeth Corse) and multiple SSNs is a scam artist with a history, a documented pattern of abuse of the judicial process.

STATEMENT OF THE CASE

Defendant was wrongly convicted and feels that there was an obvious judicial bias during both trials. The reason for that might be either or both judges' fear of Accuser's criticisms of them since she has a history of suing judges and badmouthing Officers of the Court, in writing – and/or that they oppose the political ideology of the Defendant.

Defendant is Chairman of the National Alliance, an organization with a 45 year history of advocating for the interests of the American White majority -- an unsympathetic or Politically Incorrect ideology in the minds of many, though still perfectly legal, Constitutionally protected beliefs to hold. For example, Defendant was told by his Probation Officer, Robert Tooze, that "90% of Pocahontas County residents believe the National Alliance is "Nazi." National Alliance (NA) is certainly not "Nazi," and has had a clearly stated policy for 45 years against any violence or illegality. Regardless, NA has rich and influential enemies like the Southern Poverty Law Center (SPLC) "watchdog group" which has published numerous outrageous lies about the NA and the Defendant. Accuser has worked with the SPLC during this case. Several of SPLC's widely spread articles are sourced directly from Accuser's original criminal complaint and from her interminable 250,000+ word anti-Williams blog.

1

Just one article (nearly 10,000 words) from that blog was submitted as evidence. **0235**.

After being contacted by Accuser, Heidi Beirich, the head of SPLC's Intelligence Project, called the Pocahontas County Sheriff within a half hour after Defendant's first arrest to confirm his arrest. Accuser had been taking pictures of handcuffed Defendant to publish on her blog.

Defendant arrived to the NA property in WV that is in close proximity to the house where Accuser with her co-plotter Bob DeMarais cohabitated. They called LE to execute an Arrest Warrant of which Defendant was unaware. Defendant was arrested for violating Accuser's Temporary Restraining Order (TRO), *15-S-35*. Defendant was surprised that a TRO could be in effect without any investigation or a hearing. Accuser made sure to call LE in the late afternoon so Defendant's wife Lana couldn't bring cash bond money from TN.

Defendant spent that night at Tygart Valley Regional Jail and Accuser hoped she would be granted her TRO request at the hearing the next morning, 17 December, 2015, since the Accused was incarcerated 70+ miles away. To Accuser's disappointment Lana was able to call Lewisburg, WV, attorney Paul Detch and have him appear for that hearing and request a continuance. Mr. Detch told Defendant that when he approached Accuser and DeMarais in the hallway before hearing to politely introduce himself Accuser yelled at him: "How dare you to interfere in my personal affair?"

Mr. Detch paid the cash bond for Defendant, later reimbursed, and Defendant was released from Tygart. But he was forced to hitchhike 80+ miles for over six hours back to his truck that had been moved outside NA property. That was 17 December, 2015, in an all-day, cold pouring rain, with no hat, no coat, tennis shoes, no glasses, and having had all of his money confiscated by the jailers, so not even a dollar for a cup of coffee. The kind couple who gave the soaking wet Defendant a ride from Elkins were paid $120 by him from the cash in the bank deposit bag that, fortunately, was still in his truck when he arrived back around dusk.

Defendant was forced to pick a bench trial over a jury trial at the end of 2015 when this protracted "tar baby case" began. He feared the jury pool was tainted and could not be impartial because the newspaper of record in the county, *The Pocahontas Times*, featured an article in its 23 December, 2015, edition entitled "National Alliance chairman arrested at Mill Point. The writer of that *Times* article, Janell Graham, quotes SPLC smears about the "hate group" and unsubstantiated quotes by the Accuser from her criminal complaint, but denied the Accused the right of reply to counter false claims published about him in that article. Defendant's counsel told Defendant that the biased writer of that *Pocahontas Times* article, Ms. Graham -- unaware that counsel Finch was representing the Defendant -- unwittingly gossiped to her, "That Will Williams is dangerous." It is no wonder that Pocahontas County residents perceive Defendant to be the "Pocahontas strangler" when their newspaper quotes the SPLC's smears, characterizing the Alliance as a "neo-Nazi hate group" and quotes his Accuser's claims, but denied the Accused his right of reply.

Once again, Defendant's Accuser is a documented scam artist. Defendant was aware that his Accuser-to-be had been a fellow NA member in the early 1990s. She learned Defendant had recently been appointed NA Chairman, contacted him through the NA Web site in mid-April 2015 and begged to him for urgent help because she was, in her desperate words, about to commit suicide -- was in an abusive relationship; being evicted from her home; no job, no money, no place to go.

Defendant invited her to come work and live on the NA campus in WV. Soon enough Accuser become conspiratorial, insubordinate, and defiant. Defendant could not communicate normally with her and invited another NA member, Michael Oljaca, who was an easy-going, idealistic Alliance member to come and live and work on WV property, and be between Accuser and Defendant as the Alliance Chairman's Chief of Staff. Oljaca arrived to Pocahontas County from NYC in the end of July 2015.

It soon become clear that docile Oljaca had become under Accuser's full control. Soon after the alleged incident of 09/30/15, Defendant realized that the "battery" was his Accuser's intentional pretext by which to oust Defendant as NA Chairman in a judicial coup attempt, first by being awarded TROs to keep him off NA property, then to have him jailed for as long as possible, while filing bogus civil suits against him and the NA.

From the beginning, on 31 October 31, 2015, when Defendant first heard mention of the alleged battery on 09/30/15, he has consistently denied that it happened, because it did not happen. His short statement to WV State Trooper Damon Brock on that 10/31/15 date stated that Defendant, from behind a desk, stood and extended his right arm over the desk, barely touching the Accuser's chin for a couple of seconds, after she had jumped up from a chair and charged at him in a provocatively threatening manner, screaming and wagging her finger in his face. Defendant never once touched his Accuser's -- his employee's -- neck, and he immediately left the room to defuse the situation. **0223**.

There was never any physical struggle with his Accuser. She was awarded her TRO as a result of making her battery claim. That was her intent: to keep the Defendant off of National Alliance property with her TRO. Defendant had no witness, but his Accuser had one, her boyfriend and co-conspirator Oljaca, who by then had been corrupted by Accuser, and who she got to file a second battery claim against Defendant within days of her securing an Arrest Warrant for the Defendant. Oljaca also known as Accuser #2, was also automatically awarded the second TRO, *15-S-36*, without a hearing or a proper investigation of his claim.

Before the eventual hearings for both TROs ruled in favor of Defendant, for a couple of months the Chairman of the National Alliance had been ordered to stay 1,000 feet away for two years from the offices and nearly 400 acres of NA property he was charged with managing -- a ridiculous situation! Again, DeCourcy's motive for making the battery claims was to get TROs so she and her co-conspirators could have free run of Alliance property while the Chairman was jailed twice in a five-day period for unwittingly violating those TROs for going on NA property.

Accuser, as she is known to do, appealed denial of her TRO, *16-S-AP-01*, and her appeal was soon dismissed. Accuser has been abusing and gaming the judicial system for years on regular basis while asking the Court to waive court fees for her numerous filings, due to her supposed indigence.

The court was not interested in hearing about her motives for filing a false battery claim or about her pattern of requesting TROs in another jurisdiction.

Though only evidence used during Circuit Court trial should be submitted to the Supreme Court, with his intent to help save the Supreme Court time and resources, Defendant attached with his Notice of

4

Appeal as well as with his Amendment To Motion To Use Three Documents During Appeal, a one page

cover document. It reflects Accuser's fleeing from Virginia to West Virginia in 2015 without providing

Virginia Court with her forwarding address, soon after she filed *pro se* a 172-page complaint against

three Virginia Judges and a guardian. The remainder of that Virginia case file is sealed by that Court.

Accuser's fleeing from one state for another after getting herself into trouble was repeated in

October 2018, soon after Defendant stated in open Court that he would personally question factual

inaccuracies in her Victim Impact Statement (VIS) as he is entitled under *§61-11A-3(e) (Rule 61)*.

17 days after Defendant's first sentencing hearing on 10/10/18, that was continued at least three times

to, finally, 12 February, 2019, Accuser fled WV in a 26-foot U-Haul truck on 27 October. Defense

counsel Laura Finch was informed of this exodus on 4 November, 2018, and Ms. Finch told Defendant

that she informed the Circuit Court and the Special Prosecutor of this. Ten months later, as this Brief is

prepared in August 2019, no one associated with this case seems to know or care to where the State's

claiming witness, the Defendant's fugitive Accuser, has fled.

In her VIS of 09/29/18 Accuser stated that she would like to attend Defendant's sentencing and give her

oral statement, ostensibly to reinforce her rambling 14-page single-spaced, typed statement. **0281**.

Though Defendant's legitimate post-trial motion under *Rule 61* for a hearing to question factual

inaccuracies in his Accuser's VIS, **0329**, in which she wrote that she would be at the Accused's

sentencing hearing, Circuit Court Judge Dent denied that motion. **0371**. Defendant also feels this was in

violation of his *Sixth Amendment* right to confront his Accuser (i.e. "look her in the eye") and be able

to counter the false testimony that she had submitted to the Court. Judge Dent had previously failed to

have Accuser's VIS stricken from the Court record over Defendant's strong objections to strike it.

Accuser had fled the state of WV for parts unknown several months prior to the Judge's denial of

Defendant's motion. Nothing in the Case Docket Sheet, **0001**, indicates Defendant's Accuser had

dropped out of sight, denying his right to face her and question numerous factual inaccuracies in her

VIS, as he is entitled under *Rule 61*.

5

Another issue that complicated the case is that Defendant lives about 450 miles round-trip from Pocahontas County. It was very difficult to communicate, much less meet with his attorneys during the numerous trips he was required to make from his home in Tennessee for Court hearings. Both attorneys always seemed to be overloaded with their other work and not interested in vigorously defending their wrongly accused client. Unfortunately, there are only three or so practicing attorneys in Pocahontas County and one of those represents the Accuser's roommate, Bob DeMarais.

Along with the document showing the pattern of abusing judicial process by Accuser, in the same motion Defendant requested permission to use two more documents that were not filed in Circuit Court: a one page letter of explanation correcting/clarifying transcribed portions of the testimony from Defendant's wife Lana whose first language is not English (it's Russian), and two *ex parte* letters that were sealed and then refused to be unsealed by Judge Dent.

Defendant was unaware of the 10 day period that WV State has to deny such motion. Since this Court decision is not available by the time of this mailing of the Brief to meet the deadline, Petitioner doesn't include these documents in his Appendix.

If this Court decision is going to be to grant the Motion, those three documents can be seen, if needed. The copies of those three documents have been provided to this Court and to Mr. Shannon F. Kiser as attachments to the Amendment to Motion To Use Three Documents During Appeal.

SUMMARY OF ARGUMENT

Despite guilty verdict, obtained by fraud, as described in **STATEMENT OF THE CASE,** there are several other grounds for Petitioner's appeal. To be eligible to appeal the verdict at least one possible ground is required. Defendant believes that since there were many procedural errors and violations of Defendant's rights that he has seven additional grounds to be described in his **ARGUMENT** section.

STATEMENT REGARDING ORAL ARGUMENT AND DECISION

The Petitioner requests to use Rule 19 argument in this case, because, as he understands the Rule, it's an issue of his case involving assignments of error in the application of settled law, and his claim of insufficient evidence. Defendant believes that his case is appropriate for a memorandum decision.

ARGUMENT

Defendant believes the following errors led to his wrongful conviction:

1. JUDICIAL MISCONDUCT/ Violations of *Canon 2 West Virginia Judicial Code of Conduct.*

Rule 2.2. Impartiality and Fairness,* and *Rule 2.3. Bias, Prejudice, and Harassment.

Case Docket Sheet, **0001**, reflects that every motion/request of the State/Accuser has been granted, while every legitimate motion of the Defendant has been denied. Circuit Court Judge Dent even denied Defendant 's fundamental right to self-represent. The motion for defense counsel, Laura Finch, to withdraw her representation, **0295**, states Defendant is seeking new representation, but in the transcript of the first sentencing hearing, **0305,** and in the order denying that motion, **0299**, counsel states Defendant wants to represent himself, *the actual reason* (due to her ineffective counsel to that date).

Judge Dent found Defendant guilty despite the obvious lack of sufficient evidence -- just unvalidated, untimestamped, undated selfies of "injury", **0247-0261**, provided to the Sheriff more than two months after the alleged incident, and when significant reasonable doubt had been raised about Accuser's veracity. By Accuser's testimony in trial transcript, **0028-0094**, it should be obvious to the reasonable observer that Accuser was playing dumb, not responding directly to simple "yes" or "no" questions; changing subjects, telling obvious lies, and often contradicting herself. Nevertheless, incredibly, Judge Dent stated in her final speech on 12 February, 2019, "I find Ms. DeCourcy's testimony to be credible to the extent that it has been consistent in her statements." **0208, 0207**.

At his final sentencing hearing on 02/12/19 Defendant was allowed to speak freely for the first time and listed many grounds showing due process wasn't provided to him. He mentioned *ex parte* letters, sealed without his knowledge or given the opportunity to respond *(Rule 2.9 of Judicial Code)* and question them; numerous false, defamatory and unquestioned accusations in those letters; the fact of Accuser's fleeing the State without providing the Court or anyone else with her forwarding address or contact information, etc. **0351-0362**. Regardless, each of the three legitimate post trial motions was denied. **0371**.

Before the final sentencing hearing the Judge also could see for perhaps the first time sworn Affidavit of Defendant's main witness, Fred Streed, **0319**, who couldn't be at trial to testify in person due to a sudden health problem while waiting in line at 5:30AM on 13 August, 2019, in his Oregon airport. He had an $800 round trip ticket from Oregon purchased for him by Defendant. Arrangements had been made for Mr. Streed to travel from Oregon to an earlier scheduled trial hearing for 9 August, 2019, but Judge Dent postponed that one and moved to 14 August, 2019, without consulting Defendant about his west coast primary defense witness's plans. As it was, Mr. Streed would have arrived at Lewisburg, WV, airport the evening of 13 August, be picked up and taken to a motel that night, driven to court on the morning of 14 August, and taken back to Lewisburg airport shortly after noon that same day to arrive back in Oregon airport that night. Mr. Streed had a guest arriving at his home from Canada on 16 August, but was still willing to travel to court at great inconvenience, while ill, to testify for the defense to validate his sworn Affidavit testimony and repudiate Accuser's lies about Defendant in her battery claim.

Neither of Defendant's counsels in this case, nor either of the prosecutors, nor any "investigator" from their offices, nor any "investigator" from law enforcement, ever bothered to call Mr. Streed though all of them had copies of his sworn Affidavit and were provided his phone number.

Streed was on site on 30 September, 2015, and talked to Defendant, his Accuser, and Accuser's witness Oljaca minutes after the alleged battery. His testimony for the defense was critical. He had lived and worked on the Alliance's Pocahontas County property for 11 years, had been President of the NA board of directors for years and is still executor of Alliance Founder Dr. William Pierce's estate, which is still unsettled because of the American watchdog group, the Southern Poverty Law Center's intervention in a Canadian Alliance's member's bequest to the Alliance Alliance. That NA member died in 2004; Mr Streed is still involved as Executor of that substantial 15-year-old bequest.

Motion for new trial **0311-0320**, with valid grounds, was denied along with the other two legitimate pre-sentencing motions. **0371**. Judge Dent also denied Defense request for post conviction bond, **0368-0369,** knowing full well that Defendant intends to appeal her conviction of him. Judge Dent may not have recognized back then that Defendant had grounds to appeal the verdict, but she dutifully informed Defendant about his right to appeal the sentence. **0367**. Defendant was ordered remanded to jail directly from court, denying bond while he prepared this appeal. Judge Dent likely assumed Defendant would try to retain an Appellate attorney, knowing that none would be interested in representing a misdemeanor battery conviction in the Pocahontas County Court. Defendant contacted several WV appellate attorneys and in fact none of them were interested. One did tell Defendant that he would "look at the file" for $7,500. Defendant requested an extension to file Appeal to WVSCA *pro se*. Defendant was treated like some dangerous, criminal menace to society, though Judge Dent could see in Probation Officer's Recommendation for Sentencing report, **0271-0278**, that Defendant had no criminal record, a long stable marriage, good character, and had served honorably as a U.S. military officer. In her final sentencing speech Judge Dent failed to mention that Defendant has "good character" and that probation was recommended in Probation Officer Tooze's Court-ordered report. **0365**. Defendant was 71 years old at the time and had never previously been charged with a criminal offense. For some odd reason Judge Dent ordered Defendant to submit to random drug and alcohol testing, **0366-0367**, though he neither drinks alcohol nor does any drugs, other than over-the-counter vitamins and a single Metformin pill taken for Diabetes, prescribed by his Veterans Administration doctor. Neither alcohol nor drugs were ever mentioned as a factor in the alleged battery with which he was charged.

9

Well before being fired by Defendant, his Accuser confessed to their mutual acquaintance, Meredith Kellar, that she had been diagnosed with Asperger's Syndrome (an Autism Spectrum Disorder). Defendant doesn't have written evidence of her admitted disorder, but believes that clinical symptoms of Asperger's Syndrome, like being conspiratorial, obsessively focused, repetitive, and projecting her own shortcomings onto others, are well exhibited in Accuser's *ex parte* letters and VIS, **0281**, as well as in her blog, **0235**, and also in the numerous other accusatory letters written by her that Defendant has, but that were never allowed by Ms. Finch to be put into evidence. Those letters of hers were admitted into evidence as exhibits in the two civil lawsuits against the National Alliance in Virginia, however, ***CL14-02, 2CL16-2090-01***. Those two Virginia cases were dismissed with prejudice.

It's doubtful that Judge Dent could not recognize some level of mental disability in Accuser's writings and behavior, like in her defying the Judge's explicit order to not send more *ex parte* letters, **0017**, or in Accuser's outrageous demeanor during her trial testimony. **0028-0094**. Defendant suspects the main factor for the judicial bias could have been Judge Dent's fear of Accuser's boundless criticism, but there might be other reasons, as stated earlier.

Rule 2.4. External Influences on Judicial Conduct. Accuser DeCourcy badmouths, in writing, every judge, prosecutor, or LE officer who failed to do what she demanded of them. The only two Court officers she hasn't badmouthed to date are Judge Dent and the Special Prosecutor in the Circuit Court appeal, Patrick Via. Strangely, DeCourcy sued Defendant and co-Defendant, Judge Dent, in WV Supreme Court of Appeals during the course of the trial ***(WV Supreme Court case #17-0572)***. Soon after DeCourcy's writ in that WV Supreme Court case was denied, Judge Dent dismissed Pocahontas County Magistrate Kelley's ruling that had ordered DeCourcy to return items stolen by her from Claimant Williams in the case in Magistrate Court, ***16-M38C-00109***. A reason for Judge Dent's revocation of that sound Magistrate's ruling was inexplicable, and without objections from Defense counsel Finch, who had represented Williams and easily prevailed before Magistrate Kelley in

Magistrate Court, providing receipts for each stolen item.

Kelley had denied all of DeCourcy's five outrageous motions. Magistrate Kelley could see that DeCourcy is bizarre and her testimony incredible. She didn't fear her, very nearly charging her with Contempt of Court more than once for her interruptions and courtroom antics. It's too bad Defendant didn't appear before Kelly for the battery case instead of before the biased Magistrate Wilfong.

Defendant appeared telephonically during that hearing where Dent granted DeCourcy's motion to dismiss Magistrate Kelly's Order, but was not allowed to speak, and Ms. Finch's microphone was turned off for some reason. When Defendant asked over the phone if he could say a few words after hearing the alarming adverse ruling by Judge Dent, she told him, "No, you are represented." The fact is: I was not represented at that hearing at all.

When Ms. Finch -- who handled both the criminal and civil cases for Defendant Williams, each with the same litigants -- advised Defendant that he need not travel to Court from Tennessee for that hearing because "there is no way Judge Dent will reverse Kelley's Order," Judge Dent *did* rule in favor of the Accuser, further disadvantaging Williams. Ms. Finch later told Defendant that "JudgeDent probably just wanted to get rid of that case." Judge Dent could just as easily have gotten rid of DeCourcy's Appeal of Magistrate Kelly's Order, *17-C-AP-03*, to return the items she ha stolen from Williams, by ordering her to, "Pay the man the $2,200 you owe him for the items you stole from him."

Rule 2.6. Ensuring the Right to be Heard. Judge Dent denied the Defense's motion for a pre-sentencing hearing regarding his Accuser's Victim Impact Statement (VIS), 00, in violation of Chapter *§61-11A-3(e)* of WV Code and *the* ***Sixth Amendment of the US Constitution.***

At the second sentencing hearing on 02/12/19 Defendant made clear that his Accuser had fled WV, likely to avoid being questioned about numerous factual inaccuracies in her VIS. Judge should have considered and granted Defendant's motion for a hearing for VIS questioning, **0329**, as well as Defendant's equally well-grounded motions for a new trial, **0311**, and to unseal the Accuser's

11

defamatory, exculpatory *ex parte* communications, **0325**.

Although Accuser's typically long VIS, **0281**, was an amendment to the court ordered recommendation for sentencing by Probation Officer Robert Tooze, Judge Dent told Defendant through counsel at least a half dozen times in one phone call -- witnessed by Defendant's wife Lana on an extension telephone -- that she wanted to *strike* the VIS, like it had never been submitted to the Court by the State's claiming witness, like it had never existed. However, Defendant had received his Accuser's exculpatory VIS fewer than the required ten days before his first 10/10/18 sentencing hearing, so declined all of Judge Dent's requests through counsel Finch to *strike* it. Judge Dent should have allowed Defendant to fully introduce testimony questioning numerous factual inaccuracies therein in accordance with Defendant's right under **Rule 61**.

Judge Dent denied Defendant's fundamental right to self represent granted by the **Sixth Amendment of the US Constitution**. In the transcript of the first sentencing hearing of 10/10/18 Judge Dent first said, "I am going to allow, Ms. Finch, your withdraw[al]." **0306**. Yet shortly after huddling in her private chamber with Special Prosecutor Via and Finch, Judge returned to the bench and said, on the record, "I am going to deny the motion to withdraw..." **0307**. Defendant believes that Judge Dent feared Defendant was taking control of his defense in "her courtroom" by his publicly discharging counsel; expressing his desire to represent himself going forward, and clearly and strongly asserting his statutory Defendant's Rights -- all on the transcript record of that session. **0301-0309**. She wanted him "represented," though he had made clear he had fired Finch and would represent himself.

A few days before his first sentencing hearing of 10/10/18 Defendant told Ms. Finch for the first time that he had been studying the "Rule Book"– the WV Judicial Code of Conduct WV Code – as it related to Defendant's rights, and that he might file a complaint against the Judge. No one else was told about a possible complaint. Transcript of the 10/10/18 hearing shows that just a few days later, Judge Dent stated that it had come to her attention that Defendant "may seek to file a complaint against the

12

Court." **0306.** Defendant considers his counsel's informing this to the Judge to be improper at least, and a betrayal of supposedly sacrosanct attorney/client confidentiality. Counsel Finch was working for the Court instead of for her client at this point, if not before, so had to be relieved by Defendant.

Rule 2.9. Ex Parte Communications. On 10/6/16 Accuser sent Judge Dent her first illegal private *ex parte* letter (14 pages, single spaced), telling her in the first paragraph not to share that letter with Defendant, his counsel, the County Prosecutor, or the County Magistrates. Each of the three *ex parte* letters to Judge Dent and the two VISes from both trials are extremely long -- well over 100 pages combined, single spaced, rambling, repetitive, and nearly impossible to read to the ends of them. Defendant did not receive Accuser's long VIS from Magistrate sentencing hearing until after he had been sentenced. He should have by statute received at least ten days prior to sentencing.

On 10/18/16 Accuser sent Judge Dent her second *ex parte* communication (an email, 62 pages long). The second email is not mentioned in the Docket Sheet, **0001**, except as combined with the first *ex parte* letter. Each of the three *ex parte* letters were clearly intended to influence the Judge with outrageous, unsubstantiated accusations against Defendant, accusing him of multiple murders; of hiring others to murder people for him; of rape, kidnapping, arson, being a gang leader, etc., and mentally ill, among other claims -- all false and to date unquestioned by any Court officer or investigator.

Accuser's attempts to influence the Court against Defendant appeared to be successful, when soon after receiving them Judge Dent called for a "special hearing with a extra security," **0325**, for "safety reasons," on 02/11/16. Counsel informed Defendant, that the extra security was for "safety reasons." Whose safety, Defendant wonders? The judge had obviously been affected negatively by the hysterical, and illegal *ex parte* communications from Defendant's Accuser that he was so dangerous that for safety reasons, extra security would be required for this special hearing. Defendant was informed by counsel that he did not have to travel from Tennessee to be present for this special hearing. How convenient; everyone would be safe. That special hearing with extra security for safety reasons was evidently to

13

protect everyone from the Accused who had been described as an out-of-control, Ted Bundy-like

monster by his Accuser in her illegal *ex parte* letters to the suggestible Judge.

In the first *ex parte* letter Accuser badmouthed practically every Court Officer, especially the County

Prosecutor Eugene Simmons, calling him "corrupt, lazy and senile," among other slurs, in writing! It

was doubtful that Simmons would convict Defendant in Circuit Court after evaluating the Accuser's

wild claims and actions. Accuser requested in her first private, illegal *ex parte* letter to Judge Dent that

a Special Prosecutor must be appointed to prosecute Defendant's appeal. The Court then disqualified

the County Prosecuting Attorney and his staff based in part on allegations made against them in that

first long *ex parte* letter. **0007-0011, 0326**. Patrick Via was appointed Special Prosecutor on

12/16/16. **0019**.

At that special hearing with extra security on 11/02/16 Defendant was told by counsel that he need not

appear, but that he could appear telephonically. Defendant did so and barely heard Judge Dent order his

Accuser not to *send* her any more private *ex parte* letters; nothing was heard by Defendant about the

Judge's intent to *seal* them and he never spoke. Accuser defied that oral Order, sending Judge a third,

long *ex parte* letter on 11/28/16. Why Accuser was not held in Contempt of Court is not known.

Instead, Judge Dent was, at least, then bound by ***Rule 2.9*** to send Accuser DeCourcy a formal letter on

the record, like to a disobedient child, explaining why *ex parte* communications are not allowed, and

warning her that, if received, they must be shared with Defendant's counsel.**0017**. That is how

Defendant got to see the first two *ex parte* communications from Accuser to Judge Dent before they

were sealed. He assumed from then on that they were in evidence, since they are exculpatory.

Defendant had been provided with copies of the first two *ex parte* communications, but was forbidden

by Judge Dent to be given a copy of the third one. He was only allowed to rush through a reading of the

third briefly, once, in his counsel's office minutes prior to a hearing. The only thing Defendant recalls

from that hurried reading of the third illegal *ex parte* letter was Accuser's shocking claim that the brother of her main witness to the alleged battery, Michael Oljaca, Daniel Oljaca, was dead, and that, among numerous other unsubstantiated claims, Defendant had something to do with Daniel's death. Again, more bogeyman accusations against Defendant that he has never been allowed to question.

On 12/15/16 two orders to seal *ex parte* communications were filed. **0013, 0015**. In first paragraphs Judge orders to seal *ex parte* communications; in the next ones she allows counsel and her client to discuss them for the purpose of litigation, but forbids giving copies to any person. Judge Dent could see that it would be nearly impossible to read those long, unhinged letters by counsel, much less discuss them with Defendant who lives over 200 miles away. It is Defendant's contention that counsel had no intention to use these astounding exculpatory *ex parte* communications for the "purpose of litigation."

Sealing *ex parte* communications was done without Defendant's knowledge. **0325**. Defendant was on the phone during the hearing of 02/01/17 with his wife Lana listening on an extension phone. Neither heard anything regarding sealing of *ex parte* letters. See Docket Sheet, **0002** for record for that special hearing. No transcript is available for that hearing. Defendant would certainly have vigorously objected to sealing of *ex parte* letters as they were in evidence as far as he knew, are exculpatory, and were needed for his defense as exhibits to easily impeach his Accuser's truthfulness. To repeat: Defendant has had those first two *ex parte* letters in his possession since *before* the third was mailed to Judge Dent. These first two *ex parte* communication, suppressed by the Court, were attached to Amendment To Motion To Use Three Documents During Appeal, in an envelope stamped **CONFIDENTIAL -- sealed by the Circuit Court -- Exculpatory evidence.**

Rule 2.11. Disqualification. Possible conflict of interest because Judge Dent served as Assistant Prosecutor to Prosecutor Patrick Via in Greenbrier County until she was elected to be an 11th Judicial District Judge in May 2016, while Defendant's case was already ongoing. Via was appointed to be Special Prosecutor of Defendant on 12/16/16. **0019**. Surely, if needed, a more impartial Special Prosecutor, less connected to Judge Dent could have been found. Mr. Via had run for Judge in the 11th

District also, and was defeated.

Laura Finch had clerked for an 11th Judicial District Judge in the same Lewisburg, WV, courthouse prior to starting her solo practice in Pocahontas County. Defendant was Ms. Finch's very first client, in the case *#16-M38M-693,* where Defendant was found not guilty of violating Accuser #2, Michael Oljaca's TRO.

2. INEFFECTIVE COUNSELING and Violating *Rule 8.4. Misconduct.*

Defendant's second attorney Ms. Finch never provided him with any of the Judge's orders. He saw the orders to seal *ex parte* letters of 12/15/16 for the first time more than two years after the fact, on 02/08/19, when Ms. Finch finally sent him her post trial motion to unseal *ex parte* letters. **0325.** Defendant had repeated during every conversation with Ms. Finch, with his wife Lana as witness, that those letters are in evidence and that he wants the outrageous accusations in them to be questioned and substantiated. Ms. Finch never corrected Defendant, never informed him that those letters had been sealed since 12/15/16. She would say to him and to Lana that there would be "no point to use them."

Defendant discovered for the first time that the *ex parte* communications had been sealed only after ordering the Docket Sheet from the Circuit Court Clerk, **0001**, on 08/29/18 -- two weeks after he was found guilty at his long-delayed 08/14/18 trial. **0267**. On about 10/05/18 Defendant's wife Lana asked Ms. Finch directly by telephone if she knew about the *ex parte* letters being sealed. After long pause Ms. Finch answered, "No."

Defendant believes she knew full well those illegal *ex parte*communications had been sealed, and that he was kept uninformed intentionally by her. He therefore concluded then that at some point in her representation of him Ms. Finch had begun working for the Court rather than vigorously defend her wrongly charged client. That is when Defendant decided he must represent himself going forward. When Ms. Finch first took the Defendant's case she wrote to him "This is going to be fun!" and said that it's so easy to prove that Accuser is a liar, that her undated selfies are invalid; that there is obvious

16

abuse of the judicial process by her; that there was no proper investigation by LE or by the Prosecutor. At some point, however, Ms. Finch's attitude about having "fun" defending the Accused was inverted to become so much gloom and weariness for her.

During the period between 10/10/18 and 02/12/19 Ms. Finch was extremely negligent and irresponsibly inattentive for weeks, even months at a time; delaying, obfuscating, not returning calls, not responding to Defendant's email inquiries, though their mutually agreed upon and signed motion for her to withdraw her representation had been denied by Dent. **0299**. Defendant had to prepare by himself three post trial motions because she would not. Only after sending her his own motion drafts, prepared for her approval since Dent had ruled that she still "represented" him, did she reluctantly file her motions as his counsel. **0311, 0325, 0329**. Ms. Finch's motions were still weak with serious faults, however, not even citing *§61-11A-3(e)* of WV Criminal Code or Rules of the WV Judicial Code of Conduct as he had instructed her to do to strengthen her half-hearted attempts. Defendant then had to file his own amended motion with the Clerk of Circuit Court just four days before his 2/12/19 second sentencing hearing to minimize chances for dismissals of hers. **0315**.

Ms. Finch had been ignoring her client's numerous requests to call Defendant's primary witness Fred Streed or to advise Mr. Via to do this. None of the Court Officers, including "investigators," ever called Mr. Streed to question his notarized, sworn Affidavit, dated 03/24/16, that he had prepared for the Court since he now resides in Oregon and it would be difficult for him to appear. **0319**.

Ms. Finch had finally provided Mr. Via with Mr. Streed's Affidavit only about a week or so before the 8/14/18 trial, and it was ignored by Via. Via had made clear that he had no interest in any evidence or testimony that was favorable to the Accused, that would negate this Defendant's guilt.

That sworn Affidavit by Mr. Streed, who was on the National Alliance premises where the alleged "battery" took place on 30 September, 2015, and who talked to the Defendant, to his Accuser, and to her "witness" shortly after, that same morning, and throughout that day.

Ms. Finch never bothered to call her client's primary defense witness, Mr. Streed, though she had his telephone number and he had expressed that he was willing to be the key witness for the Defense.

During Accuser's testimony at the trial, **0028-0094,** Ms. Finch repeatedly failed to object to Accuser's refusal to respond to her questions during cross- examination. She also failed to point out Accuser's obvious and numerous lies and contradictions in her written descriptions of the alleged incident and those by her main witness in Magistrate Court, boyfriend Michael Oljaca. **0232, 0233.**

There is no transcript of the Magistrate trial, *15-M38M-00687,* but there is boyfriend Oljaca's written statement, **0233,** that is considerably different from Accuser's and nearly opposite of the Defendant's short statement made to WV State Trooper Damon Brock on 31 October, **0223.** the first day Defendant had heard of his Accuser's imagined "choking" incident on 30 September, 2015.

According to Accuser's trial testimony, **0040-0044,** there was a long physical fight, with Defendant beating her with his fists, choking her with both hands around her neck, forcefully pushing her up in a corner of the room against a sharp filing cabinet and bookshelves, then fighting with her on the floor. Oljaca's coached, untruthful written statement was nothing like that; he and his coach had not been careful to get their story straight. Ms. Finch should have been all over the contradictions in Accuser's claims and those of her boyfriend.

When Accuser blurted out under cross examination that she had "a date stamp on mine [photographs]" **0049,** Ms. Finch failed to ask her, "Where are these time-stamped photos? Why have you not submitted this essential evidence?" – or a series of other probative questions to demonstrate to the Court that Accuser prefers to make up lies, even when not asked.

Defendant's stated defense strategy from the beginning was, *falsus in uno, falsus in omnibus.* Both of his counsels in the case, however, were unable or unwilling to follow that simple, time-honored legal maxim.

18

When Defendant was cross examined by Mr. Via about his response to Oljaca's September 2016 email
to him, characterizing it as "witness tampering," Defendant responded, showing how ridiculous was
Via's accusation: "He contacted *me*. And they call that witness tampering? I don't generally, when I
tamper with witnesses, I don't wait until they contact me first, you know." **0148.**

Later Defendant clarified that his flip response was an unfortunate joke, **0169**, said to make his point
that "witness" Oljaca had contacted *him*, not *vise versa*. In her closing argument Ms. Finch stated, "Mr.
Williams lied when he was asked if he had tampered with witnesses. And he was impeached on it."
0202. What kind of defense lawyer would make such an offensive and false statement in defense of her
client?

Ms Finch could have instead pointed out that in State's "witness" Michael Oljaca's leadoff email to
which her client had responded (since she was on vacation at the time and unavailable), the lines, "If
Bob [DeMarais] and Gael [DeCourcy's alias] find out I have written to you, there is no telling what
they would want to do to me, I shudder when I think about this." **0265**. The fact is, "witness" Oljaca
initiated the contact, writing to Defendant first, informing him that he wanted to drop the lawsuit he'd
filed against Defendant and the National Alliance at co-conspirators Bob's and Gael's urging. A
reasonable person reading Defendant's testimony should see that he was scrupulously honest and never
evasive at every step of his sworn testimony.**0120-0170**.

At Defendant's request Ms. Finch had what she described to Defendant as an hour-long telephone
conversation with Indiana attorney Tim Kalamaros, a friend of the Defendant. Accuser claimed in
several documents, including in the sealed *ex parte* communications, that Mr. Kalamaros has been
appointed as Defendant's fiduciary guardian, because Defendant has been adjudicated by two federal
agencies to be mentally ill and incapable of handling his personal finances, much less to serve as
Treasurer of the National Alliance. **0239.**

That claim is outrageous, and Kalamaros explained to Ms.Finch just how outrageous it is, yet she made

19

105

no effort to inform the Court of this bald-faced, easily refutable false claim made against her client *in writing* by his Accuser. That, nor other exculpatory facts never were brought up by Ms. Finch to the Pocahontas County Sheriff or to his Deputy who supposedly "investigated" the battery claim -- repeatedly characterized by Accuser as an "attempted homicide" – and they they never once bothered to interview the Defendant. However they had interviewed his Accuser, her boyfriend "witness," her employer "witness," and her landlord/roommate "witness" several times to establish probable cause to arrest her innocent client. A search for truth about the alleged 9/30/15 battery was not being pursued in the Pocahontas County courthouse; obvious facts that would lead to a conclusion of false reporting by Accuser and her co-conspirators and innocence of the Accused were never investigated.

Despite Accuser's putting so many outrageous lies in writing Ms. Finch stated that most of the Accuser's long writings can't be used as evidence since they are irrelevant. Ms Finch still submitted just a few documents that she failed to read, comprehend, and use effectively to impeach Accuser. For example, she was questioning Accuser regarding the short Termination of Contract, **0219**, that was sent both by email and certified/return receipt regular mail to Accuser by Defendant in October 2015.

Accuser had been lying, saying that there were demands in the Agreement that Accuser wouldn't go to the police, to media; that she wouldn't testify against Defendant. **0076**. If Ms. Finch had read the contract she could easily have caught Accuser in several of her lies by having her read the standard Non Competitive/Non Disclosure clause for this sort of Termination Agreement, or even the entire, short Agreement. **0219**.

Ms Finch could have used much more effectively the email from Defendant's wife Lana to Accuser, **0213**, with the description of the alleged incident that was sent almost two months prior to Accuser's filing her Criminal Complaint. Even supposing that Mrs. Williams could be misinformed by her husband, or not completely honest for his sake during her testimony, there is contemporaneous written confirmation in that email that Mrs. Williams and Accuser had been talking about the ongoing civil suit, *CL14-2*. **0178**, **0216**, during their 20-25 minutes conversation on 30 September, 2015.

Ms Finch shortly mentioned this fact in her closing arguments, but failed to point out that a woman who later claimed that she was beaten up by a large man just a half hour before that phone conversation could not discuss rules of process service, etc., without any change in her mood or in her voice being noticed by the listener/Mrs.Williams. **0173**.

Another example, in the article from Accuser's blog she wrote: " ...the Williams' are totally insane and incompetent...Which is why the US Veterans administration mandated Williams can't get his monthly crazy checks..., unless Williams has a guardian & fiduciary...surprise [*sic*] it is corrupt business partner Tim Kalamaros..." **0239**. As stated above Mr. Kalamaros, as a respected Officer of the Court in Indiana and Illinois, made clear in a phone conversation with Ms.Finch that it was an outrageous lie.

That entire article, especially it's last paragraph with Accuser's link to the agitating YouTube video (since removed), also clearly shows Accuser's ulterior motive for making her Criminal Complaint of battery against Defendant. **0241**.

Despite his living over 200 miles away from Pocahontas County, Defendant and Ms.Finch had many long conversations in person and by phone during the more than three years of her representation of him. Defendant and his wife Lana also have sent counsel close to a hundred long emails with legal research and vital proving documents attached. Most were unacknowledged by Ms Finch. It became apparent that Ms. Finch ignored many of those helpful emails.

For example, Defendant explained to Ms. Finch so many times that Accuser is delusional, believing and stating that two of her coup-plotters and "witnesses," Michael Oljaca and John McLaughlin, are the "true" NA Board while claiming Defendant's duly appointed Chairmanship and National Alliance Board Presidency is false. Ms. Finch was communicating with NA's Corporate attorney in Virginia, Andrew Bury, on that subject and was provided with, among other corporate documents – such as Annual Reposts, etc. -- NA's By-Laws, stating the President's (Defendant's) absolute authority to add

21

and remove Directors at his pleasure. Ms. Finch was given copies of the official certified, return receipt letters, that removed Oljaca and McLaughlin from NA Board on 10 March, 2016, by the NA Chairman, that were mailed to Accuser's co-conspirators after getting Mr. Bury's approval – and were signed for by both recipients.

Nevertheless, despite Accuser's numerous lies about her "real board" and it's phantom board meetings, phantom minutes, etc., during her examination of Accuser, **0074**, Ms. Finch failed to ask probative questions on this subject to easily trap Accuser in her outrageous lies.

In Accuser's rambling trial testimony complaining about how scared she was that Defendant will "get even" and kill her. Ms Finch failed to ask questions and point out in her closing arguments that a person who is so scared for her life would certainly move away, especially when offered $3,000 severance, according to the Termination of Contract. **0219**. How many casual contract employees, fired for outrageous insubordination, are offered such generous severance to vacate when fired? Besides her revenge against Defendant for being fired by him, Accuser had another obvious motive to accuse Defendant of battery. She has participated to a great extent in three coup attempts, using her three puppets -- a boyfriend, a roommate and a new employer – as her "witnesses" in the alleged battery, as well as their involvement in the three civil lawsuits against Defendant and the National Alliance, *CL14-2, 16-C-12, CL16-2090-01*. All three actions were finally dismissed with prejudice at great expense to the Defendant. Ms. Finch often said that facts of these judicial coup attempts to seize NA assets were not relevant while the Defendant has said all along that introducing his Accuser's motives for making a false claim of battery to get TROs against Defendant most certainly *are* relevant. On the date of Defendant's second arrest within five days at the hands of Accuser and her co-conspirators, on 21 December, 2015, Accuser was arrested that same day by Pocahontas County Sheriff's Deputy B.A. Shinaberry, *16-M38M-00002*, for her "falsely reporting an emergency incident" under *§ 61-6-20(3)* of WV Code, about Defendant's arrest that afternoon. In Deputy Shinaberry's Criminal Complaint of

Defendant DeCourcy he states that Accuser "had no business [being involved] in the incident [of Defendant's arrest for violating her boyfriend's TRO, called in by her roommate DeMarais]." She had orchestrated Defendant's false arrest for "breaking and entering" NA property. Then had been told to cease calling 911 about this, but kept calling anyway, so was arrested.

Defendant was never informed of the arrest of his Accuser by counsel, learning about it only ten months later in Accuser's first personal *ex parte* letter to Judge Dent. Defendant requested more than once to Ms. Finch to include Deputy Shinaberry on his list of defense witnesses – another request that was ignored by Ms. Finch. Shinaberry would have made an excellent, reliable defense witness.

Oljaca was eventually evicted from the NA residence on NA property that he had illegally squatted in for five months the NA residence that he, his Accuser/girlfriend and her roommate DeMarais had falsely claimed to law enforcement and in Court filings belonged to Oljaca.

3. IMPROPER EXCLUSION OF EVIDENCE.

*Sealing three illegal *ex parte* letters. Counsel did not inform Defendant or allow him to object to the sealing.

*Denial of the Motion by Judge Dent to unseal them.

*Judge's attempt to strike VIS.

*Refusal and failure by Ms. Finch to enter as evidence the Accuser's obvious motive for her battery claim.

*Refusal of Patrick Via to contact Defendant's primary witness despite having his sworn Affidavit in hand. Suppression of exculpatory evidence.

4. LACK OF SUFFICIENT EVIDENCE.

During both trials the State's *only* evidence was eight undated, un-timestamped selfies with very slight pink spot on Accuser's neck, submitted by Accuser to law enforcement more than two months after the alleged 9/30/15 battery. **0247-0261**. In the transcript of Ms. Finch's short closing arguments, **0200-0204**, counsel did not mention the important fact that Accuser failed to ever seek medical attention, despite what she repeatedly describes in her various documents as a very brutal physical beating and "attempted homicide" by the Accused.

Ms. Finch did not mention that in Accuser's original claim she described "punching, pulling, choking and holding down" by the Defendant, yet Accuser waited more that two months to file her Complaint against the Accused Defendant. **0200-0204**.

In Circuit Court trial the State introduced Defendant's response to the desperate email from Accuser's ex-boyfriend, Michael Oljaca, who had perjured himself as Accuser's witness at the Magistrate Court trial. Accuser had cajoled him to file his own battery claim against Defendant to get that second TRO in order to wrongfully keep Defendant off of NA property. Defendant was later found not guilty of violating that protective order at his 25 April 2016 Magistrate trial, *15-M38M-693*. Accuser cornered Assistant County Prosecutor McMillion in the hallway after that ruling, argued loudly with him, trying to appeal the Judge's ruling. McMillion informed her, "Listen, lady, this case is over!"

Accuser also cajoled boyfriend Oljaca to file the four-part frivolous civil suit, *16-C-12*, against Defendant Williams and the National Alliance, the corporation of which Defendant was Chairman then, in 2015, and is still Chairman today. Co-conspirator DeMarais paid the Lewisburg, WV, attorney Kris Faerber a reported $4,000 to file that bogus action for him. Oljaca soon moved back to NYC after becoming seriously depressed by what he described as his "nightmare." Oljaca's bogus criminal complaint failed, then his bogus civil suit was dropped. Defendant and NA dropped the counterclaim against Oljaca. Then Mr. Oljaca was not available to testify as a prosecution witness in the Circuit Court appeal of the battery conviction. There had absolutely been no "witness tampering."

Defendant responded to Mr. Oljaca's email, stating that he wanted to drop the civil case against

24

110

Defendant. Oljaca was told by Defendant in that email response that he should tell the truth: that he should inform the Court that he was coached to lie by Accuser. **0265**. That does not constitute "witness tampering," but Special Prosecutor Via based his battery prosecution on that email response by Defendant, on Accuser's lies and on her phony selfie photos. **0247-0261.**

The State's plan was to use only Defendant's email response to "witness" Oljaca, out of context, as evidence, describing it as "witness tampering," but Defendant was able to go off the Special Prosecutor's script to read the part of Mr. Oljaca's initial email to Defendant, showing his great fear of the Accuser and of her co-conspirator/landlord/roommate and financial supporter, Bob DeMarais. **0165**.

The State's only "witness" of the alleged battery during Circuit Court trial was Accuser's landlord/cohabitant/benefactor and financial supporter DeMarais who stated that he "saw the bruises." A Defense exhibit used during cross examination of "witness" DeMarais was an Internet forum posting by him, **0244,** that revealed his immoderate hatred of the Defendant, that should have impeached his testimony. He was not present to witness any battery and the selfie "evidence" showed no "bruising" whatsoever.

That a documented scammer could and would pinch her own neck, creating a small red mark, then take a selfie of it as "evidence" of what she claims is a "strangulation," is not outside the realm of possibility. Doing so would not be the first time a "victim" self-inflicted "evidence" of a battery. All along Defendant swore he never touched his Accuser's neck, because he never did. **0223, 0126-0127**.

Defendant desires that Accuser's entire trial testimony during her direct and cross examination, **0028-0094**, be read for this Court to see her many unresponsive, rambling answers, and attempts to fool Officers of the Circuit Courtroom by lying, contradicting herself, feigning confusion, playing dumb, repeating "I can't hear, I can't see, I can't remember," and constantly interrupting and talking out of turn.

111

Here are just a few more examples not mentioned in **INEFFECTIVE COUNSELING** section:

Accuser lied about Trooper Brock preparing her written statement himself and impelling her to sign it by promising her he would stop Defendant's "ongoing crime" against her if only she would sign it. **0058-0062**. Trooper Brock's sworn testimony contradicting Accuser's on page **0186-0187**. Defense witness Brock had been sequestered during Accuser's previous testimony to the contrary.Brock wrote in his own statement that day, 10/31/15, that he called Mr. Oljaca in New York City asking him for his version of events, and that Oljaca told him he would contact him later with that, but never did. **0228**. He would have needed to speak with his coach, Defendant's Accuser first. While testifying in Magistrate Court, Oljaca requested a bathroom break and was instructed by the Judge to not talk with Accuser while out of the room, and was escorted to the restroom and back by Bailiff.

Accuser lied that she had never been asked to separate from her employment by Defendant. **0072-0076**. Later Accuser DeCourcy contradicted that sworn testimony and admitted that she *had in fact* received the Termination of Contract document, **0219**, from Defendant, her former employer. **0079-0082**.

Accuser's contradicts herself when asked if she had been paid for the month of September 2015: In line 9 of page **0068** she said, "No." In line 13 of the same page she admits, yes, " I did (get paid)." Then she lied that she was paid a day or two before 30 September, 2019, **0069**, while in actuality she (and her "witness," Oljaca) were paid in cash for September, as was customary at the end of each month, by the Defendant just 10 minutes, or so, after the alleged incident. **0128**. Her response as to how much she had been paid for her work for the NA was outrageous. **0069**. She had been paid $800 per month by the Defendant at the ends of each of the previous four full months of employment with the National Alliance **0122**.

Nearly the Accuser's entire testimony was based on one lie after another, even when lying would not help or make any sense for her case. It's difficult to understand why, for example, that she lied that Oljaca was outside the room, **0083**, while he actually was sitting three feet to the left of the Defendant, who was sitting behind the office desk. **0125**. Oljaca was being interviewed by Defendant at the time,

26

112

not she, as Accuser claims. She would not let Oljaca, who was Defendant's Chief of Staff, answer any

of the questions he was being asked by his employer, the Defendant. She interrupted them the entire

short time and talked over her employer, the Defendant, and was out of control. **0126-0127**.

Accuser's trial testimony described a drawn out, violent beatdown fight she and Oljaca had with the

Defendant, **0040-0044**, while in her and Oljaca's earlier written sworn statements, **0232, 0233**, -- in

which they contradicted each other -- they had described different versions of a short "choking" and of

a fantastic, contrived dialog by Defendant of, "She knows too much. She has to be dealt with, etc.,"

with no regard for reason or reality. These same rehearsed quotes attributed to Defendant were repeated

in Defendant's Magistrate trial by her other "witness," John McLaughlin, who became her employer

after she had been fired by Defendant and who happened to be in Illinois at the time of the alleged

battery. So McLaughlin "witnessed" nothing, and heard none of those rehearsed quotes that Defendant

supposedly uttered while he was allegedly "choking" his new employee, his co-conspirator, the

Accuser. Accuser's other "witness" and co-conspirator, Michael Oljaca was also employed by John

McLaughlin after he had been fired by Defendant.

Accuser has been describing serious deep bruising and other injures on her "shoulder and the back of

the legs", **0070**, but only took pictures of slight pink spots on the side of her neck from different angles.

She testified how Defendant dug his fingernails into her neck, leaving scratches. **0085**. Anyone can see

Defendant has no fingernails long enough to scratch anything. He held up his fingernails to show Ms.

Finch as soon as Accuser told that whopper, but Finch didn't point out to the Court that the Defendant

could not have "dug nails" into the Accuser's throat because the ends of his fingers are soft nubs.

Ms. Finch failed to ask what Accuser's reason was for failing to take pictures of her other injuries (on

shoulder, legs) and the spots on the neck after discoloring, **0070, 0086**, but at least stated in her closing

arguments that "There is no evidence of the injures...by being pushed against filing cabinets or

bookshelves. And we know she [Ms DeCourcy] knows how to take photographs of herself." **0203**.

Remarkably, though, Judge Dent stated, "the Court believes that the photographs are consistent with the type of injury that was described by Ms. DeCourcy in her testimony." **0206**.

Accuser is not stupid, but one must read the transcript of her testimony to see how she was either playing dumb, has serious mental issues, or both. For example:

Note the number of times Accuser began giving long unhinged, off-topic answers before Mr. Via or Ms. Finch could finish formulating their questions. **0039, 0043, 0044**.

Or note the number of times Accuser would not stop running her mouth while Judge Dent was ruling on Ms. Finch's objections. **0036, 0038, 0040**.

She was advised by Mr. Via, by Ms. Finch, and ordered by Judge Dent to listen attentively and give short answers to yes or no questions instead of running her mouth. She was unable to do so and, instead, would make more unsubstantiated accusations against the Defendant. **0036, 0057, 0061, 0064, 0079**. Examples of when even the simplest questions like requests to name the document/exhibit she had been handed would need to be repeated several times. **0030-0031, 0057-0060, 0064-0065, 0066-0067**. Defendant could give several more examples citing lies and outrageous demeanor of Accuser, but worries that he will exceed the 40-page Brief limit. He feels he has provided enough to raise reasonable doubt that no battery was perpetrated by him on 9/30/2015.

Despite all episodes described above, Judge Dent found Accuser's testimony "credible," **0205-0209**, and Mr. Via stated in his sentencing speech "... But this Court made the finding beyond a reasonable doubt that the offense of battery was committed." **0364**.

5. PROSECUTORIAL MISCONDUCT. Violation of *Rule 3.8 (Special Responsibilities of a Prosecutor) and Amendments of the U.S. Constitution*.

Fourth Amendment of the U.S. Constitution, and Rule 3.8. Special Prosecutor Via began prosecuting Defendant in Circuit Court, having an unprofessional bias and lack of probable cause. He never cared to have his office investigate Accuser's claim, nor have law enforcement look into the abundance of

28

facts that would lead to the truth; never interviewed Defendant, accepted every lie of Accuser as being truthful. He never called Defense's very reliable primary witness, Fred Streed, though he had in hand that witness's sworn Affidavit, **0319,** and his contact information prior to trial. Via therefore suppressed exculpatory evidence that even TV Judge Judy would have followed.

Defendant never enjoyed any presumption of innocence, and SP Via, as a state actor, seemed intent on depriving Defendant of his liberty without due process of the law -- not only in violation of WV law but in violation of both the *Fifth and Fourteenth Amendments of the U.S.Constitution*.

Sixth Amendment of the U.S.Constitution Despite Defendant's motion requesting a hearing to question Accuser regarding her VIS, **0329,** Mr. Via stated that Accuser "is not available here today for cross-examination, nor should she be" at the 02/12/19 sentencing. **0346.** That appears to be yet another violation of *§61-11A-3(e)* of WV Code, since she had stated in writing in her VIS and on the telephone to Probation Officer Tooze that she wished to attend Defendant's sentencing to give an oral statement reinforcing her written VIS. **0281.** As Accuser's scheme unravelled she fled the state rather than appear at Defendant's sentencing and risk being charged with harassment, perjury, filing false reports, contempt of court, abuse of process, or whatever else she has been guilty of perpetrating on the Court all along.

Eighth Amendment of the U.S.Constitution On presentation of the Defense's request for post-sentencing bond Mr. Via stated that Defendant is going to be at the jail for just 18 days, so he will have plenty of time to take care of his appeal **0368**. Actually, it took Defendant more than three weeks after being jailed to partially restore his health and become capable enough for clear thinking and working. The 71 year old Defendant, now 72, was handcuffed for the third time during this protracted ordeal, and remanded from court directly to the Tygart Valley Regional Jail again while that facility was locked down, under quarantine due a serious flu epidemic. The Defendant was infected with the virus, became seriously ill and lost 12 pounds he did not have to lose.

29

It took Mr. Via two weeks to prepare and file the final order which combines the Court's denials of the three post trial motions.**0371**. Later it was discovered that the order denying Ms. Finch's Motion to withdraw of 10/10/18 is missing, as well as the order regarding Defendant's bond. Mr. Via was responsible for those orders and for over a week had been ignoring Defense's urgent requests for those documents due to the, by then, shortened deadline to submit his Notice of Appeal. Defendant's wife Lana had to make several calls to the Circuit Court Clerk after emailing Mr. Via and leaving several telephone messages with his Clerk with no responses. Very unprofessional.

Defense counsel Finch and SP Via couldn't decide who was responsible for filing the order denying Ms. Finch's motion to withdraw. It was finally filed at Defendant's request by Finch, signed by Judge Dent on 3/20/19, **0299**, five months after its denial, and on the *very last day* before the Notice of Appeal was mailed in order to meet the required deadline. Recall that Special Prosecutor Via had spitefully remarked at sentencing that Defendant did not need bond to prepare his Notice of Appeal because he was only going to jail for 18 days. **0368**.

6. PRESERVING AN ERROR FOR APPEAL. Each of the four legitimate post trial motions by Defendant, pointing to Court errors, ineffective counsel, and violations of Defendant's rights were denied. **0299, 0311, 0325, 0329**.

7.PROCEDURAL ERRORS DURING MAGISTRATE COURT TRIAL.

Rule 2.11. Disqualification. Magistrate Carrie Wilfong stated in an extremely emotional statement before sentencing Defendant to to an unprecedented six months in jail for a first offense that she "had been abused herself" and that "there would be no battering of females in her county." Both of Defendant's defense attorneys in this saga were in the courthouse that day and told Defendant immediately after the emotional sentencing that Magistrate Wilfong should have recused herself. Her biased, unrestrained outburst, affected by Accuser DeCourcy's courtroom theatrics, sobbing, shaking and claims of an "attempted homicide" on her by Defendant, would indicate that Wilfong should not hear and sit in judgment in criminal cases involving claims by females against males of battery, if there is to be a presumption of innocence.

Rule 2.14. Disability and Impairment. By Magistrate Wilfong's disorderly behavior when she sentenced Defendant, he sensed that she was somehow impaired. The intemperate intensity of her sentencing of him did not show the reasonable impartiality one would expect from a judge in a criminal case. Defendant has since learned that in 2018, this West Virginia Supreme Court of Appeals suspended Magistrate Wilfong without pay in Case No. *18-0891*, following allegations that Magistrate Wilfong missed an excessive amount of work and had been intoxicated both at a 2015 Magistrates' conference and while on the bench. The integrity of the judiciary is certainly placed into question by such conduct by a judge. Wilfong had a judicial hearing wherein she apparently admitted she "has suffered from addiction to drugs legally prescribed to her over a period of approximately fifteen years and that this prescription drug addiction had negatively impacted the performance of her judicial duties." In the interest of brevity, summarizing Magistrate Wilfong's later case before WVSCA, No. *19-0170*, Petitioner notes that the monitoring agreement that Wilfong had agreed to was suspended "due to noncompliance following drug tests showing significant increases in hydrocodone and benzodiazepines..." Apparently Magistrate "backslid" and was suspended without pay again, following a finding of probable cause that she engaged in a serious violation of West Virginia's Code of Judicial Conduct. On March 13, 2019, Magistrate Wilfong requested a hearing, and the matter was heard by this WVSCA on May 15, 2019.

Defendant is unaware of details of Magistrate Wilfong's unfortunate case but apparently this WVSCA was satisfied on 3 June, 2019, "that probable cause currently exists to believe that Magistrate Wilfong has failed to comply with the terms and conditions set forth in the Board's November 20, 2018 order that was adopted by this Court's January 10, 2019 order."

The final disposition of Magistrate Wilfong's future as a judge is unknown to Defendant, but he has

31

seen enough about her admitted alcoholism and drug addiction, especially that she has been found to be "intoxicated while on the bench" during the same period when she heard his case of misdemeanor battery, found him guilty and sentenced him to six months in jail, that more than her personal history of being battered comes into question as far as her judicial temperament under ***Rule 2.14, Disability and Impairment.***

Perhaps Magistrate Wilfong's conviction of Defendant can be reviewed in light of her recent suspension from judicial functions for alleged violations of Judicial Code of Conduct.

Defendant 's first defense counsel before Magistrate Wilfong, attorney Paul Detch, failed to inform Defendant that he could have petitioned for a new trial, only that he could appeal Wilfong's decision to Circuit Court. Mr. Detch hardly defended the Accused at all. He even failed to notice an obvious contradiction in short written descriptions of the incident by Accuser and her main witness in Magistrate Court, Mr. Oljaca. **0232, 0233**. Mr. Detch's stated strategy was, "Don't say anything. Let DeCourcy run her mouth and she will reveal that she is crazy." His entire closing argument was described to Magistrate Wilfong with just two words: "raging paranoia," Upon hearing of that Ms. Finch, who replaced Detch as defense counsel told Defendant, "That's no defense." She was correct.

Mr. Detch also failed to object to Accuser's co-conspirator and new employer, John McLaughlin, being her "witness" in Magistrate Court. That "witness" was in Illinois at the time of the alleged battery so could not have "witnessed" anything.

Mr. McLaughlin died of a massive heart attack in February 2017, just after his Plaintiff's counsel withdrew representation of him in *McLaughlin vs. NA, **CL16-2090-01.*** That was the second civil lawsuit filed against NA in Virginia with the intent to dissolve the NA corporation and somehow receive its assets. Plaintiff McLaughlin's employee by then, Accuser DeCourcy, was his "Legal Liaison" and "Executive Administrative Assistant,'" and orchestrating that bogus action.

Mr. McLaughlin, who was not judgement-proof, having an estate worth in excess of $4,000,000, then

32

118

realized the serious trouble Accuser had gotten him into, cajoling him to become Plaintiff in the third baseless, harassing civil suit against the NA (including *Oljaca v. NA and Will Williams* in WV) NA presently has an active, sound $850,000 counterclaim in Virginia against the co-administrators of the estate of Mr. McLaughlin, *CL16-2090-01*, based on Mr. McLaughlin's breach of fiduciary duties for working against NA while he was still serving as an Officer of the NA Board -- of which Ms. Finch is well aware -- wherein Defendant's Accuser DeCourcy is prominently named for her role in *McLaughlin v. National Alliance* as the Plaintiff's "Legal Liaison" and "Executive Administrative Assistant."

In Magistrate Court Defendant believes there was also a violation of Chapter *§61-11A-3(e)* when Accuser's long VIS in that lower Court -- with many of the same easily-refuted lies contained in the sealed Circuit *ex parte* letters and VIS -- was provided to him only *after* he was sentenced, denying him the opportunity to question the many factual inaccuracies therein. Counsel Detch did not object.

In the Magistrate Court case Assistant Prosecutor McMillion never interviewed Defendant nor Mr. Streed. McMillion's closing argument was, "The pictures tell the whole story." A couple of plea offers arranged between McMillion and Detch, without Defendant's consent, were declined by the Defendant because the alleged battery of Accuser never happened and by his accepting those plea arrangements Defendant would have essentially been admitting guilt that he battered his Accuser. When he did not.

Defendant was an innocent victim in this four-year-old saga. He was a passive Defendant who had trusted the legal process and his two defense attorneys to disprove the State's case. When that failed, he found the Rule Books online that clearly state Defendant's rights. He studied and learned the law as best he could as a layman, realizing at that point that he would have to self-represent if he was to finally achieve legal relief, clear his name and be made whole again.

Unedited from Defendant's Notice of Appeal:

A jurist's gender should make no objective difference in deciding how he or she interprets the law, but after having two female judges convict him in the questionable charge of battery against a female -- in

33

this "me, to" era when an accusation by a female against a male often leads to a conviction, without presumption of the Accused's innocence – Defendant is reticent to admit, but is somewhat encouraged, nevertheless – with no offense intended toward the female justices -- to learn that the majority of judges sitting on the WVSCA are male. Ms. Finch had actually advised him, "Do not let the Court know that you served two combat tours in Vietnam as a Green Beret Captain, because that indicates a violent tendency." Defendant honorably served in the military and is disabled, resulting from that combat experience. He does not have a violent personality. Defendant believes errors mentioned in section ARGUMENT are what led to a wrongful conviction.

CONCLUSION

Being wrongfully convicted of battery of a female, Defendant needs to clear his name and be made whole. He prays that this last avenue of judicial relief in West Virginia will assist him in removing the false stigma of "convicted woman beater" imposed on him in the 11th Judicial District of WV. Defendant has no interest in having this highest Court send his case back to the Pocahontas Court for retrial. He has already "served his time," and "paid his debt."

As far as Defendant understands there are three rulings possible in an appellate case- Affirmed, Reversed, or Remanded. To quote **_Rule 21_** of WV Revised Rules: *(d)Reversal. A memorandum decision reversing the decision of the lower tribunal shall contain a concise statement of the reason therefor and a concise statement of the reason for issuing the memorandum decision instead of an opinion. A memorandum decision reversing the decision of a circuit court should be issued in limited circumstances.* Defendant feels that his case fits "limited circumstances."

Should Defendant's conviction be remanded back to the Pocahontas County Court, the State will have no witnesses of the alleged battery, no evidence of that alleged battery, and its claiming witness, Accuser DeCourcy, has long fled WV. Besides that, the County Prosecutor's Office was DISQUALIFIED **0011.**

34

For the four years this misdemeanor criminal case has dragged on nearly *all* Court Officers have seemed to have some degree of conflicts of interest. It is apparent to anyone who knows the Defendant well that from the rulings, the denials of all of Defendant 's motions, and from evidence in the Court transcripts that due process was not accorded him. Perhaps Defendant was being punished because he quickly declined the several plea bargains offered to him from both prosecutors, or perhaps for who he

is. Either, if true, should bring shame on the 11th Judicial District of West Virginia and perhaps investigated by a higher authority.

It was stated by both the Circuit Court Judge and the Special Prosecutor that Defendant should be sentenced to six months in jail because he "refused to accept responsibility for the crime." **0366, 0364**. Of course Defendant was not going to accept responsibility for a false claim about an incident that never happened. Also Defendant understands that his acceptance of a plea would be accepting guilt for a false charge where no guilt by him exists.

Special Prosecutor Via expressed that he wanted to recommend one year in jail for Defendant, except he was limited by the six month sentence given by Magistrate Wilfong, **0364**, the same Judge who has since been suspended without pay by this same WVSCA for what it ruled was her Judicial misconduct. Again, Defendant is an honorable, law-abiding citizen with a clean record and, more than that, Chairman of a respected organization, the National Alliance, and Trustee of a long-established Church. His name matters a lot to him. Defendant put his faith in the judicial process to prove his innocence and to date that process has failed him.

If he isn't granted a reversal for his wrongful conviction by the Highest Court where he and his wife can put this experience behind them, to clear his name he will have no other recourse, but to take the story of his shocking experience with 11th Judicial District to the court of public opinion.This is not a threat. Defendant has a voice and he will use it.

35

Defendants hopes, though, that his experience with the Pocahontas County Court is exceptional -- like nowhere else in West Virginia -- perhaps because the county is remote and difficult to monitor by higher authorities.

That's why Defendant has persistently pursued his right to appeal to WVSCA despite serious obstacles like refusals from several appellate attorneys he had tried to retain. Defendant prays that Supreme Court will be considerate about lawyerless imperfections in the Petitioner's Brief due to *pro se* representation as a layman.

If this Court can not reverse lower tribunal decision without remanding the case to Pocahontas Court, maybe it can vacate the conviction. Defendant can not imagine dealing with Pocahontas Court again which he has lost all trust for a fair trial. There was an obvious judicial bias before, and it will probably become even worse after Defendant revealed numerous violations of that Court to the WVSCA.

Unlike the Magistrate who sentenced him to jail, Defendant would add that he neither drinks alcohol nor does any illegal drugs, yet he was ordered to submit to random alcohol and drug testing by Judge Dent. **0366.** Neither alcohol nor drugs were ever claimed to be involved in his alleged "crime." That alleged battery was not by definition "domestic," and the final disposition of the case has not yet been reached since it is still under appeal, yet Homeland Security revoked Defendant's duly obtained permit to carry a concealed handgun under threat of arrest and one year in prison had he not turned in his permit to those authorities within 10 days of their notification to him. A first offense of non-domestic, simple misdemeanor battery should not have called for revocation of a duly-obtained concealed-carry permit in WV, especially in a case that has not yet come to a final disposition.

Defendant can see why an Anger Management course was ordered in a battery conviction. **0367.** He completed the nine-week AM course, as ordered, but he would appreciate if this Court will officially repeal his remaining probation restrictions and order his improperly revoked concealed-carry permit reinstated without penalty. It is a dangerous world and Defendant is a responsible, trained firearm user,

122

the sort of user one would want armed in an "active shooter" situation when there are no trained law enforcement personnel on scene.

Defendant prays that grounded on his ARGUMENT herein that this highest State Court will decide to conclude this case of the out-of-state Accused in his favor. This four-year-long ordeal has unnecessarily burdened the Defendant as well as the State with an enormous waste of both time and resources,

leading to a wrongful conviction, he argues, based on a false claim of a crime that was never committed.

Respectfully submitted,

William White Williams
1XXX XXX Road
Mountain City, TN 37683
PHONE: (423)XXX9, (423)XXX1
FAX: (423)XXX9

37

Appendix 32: Summary Response by the State of West Va.

Respondent State of West Virginia, by counsel, Holly M. Flanigan, Assistant Attorney General, respectfully responds to Petitioner's Brief. Because Petitioner fails to demonstrate the existence of reversible error, this Court should affirm the Circuit Court of Pocahontas County's February 25, 2019, Order.

I. STATEMENT OF THE CASE

On August 14, 2018, Petitioner received a *de novo* bench trial in the Circuit Court of Pocahontas County on his appeal from a conviction of battery in a magistrate court bench trial. Appendix Record ["AR"] 25. The State's witnesses were the victim, Garland DeCourcy, and Robert DeMarais. AR 22. Petitioner's witnesses were himself, his wife, Svetlana Williams, and State Trooper Damon Brock. AR 22. The battery charge arose from events occurring on September 30, 2015. In September of 2015, the victim in this case, Garland DeCourcy, was employed by National Alliance at its location in Mill Point, Pocahontas County.[1] AR 28, 30, 75, 91, 95, 103. Petitioner was her boss or supervisor. AR 29-30. Although Petitioner lived in Tennessee, he made regular trips to the Mill Point property where DeCourcy lived and worked. AR 31. September 28, 2015, and the following days involved one of these trips. AR 32-33. Petitioner arrived in town and DeCourcy saw him shortly thereafter. AR 32.

On September 29, 2015, DeCourcy received a phone call while she was at work and "[Petitioner] went ballistic and started going crazy. AR 33-34, 37. And, then he wouldn't let me leave the building." AR 34. DeCourcy eventually left, and returned the following day before 9:00 a.m., which was earlier than usual, because Petitioner demanded she come make him coffee. AR 34. After DeCourcy arrived at work and made Petitioner coffee, AR 35-36, she went back to her

---

[1] DeCourcy and Petitioner disagreed as to whether it was Petitioner who employed her or National Alliance who employed her. AR 30, 75, 91, 95, 103, 121.

office to avoid him. AR 36. Petitioner came in to her office and swore at her, demanding to sit behind her desk. AR 36. She complied and sat on the other side of her desk while Petitioner badgered her with questions about the telephone call she received the previous night while working. AR 37. DeCourcy described Petitioner as going crazy and repeatedly demanding to know what people said about him. AR 37. When she told Petitioner she had talked to "him" last night (referring to the telephone call), Petitioner got up and slammed his hand on her desk, calling her a "liar, liar liar." AR 37. Mr. Oljaca was standing outside DeCourcy's office door monitoring the situation and letting DeCourcy know he was there because each visit "Williams was getting more violent." AR 37. DeCourcy stated Petitioner was going nuts, slamming his hand on the desk again and demanding she tell him what people say about him. AR 37-38. When she tried to leave her office, Petitioner demanded she stay right there, saying "Don't you walk away from me. Don't you know who I am[?]" AR 39. It was when DeCourcy moved to get one of her purses that Petitioner told her he was not done with her and came across the room with a hand fisted and hit her in the neck, which knocked her into chairs. AR 39-41. Petitioner then choked her using both hands around her neck, and screamed about her knowing too much. AR 41, 42. Petitioner pushed her toward a corner, she tripped over a file cabinet, and he continued to push her toward bookcases. AR 41. DeCourcy described trying to fight off Petitioner, but was stunned and off-balance. AR 41. Oljaca came into her office yelling for Petitioner to stop. AR 41. Petitioner did not stop. AR 41. Oljaca rammed Petitioner with his body to knock him off of DeCourcy. AR 41-42. Petitioner yelled and swore at Oljaca about DeCourcy needing to be "shut up for good. She knows too much." AR 42. DeCourcy described trying to catch her breath after Petitioner was knocked away and how Petitioner kept trying to skirt Oljaca and grab her neck. AR 43. She was stunned and frozen in fear, and Petitioner was fighting Oljaca. AR 43-44. DeCourcy got her voice back and screamed she was

2

calling the police. AR 44. The fight broke up and DeCourcy and Oljaca left the building through the back door. AR 45.

Oljaca snapped photographs of DeCourcy's neck once they were outside the building. AR 45.[2] They reentered the building a short time later. AR 45. DeCourcy went to the restroom to splash water on her face and clean up, and she took photographs of herself in the bathroom mirror. AR 46-47. The State used a selection of these photographs at trial, marking them as State's Exhibits 1-8. After DeCourcy authenticated the photographs, they were admitted into evidence without objection. AR 54. DeCourcy and Oljaca left shortly thereafter and went to the nearby home of Mr. DeMarais, where DeCourcy rented a room. AR 51-52; 96. DeCourcy immediately informed DeMarais what had occurred, and DeMarais urged DeCourcy and Oljaca to call the police. AR 52. DeCourcy waited to contact the police until after Petitioner left town, out of fear Petitioner would kill her and Oljaca. AR 52-53.

Robert DeMarais testified that DeCourcy and Oljaca arrived at his home on September 30, 2015. AR 94-96. He learned Petitioner had attacked DeCourcy, and advised her to call the police. AR 99. DeMarais described DeCourcy as very nervous and frightened and she had two bruises on the left side of her neck. AR 99. Each bruise was about half an inch wide and two inches long. AR 99-100. DeMarais also saw an injury on the right side of DeCourcy's neck, but it was not significant compared to the injury on the left side. AR 100. He described that in the following weeks, DeCourcy continued to work as usual, although she was "a lot more alert, you know. She was afraid of Mr. Williams and expressed that." AR 100. DeMarais confirmed DeCourcy spoke

---

[2] Petitioner included photographs on pages 247-261 of the Appendix Record. These photographs may be the photographs marked at trial as State's Exhibits 1-8, *see* AR 47, and which DeCourcy authenticated at trial as accurately representing the injuries Petitioner inflicted. AR47-51. However, the photographs in the Appendix Record lack the court reporter's exhibit markings, leaving Respondent unable to determine whether the photographs are part of the underlying record. For the sake of this Brief, Respondent presumes they are the photographs from trial.

3

126

with Trooper Brock on October 4, 2015, AR 107, 115, and he believed DeCourcy called the police the day following Petitioner's attack. AR 115.

Petitioner's wife, Lana, testified about DeCourcy's aspirations at work, which she learned through their many telephone conversations. AR 171-173. On September 30, 2015, at the end of one such conversation with DeCourcy around 10:00 a.m., DeCourcy told her she and Petitioner had argued and Petitioner tried to choke her. AR 173, 179. Lana stated DeCourcy's "voice sounded like it was a joke, like there was [a] big smile on her face." AR 173.

West Virginia State Trooper Damon Brock testified to being called to the National Alliance property at Mill Point on October 31, 2015, in regard to Petitioner removing DeCourcy's property from the building. AR 181-182. He recalled DeCourcy previously reporting Petitioner's battery to law enforcement and having a conversation with her about it. AR 182-183. On October 31, 2015, he spoke with DeCourcy and Petitioner about the allegations, took DeCourcy's statement, AR 225-226,[3] prepared a report, and handed the matter over to the prosecuting attorney. AR 183. He did not file a criminal complaint against Petitioner himself, because DeCourcy had spoken to law enforcement a couple of times about it and he wanted to let the prosecutor decide how to proceed. AR 189, 192. He did not complete the investigation or determine whether the charges were actionable because the case ended up with the Sheriff's Department. AR 190.

Petitioner testified about the September 30, 2015, incident. AR125-127, 129. He confirmed he sat behind her desk. AR 125-126. He confirmed his hand made contact with her chin when he held his arm out across the desk to stop her from shaking her finger in his face. AR 126-127. He confirmed he told her to "shut the fuck up." AR 140. He confirmed he left the room. AR 127. He confirmed he told her to shut up. He confirmed DeCourcy and Oljaca left out the back of the

---

[3] Petitioner included a copy of the Statement on pages 225-226 of the Appendix Record. Although the Statement lacks the court reporter's exhibit markings, for the sake of this Brief, Respondent assumes the statement is the one admitted at trial.

building, came in a few minutes later, and he paid them for the month. AR 128. He testified he did not believe she was going to hurt him, AR 141, despite telling the state trooper he was acting in self-defense. AR 141. He confirmed his actions to fire her occurred after the September 30, 2015, incident. AR 131-132, 142-143. He confirmed that prior to the incident DeCourcy had challenged his authority in the National Alliance. AR 162-163.

The determination of guilt

In adjudging Petitioner guilty of battery, the circuit court assessed the credibility of the witnesses, AR 208-209, and found DeCourcy's testimony to be credible to the extent it was consistent with her statements; the photographs depicting redness and swelling of DeCourcy's neck were consistent with the type of injury DeCourcy described; DeCourcy's October 31, 2015, statement to Trooper Brock were consistent with DeCourcy's testimony; and found DeMarais's testimony corroborated DeCourcy's testimony, and he personally saw injuries to DeCourcy's neck. AR 206-207. What the Court found most telling of the event was Petitioner's wife's testimony in that Mrs. Williams testified that on September 30, 2015, shortly after the time frame in which DeCourcy identified as the time of the attack, DeCourcy told her Petitioner had choked her. AR 208. The circuit court stated Mrs. Williams' testimony leads to the conclusion that DeCourcy's allegations "had nothing to do with some of the ancillary information that's come into this case with regard to terminations or who worked for whom and when they were terminated or if they were paid." AR 208.

The Sentencing

Prior to sentencing, the circuit court received multiple ex parte letters from DeCourcy and held a hearing during which it sealed the ex parte communications after providing a copy to all counsel and prohibiting them from making copies. AR 332, 337-339. In response to Petitioner's motion at sentencing regarding the propriety of sealing those letters, the circuit court explained it

5

128

dealt with the ex parte communications as required, that it did not consider them, and sealed them and cast them from the record. AR 334.

In addition to a motion to unseal the ex parte letters, Petitioner filed a variety of post-trial motions, including motions relating to Judicial Code of Conduct Cannon 2.9, AR 337-339, cross-examining the victim on her Victim Impact Statement, the credibility of the victim, the availability of an out-of-state witness and other evidence not presented at trial. AR 340-349. Although the circuit court would not permit Petitioner to argue the motions because he was represented by counsel, AR 335, it gave Petitioner the opportunity to be sworn and respond to any aspect of the Victim Impact Statement as it related to the offense when the sentencing proceeding reached that point. AR 349, 351-361. The circuit court also advised the parties that it considered the Victim Impact Statement only as it related to the offense of battery and the information permitted by W.Va. Code §61-11A-3. AR 349.

Ultimately, the circuit court sentenced Petitioner to six months of incarceration and suspended all but twenty days of the sentence, with credit for the two days Petitioner had already served. AR 366. It also placed Petitioner on probation for eighteen months with the usual terms and conditions. AR 366. Special conditions of probation included anger management counseling and no contact with DeCourcy. AR 367.

The appeal

In the Assignment of Error section of his Brief, Petitioner identifies the following errors: (1) no presumption of innocence; (2) no proper investigation; (3) insufficient due process; (4) insufficient evidence; (5) unreliable witnesses; (6) significant reasonable doubt; (7) ineffective assistance of counsel in magistrate court; (8) ineffective assistance of counsel in circuit court; and (9) verdict obtained by fraud. Pet'r Br. 1. In the Argument portion of his brief Petitioner advances the following issues: (1) judicial misconduct by violations of Cannon 2 of the West Virginia

6

Judicial Code of Conduct, Pet'r Br. 7-16; (2) ineffective counseling, Pet'r Br. 16-23; (3) improper

exclusion of evidence, Pet'r Br. 16; (4) lack of sufficient evidence, Pet'r Br. 23-28; (5)

Prosecutorial misconduct, Pet'r Br. 28-30; (6) "[p]reserving an error for appeal," Pet'r Br. 30; (7)

procedural errors during magistrate court trial, Pet'r Br. 30-34; and (8) "[u]nedited from

Defendant's Notice of Appeal."

II. <u>STANDARD OF REVIEW</u>

The findings of fact and conclusions of the underlying circuit court are subject to a two-

pronged deferential standard of review. Syl. Pt. 1, *State v. Mechling*, 219 W. Va. 366, 633 S.E.2d

311 (2006) (citing Syl. Pt. 1, *Pub. Citizen, Inc. v. First Nat'l Bank in Fairmont*, 198 W. Va. 329,

480 S.E.2d 538 (1996)). "The final order and the ultimate disposition are reviewed under an abuse

of discretion standard, and the circuit court's underlying factual findings are reviewed under a

clearly erroneous standard." *Id.* "Questions of law are subject to a *de novo* review." *Id.*

III. <u>ARGUMENT</u>[4]

Fatally problematic for Petitioner are the substantive deficits in his brief in regard to the

assignments of error and argument. Rule 10 of the West Virginia Rules of Appellate Procedure

sets forth requirements designed to ensure that a petitioner makes an argument sufficient for

appellate review by including direct factual and legal support for each claim of error committed

by the lower tribunal. Specifically, Rule 10(c)(7) requires that

> The brief must contain an argument exhibiting clearly the points of fact and
> law presented, the standard of review applicable, and citing the authorities relied
> on, under headings that correspond with the assignments of error. The argument
> must contain appropriate and specific citations to the record on appeal, including
> citations that pinpoint when and how the issues in the assignments of error were

---

[4] In addition to the specific arguments set forth below, the State notes that "[t]his Court may, on appeal, affirm the judgment of the lower court when it appears that such judgment is correct on any legal ground disclosed by the record, regardless of the ground, reason or theory assigned by the lower court as the basis for its judgment." Syl. Pt. 3, *Barnett v. Wolfolk*, 149 W.Va. 246, 140 S.E.2d 466 (1965).

7

presented to the lower tribunal. The Court may disregard errors that are not adequately supported by specific references to the record on appeal.

W. Va. R. App. P. 10(c)(7)[2010]. Additionally, in an Administrative Order entered December 10, 2012, "Re: Filings That Do Not Comply With the Rules of Appellate Procedure," Chief Justice Menis E. Ketchum specifically noted that "[b]riefs that lack citation of authority [or] fail to structure an argument applying applicable law" are not in compliance with this Court's rules. Further, "[b]riefs with arguments that do not contain a citation to legal authority to support the argument presented and do not 'contain appropriate and specific citations to the record on appeal, ...' as required by rule 10(c)(7)" are not in compliance with this Court's rules. *Id.*

In direct contravention of Rule 10, Petitioner's Argument section contains a mere paucity of citations to the Appendix, refers to matters and conversations outside the record, utterly fails to cite legal authority to support the claims, and does not structure an argument applying applicable law. This Court has stated that "appellate courts frequently refuse to address issues that appellants . . . fail to develop in their brief." *State v. Lilly*, 194 W. Va. 595, 605 n.16, 461 S.E.2d 101, 111 n.16 (1995). "The [Petitioner's] mere assertion, without supporting case law, is inadequate to preserve the assignment of error. *State v. Ladd*, 210 W. Va. 413, 424 n.1, 557 S.E.2d 820, 831 n.1 (2001).

Moreover, Petitioner does not cite the Appendix demonstrating where he raised the issues below or where the Circuit Court addressed it, and makes no real argument much less an argument relevant to the appeal and supported by legal authority with a discussion thereof. This Court's clear precedent is that, while briefs are liberally construed, particularly for *pro se* litigants, issues "not supported with pertinent authority are not considered on appeal." *State v. LaRock*, 196 W.Va. 294, 302, 470 S.E.2d 613, 621 (1996); *see, e.g.*, *State v. Corey*, 233 W. Va. 297, 309, 758 S.E.2d 117, 129 (2014) (finding an assignment of error was not properly briefed where Petitioner recited facts but failed to cite to legal authority or make a legal argument in support of his desired relief).

8

Per the Rules of Appellate Procedure and the dictates of West Virginia jurisprudence, each of Petitioner's assignments of error and argument sections fall woefully short of setting forth a reviewable claim. This Court has consistently refused to consider inadequate briefs, and it likewise should do so here. *See, e.g., Hayes v. Brady*, No. 15-0518, 2016 WL 3197435, at *6 (W. Va. June 8, 2016)(declining to address claim of denial of due process and equal protection, where the petitioner's "argument" consisted solely of typing out the texts of the Fifth and Fourteenth Amendments to the United States Constitution.). Error will not be presumed, all presumptions being in favor of the correctness of the judgment." *State v. Myers*, 229 W.Va. 238, 241, 728 S.E.2d 122, 130 (2012) (internal quotations and citations omitted). It is Petitioner who "must carry the burden of showing error in the judgment of which he complains[,]" *Myers*, 229 W.Va. at 241, 728 S.E.2d at 130, and he has not done so for any of his claims. Because this Court will not reverse the judgment of a trial court unless error affirmatively appears from the record, this Court should affirm the circuit court's Order. *See id.* For the sake of thoroughness, Respondent addresses each section of Petitioner's argument below.

A. Judicial Misconduct.

This ground is based on Petitioner's disagreement with his conviction, the sufficiency of the evidence against him, the credibility of DeCourcy for a variety of reasons that have no basis in the record, law enforcement's investigation, and the circuit court's denial of various motions. Pet'r Br. 7-16. He also disliked the sentence imposed and the Judge not stating "that Defendant has "good character." Pet'r. Br. 9. Petitioner launches the majority of attacks on the trial court judge based on Petitioner's self-serving speculations, conclusory suppositions, and conversations and dealings outside the record of this proceeding. Pet'r Br. 7-16. A review of Petitioner's "argument" here shows it fails to satisfy the Rule 10 pleading requirements because much of it is based on matters outside the record, it lacks citations to legal authority, and it fails to structure an argument applying applicable law. In the ten pages he devotes to this issue, the only authority Petitioner references is Cannon 2 of the West Virginia Judicial Code of Conduct and the 6th Amendment, and he did not bother to include the text of either one. Petitioner's first ground is insufficient and relief should be denied.

B. Ineffective assistance of counsel in magistrate court[5]; ineffective assistance of counsel in circuit court; and ineffective counseling.

First and foremost, this Court has long held that "[t]he very nature of an ineffective assistance of counsel claim demonstrates the inappropriateness of review on direct appeal." *State v. Miller*, 194 W.Va. 3, 14–15, 459 S.E.2d 114, 125–126 (1995). This Court's review function, requires matching "applicable principles of law to the discerned facts and circumstances of the litigated case. When those facts are not properly furnished to this Court, we are denied the basic tools necessary to carry out our function." *Id.* Intelligent review of cases involving ineffective assistance claims on direct appeal is rendered impossible because the most significant witness, the trial attorney, has not been given the opportunity to explain the motive and reason behind his or her trial behavior. *Id.* For this reason, the WVSCA has "held with a regularity bordering on monotonous that if the record provided to us on direct appeal proves to be so deficient as to preclude us from reaching a reasoned determination on the merits of the ineffective assistance claim, it is the defendant who must bear the brunt of an insufficient record on appeal." *Id.* (internal citations omitted).

Here, because ineffective assistance of counsel issues are raised on direct appeal, a developed record does not exist, depriving both Respondent and this Court of the necessary tools to address Petitioner's claims.[6] The appropriate forum for bringing a claim of ineffective assistance

---

[5] Petitioner's allegations of ineffective assistance of counsel in magistrate court are set forth in the section entitled "Procedural Errors during Magistrate Court."

[6] The majority of Petitioner's assertions are based on matters not contained in the record, such as purported conversations and emails between him and his wife and counsel, telephone calls,

of habeas counsel in the first instance is in circuit court where a record can be developed for appellate review. *See, e.g., Smith v. Mirandy*, No. 12-0374, 2013 WL 6184038, at *2 (W. Va. Nov. 26, 2013) (memorandum decision) ("the preferred way of raising ineffective assistance of habeas counsel is to file a subsequent petition for a writ of habeas corpus raising this issue in the court below.").

Additionally, Petitioner's "argument" fails to satisfy the Rule 10 pleading requirements, as it lacks citations to legal authority, it fails to structure an argument applying applicable law, and much of his contentions arise from matters outside the record. Petitioner's second ground for relief therefore, is insufficient and relief should be denied.

C. Improper Exclusion of Evidence.

Petitioner titles his next contention the "Improper Exclusion of Evidence." Pet'r Br. 23. This so-called error consists of five bulleted items, only one of which contains a complete sentence. Pet'r Br. 23. No aspect of this claim complies in any fashion with the requirements of Rule 10 and thus falls woefully short of a reviewable claim. Preserving an issue in an appellate brief requires more than simply raising it in a "perfunctory manner unaccompanied by some effort at developed argumentation." *Id.*, 461 S.E.2d at 111 n.16. "Indeed, '[i]t is . . . well settled . . . that casual mention of an issue in a brief is cursory treatment insufficient to preserve the issue on appeal.'" *Id.*, 461 S.E.2d at 111 n.16 (quoting *Kost v. Kozakiewicz*, 1 F.3d 176, 182 (3rd Cir.1993)). This ground is insufficiently pled, and relief should be denied.

D. Lack of Sufficient Evidence.

Petitioner contends that "the State's only evidence was eight undated, un-timestamped selfies with [a] very slight pink spot on Accuser's neck, submitted by Accuser to law enforcement

---

other litigation between Petitioner and the victim, counsels' alleged actions and inactions during the course of their representation, and a number of other assertions lacking support in the record below. Pet'r Br. 16-23.

more than two months after the alleged 9/30/2015 battery." Pet'r Br. 23-24. He attacks witness credibility, the evidence, and counsel's representation of him. But Petitioner cannot satisfy the heavy burden of proof required to set aside a conviction.

This Court has long held that a petitioner who challenges the sufficiency of the evidence underlying their conviction faces a heavy burden. Syl. pt. 3, *State v. Guthrie*, 194 W. Va. 657, 461 S.E.2d 163 (1995). To prevail, a petitioner must establish that "no rational trier of fact could have found the essential elements of the crime beyond a reasonable doubt." *LaRock*, 196 W.Va. at 303, 470 S.E.2d at 622 (1996). While undertaking its review of the record, this Court must "review all the evidence . . . in the light most favorable to the prosecution and must credit all inferences and credibility assessments that the jury might have drawn in favor of the prosecution." *Guthrie*, 194 W. Va. at 669, 461 S.E.2d at 175. This Court has ruled that it may accept any adequate evidence, including circumstantial evidence, as support for a conviction. *State v. Spinks*, 239 W. Va. 588, 611, 803 S.E.2d 558, 581 (2017) (citing *Guthrie*, 194 W.Va. at 668, 461 S.E.2d at 174). As the Court explained in *Guthrie*, it will not overturn a verdict unless "reasonable minds could not have reached the same conclusion." 194 W. Va. at 669, 461 S.E.2d at 175. Finally, "[t]he evidence need not be inconsistent with every conclusion save that of guilt so long as the jury can find guilt beyond a reasonable doubt." *Id.* Instead, a verdict will be set aside only when "the record contains no evidence, regardless of how it is weighed, from which the jury could find guilt beyond a reasonable doubt." *Id.* at 663, 461 S.E.2d. at 169.

Here, the record reflects ample evidence to support the conviction. A "battery" occurs when a person unlawfully and intentionally makes physical contact with force capable of causing physical pain or injury to the person of another or unlawfully and intentionally causes physical pain or injury to another person. AR 205; W.Va. Code §61-2-9 (2014). DeCourcy testified that Petitioner came across the room with a fist, knocked her back into chairs, choked her using both hands around her neck, screamed he was not done with her, she knew too much, and pushed her into a corner with bookcases. DeMarais's testimony corroborated DeCourcy's testimony in that DeCourcy and Oljaca arrived at his residence, told him of the attack, DeMarais personally saw twin bruises on DeCourcy's neck and described her as being nervous or afraid. The photographs admitted into evidence depicted redness and swelling of DeCourcy's neck and were consistent with the type of injury DeCourcy described. What the Court found most telling of the event was Petitioner's wife's testimony. Mrs. Williams testified that on September 30, 2015, shortly after the time frame in which DeCourcy identified as the time of the attack, DeCourcy told her Petitioner had choked her. The circuit court stated Mrs. Williams' testimony leads to the conclusion that DeCourcy's allegations "had nothing to do with some of the ancillary information that's come into this case with regard to terminations or who worked for whom and when they were terminated or if they were paid." And lastly, DeCourcy's statements to law enforcement in October 2015, was consistent with DeCourcy's testimony. The statement described Petitioner coming across the room toward her, placing his hands on her neck, and causing her to lose her balance. AR 226. She fell into the corner, where Petitioner began choking her with both hands. AR 226. Oljaca witnessed it and forced Petitioner away from DeCourcy, and Petitioner was yelling that he needed to shut her up because she knew too much. AR 226. DeCourcy did not pursue charges because she was scared of Petitioner and afraid for her life. AR 226.

While Petitioner characterizes the evidence as not credible, credibility determinations are made by the trier of fact, and review of those determinations "is not a legitimate function of this Court." *State v. Trail*, 236 W. Va. 167, 187, 778 S.E.2d 616, 636 (2015). As this Court has long stated, "we will not weigh evidence or determine credibility." *Guthrie*, 194 W.Va. at 669, 461 S.E.2d at 175. It follows that because "a verdict will be set aside only when "the record contains no evidence, regardless of how it is weighed, from which the jury could find guilt beyond a reasonable doubt," *Guthrie*, 194 W. Va. at 669, 461 S.E.2d at 175, the evidence was sufficient to convict Petitioner of battery.

E. Prosecutorial Misconduct.

The Petitioner's cursory treatment of this claim is insufficient to have raised an error sufficient for appellate review. According to Petitioner, the prosecutor violated the 4th, 6th, and 8th Amendments to the US constitution and Rule 3.8 of the West Virginia Rules of Professional Conduct. As with Petitioner's claim of judicial misconduct, Petitioner did not include the text of any legal authority or discussion thereof. Instead, he merely referenced by number the Constitutional Amendments and the Rule of Professional Conduct pertaining to prosecutors. Once again, he rests upon on a variety of self-serving proclamations and his own credibility determinations based on telephone calls, emails, and actions that are absent from the record. Pet'r Br. 28-30. While Petitioner does include some citations to the record, he fails to explain how any of it correlates with the elements of prosecutorial misconduct. Again, this Court should deny relief.

F. Preserving an Error for Appeal.

No aspect of this single-sentence assertion of error complies with the Rule 10 pleading requirements and thus, falls critically short of a reviewable claim. While briefs are liberally construed, issues "mentioned only in passing but [ ] not supported with pertinent authority, are not considered on appeal." *LaRock*, 196 W.Va. at 302, 470 S.E.2d at 621. This ground is insufficiently pled, and relief should be denied.

G. Procedural Errors During Magistrate Court.

Petitioner lastly slings a stream of accusations against Magistrate Wilfong. Pet'r Br. 30-33. As with his other contentions in this appeal, here, too, Petitioner fails to point to anything in the Appendix supporting his claims, and though he references Cannons 2.11 and 2.14 of the Judicial Code of Conduct, he does not include any portion of the Cannons themselves, develop an

14

argument, demonstrate how the Cannons were violated, or incorporate legal authority to support his contentions. And, again, Petitioner's "argument" refers almost entirely to matters outside the record. Petitioner fails to show error, and relief should be denied.

H. Unedited from Defendant's Notice of Appeal.

Petitioner's last statements have no point other than denigrating women who have earned a place in the judiciary, and warrant no consideration or response.

I. Any Assignments of Error Not Otherwise Addressed.

Any other issues Petitioner may have mentioned in his brief were skeletal arguments at best and thus fall short of the Rule 10 pleading requirements, and should not be considered.

IV. <u>CONCLUSION</u>

For the foregoing reasons, Respondent respectfully requests that this Court affirm the Circuit Court of Pocahontas County's February 25, 2019, Order.

Respectfully submitted,

STATE OF WEST VIRGINIA,
Respondent,
By counsel,

PATRICK MORRISEY
ATTORNEY GENERAL

Holly M. Flanigan [WVSB No. 7996]
Assistant Attorney General
812 Quarrier Street, 6th Floor
Charleston, WV 25301
Telephone: (304) 558-5830
Email: Holly.M.Flanigan@wvago.gov

138

Appendix 33: Reply Brief by Williams

RESPONDENT'S SUMMARY RESPONSE

Respondent (Resp.) states : "Because Petitioner fails to demonstrate the existence of reversible error, this Court should affirm the Circuit Court of Pocahontas County's February 25, 2019, Order." SUMMARY RESPONSE (SR), Page 1, Paragraph 1 **(SR1(1))**. Defendant (Def.) strongly disagrees with this statement by the State and will make his arguments below.

As stated in his Petitioner's Brief (PB) Def. is a non- lawyer; he asked the Court to consider that. **PB36**. To repeat, Petitioner was forced to represent his appeal *pro se*, since none of the several appellate attorneys he had tried to retain were interested in a misdemeanor battery case. **PB9**. Defendant was told by the Office of the Clerk that WVSCA is usually considerate to *pro se* petitioners as long as general requirements are met.

Asst. Attorney General, Mr. Shannon F. Kiser, who represented the State up until six days before Respondent's Brief due date, also told Def. that he tries to be considerate with *pro se* petitioners. In her SUMMARY RESPONSE (SR) Ms. Holly Flanigan, who replaced Kiser, concentrates on finding fault with Def.'s inexperience in the law while ignoring many facts pointed out by him that would lead to justice. Resp. also failed to respond to the several *assignments of error* in Def.s 37-page PB .

Def. wishes he had more than the 20 pages to comment on Resp.'s SR in this REPLY BRIEF (RB).

I. STATEMENT OF THE CASE

SR1(2): The *alleged* victim in this case, Ms. DeCourcy, was employed, supervised and paid in each of the five months of her employment contract by the Petitioner, not by her phantom National Alliance board of directors, consisting of her boyfriend Michael Oljaca and her new employer John McLaughlin. The footnote on page one of SR is inaccurate and misleading. Petitioner has been and is currently the duly-appointed Chairman of the National Alliance, Inc., as well as President, Treasurer, and one of the Directors of the National Alliance board since 24 October, 2014. **PB21,22. AR121.**

SR1(3): Respondent retells and selectively quotes Accuser's testimony as unquestioned truth. Ms. Flanigan could not miss the numerous bizarre lies of Accuser, sworn to under oath, that were

1

clearly cited and proven in **PB20, 21, 22, 26, 27, 28.** Yet every word of this proven liar, DeCourcy, as well as her corrupted co-conspirators and "witnesses," Michael Oljaca and John McLaughlin, in Magistrate Court (MC), and Bob DeMarais in both MC and Circuit Court (CC) is presented as the unquestioned truth throughout Summary Response, in **SR1, SR2, SR3, SR4, SR5, SR13**, for example.

The doctrine of *falsus in uno, falsus in omnibus* is recognized as a valid legal maxim that should be considered by courts in searching for trustworthy evidence, leading to truth and justice. Petitioner wrote about this in **PB18**. This was *his* personal defense strategy all along but not of his ineffective counsels.

Respondent repeatedly criticizes "lack of citations," yet completely ignores long quotes in PB that are favorable for Def. Example: quote from Oljaca's email to Def.: "If Bob [DeMarais] and Gael [DeCourcy alias] find out I have written to you. there is no telling what they would want to do to me, I shudder when I think about this." **PB19, AR165, AR265**, clearly shows that Oljaca is fearful of Accuser and her roommate DeMarais, their other co-conspirator.

Def. didn't give the exact quote, but cited the page from DeMarais internet forum post, "that revealed his immoderate hatred for Def, that should have impeached his testimony." **PB25**. Def. quotes that now: "I am prepared to fight Williams' wrongs for 11 years and two months. He and I will both be over 80 then... I've got more money than Wee Willie, more brains, more endurance, and I work one heck of a lot harder." **AR244**. At counsel Finch's request DeMarais read a part of this quote during his testimony, **AR112**, and confirmed that it was his writing. **AR111**. He admitted switching from " 80 percent not liking Will Williams to 98 percent not liking him." **AR109.** He lied for Accuser, his tenant/roommate.

Another example of ignoring a long quote in PB is about "a guardian & fiduciary." **PB21**. Did Ms. Flanigan truly believe after reading Def.'s Brief, filed *pro se,* that Def., who introduced himself as the Chairman of a corporation on **PB1,** and supposedly reading his 52-page testimony, **AR120-171**, had been appointed "a guardian & fiduciary" due to an incapacity to handle his own finances? **PB19**.

Resp. has been pretending not to see Accuser's obvious lies and "some level of mental disability", commented on **PB10**, despite numerous cited examples of them on **PB20, 21, 22, 26, 27, 28.** Def.

2

hopes that Supreme Court justices will, at least, read just four pages of Accuser's description of the alleged incident, **AR40-44**, and scan through two examples of her writings in the record – Victim Impact Statement (VIS), **AR329**, and one article from her 250,000+ word blog, **AR235** – to see obvious confirmation of "some level of mental disability," showing symptoms of her self-admitted Asperger's disorder. **PB10.** Resp. also feigns ignorance of the possibility that the State's claiming witness, especially one with an obvious motive to lie, would intentionally lie under oath. Ms. Flanigan completely ignores Accuser's well explained motive to claim a battery that never happened. (TRO to keep Def. off NA property in coup attempt) explained in **PB3, 4**, **AR360.**

SR2: Resp., quoting Accuser liberally, describes the alleged battery as a brutal fight. Def. is 6', 220 lbs. If he "hit [Accuser] in the neck, which knocked her into chairs," surely there would be significant visible damage to Accuser's neck besides two little pink spots that were declared as result of that. After Def. allegedly hit Accuser in her neck with his fist "...[he] then choked her using *both* hands around her neck." If *both* hands were used for the alleged "choking," there would certainly be more than two little pink spots seen on the eight *undated, untime-stamped* photographs that Accuser and her "witness" Michael Oljaca said were taken right after the alleged incident. **AR247-261**.

SR3: Another State witness Bob DeMarais would also see additional spots after "*hitting [my]neck,*" **AR40,** besides "two bruises on the left side of her neck. AR99. Each bruise was about half an inch wide and two inches long. AR99-100." Right after the alleged incident there couldn't be any "bruises" seen, only pink spots. According to DeMarais's and Accuser's testimony he met DeCourcy and Oljaca very soon after Oljaca and DeCourcy supposedly took their evidence photographs. **AR51.** Those photos, **AR247-261**, contradict the color and size of the spots described by DeMarais. To SP Via's question: "Were you able to make any observations at that time different or in addition to the ones you've made previously?," DeMarais answered, "No. I didn't look..." **AR100**. Accuser and DeMarais are roommates, share same kitchen, and spent a lot of time together, day and night. It's not reasonable that he wouldn't notice "bruises" and scratches after discoloring when these alleged "bruises" are the

3

main evidence in her claim of battery or "attempted homicide," **AR92,** as Accuser often described the alleged incident. It's also not believable that DeCourcy, who took at least eight pictures of two pink neck spots, would forget to take photographs of her other serious "injures" from "being pushed into stuff, sharp things, blunt things, up against the phone and the cabinet, filing cabinet, blunt compression." **AR42**, and fail to show those several other "injuries" to DeMarais. Accuser also testified that "[DeMarais] asked if we had pictures. And he was going to take pictures. And he wanted us to call the police... but we didn't want [Defendant] to then kill us for that."**AR52, 53.**

The footnote on SP3: Def. stipulates that the eight (8) photos submitted in **AR247-261,** are the same photographs from trial.

In what follows Def. will present every quote from the statements on the record, showing contradictions in the descriptions of the alleged incident by Accuser and her main witness Oljaca.

1st description of 10/31/15. Trooper Brock wrote in his report from the words of Accuser in her presence, which she read and signed: "...Will Williams, the accused, jumped across the room toward her and made contact with her throat area causing her loose [*sic*] her balance and fall backwards into the corner. Mrs.[*sic*] DeCourcy further stated that the accused then followed her and began choking her with both hands." **AR229**. Brock's hand-written version that his report was based on is at **AR225**.

Regarding main witness Oljaca's version of the alleged incident Brock wrote: "On this same day, this officer spoke to Michael Oljaca via telephone. Mr. Oljaca stated that he had recently traveled to New York. (Oljaca actually got to NYC from WV around 10/17/15 - about two weeks before Brock's call). Mr. Oljaca stated that he would provide this officer with a statement concerning this incident at a later time. This officer has not received anything from Mr. Oljaca since this discussion." **AR229, 185**.

Def. commented on Oljaca's need "to speak with his coach, Defendant's Accuser, first" in **PB26**.

2nd description of 12/02/15 to Deputy Kelly. DeCourcy hand wrote "...he began abuse, it resulted in him threatening me & then lunging towards me hand in fist to smash me In face or head and then began to choke me." (No mention of first hitting her neck with fist before following her to choke her).

4

"The force of the attack knocked me back onto area of corner to room away from door. Mr. Michael Oljaca was present at the door listening & waiting & jumped in & with great effort and force and had to push back & pry him off my neck. Williams fought him and continued to come after me shouting he needed to finish it..." **AR232**.

Oljaca's handwritten description of 12/2/15 to Deputy Kelly. "...Mr. Williams, sitting at her desk... got up from the chair [from behind the desk?], lunged at Ms. DeCourcy, made a motion w/his left hand to smack her [not with fist], then Mr. Williams took his right hand and started choking Ms. DeCourcy. [choking with the *right* hand, no mentioning of *hitting the neck* with the fist before choking] As soon as this happened, I quickly jumped in to pull Mr. Williams off of her, and physically restrained him so he would not do any further damage." **AR234**.

3rd description from 8/14/18 trial transcript. "...when he [Def.] started across the room, he had a fist that was going to smash me in the head. And when he came across, he is aiming and he is hitting my neck [more than once?]. I got knocked back into chairs." [not "into corner away from the door."] **AR40**. Def. hopes that Accuser's entire description of the fabricated "battery" incident as a long fight, **AR41-44,** will be read by the Justices to make note of Accuser's over-the-top theatrics and the obvious contradictions between her and her "witness" Oljaca's earlier versions of the incident. Quoted above, Oljaca "physically restrained" Def., mentioning no long and brutal fighting whatsoever. **AR234.**

Accuser describes the injuries on the photographs as "the swelling and the scratch marks." **AR49**. Photographs, **AR247-261**, do not show either swelling or scratch marks, just tiny pink spots.

On **AR85** Accuser testified when asked "if the red marks [in the photos of her neck] could easily have been made by pinching oneself?," she replies, "Oh no. You can see in the photo. It's from [Def.'s] nails pulling on me. The nails start here. And then it pulls. And then it's raised." The selfie photos of little red marks show nothing of the sort, and the marks *could have been self inflicted* by pinching.

Def. commented on the photographs, "it doesn't look to me like somebody was choking her, lifting her up off the floor and slamming her in the corner." **AR161-162.** DeCourcy didn't mention lifting off

5

the floor in any of her three statements on the record, but wrote in the last paragraph of the second page of her 5-page "Affidavit" as an EXHIBIT to her TRO request, *15-S-35*, hearing "...Williams unprovoked jumped out at DeCourcy [from behind the desk?], arm ready to strike, in fist hit about the face/head, & went to strike her harshly, & then while lunging across the room did with such force grab and wrap around her neck, that she was moved off her feet further into the room towards far corner."

There is little consistency in the three descriptions cited above regarding where Accuser was "forced knocked" into the cabinets, the book shelf, the chairs, or into the corner. By Accuser's and Oljaca's contradictory descriptions it sounds like the cramped office is roomy with a lot of furniture, while the size of the room is about 10'x10' with a large desk, 3 chairs, a file cabinet and a bookshelf.

Well before submitting her "Affidavit" as an EXHIBIT to her TRO request, *15-S-35*, on 10/7/15 DeCourcy emailed the same 3,634 words "Affidavit" to NA member Chris Larsen. That's when it became apparent that DeCourcy had begun her coup attempt. Larsen forwarded that email to Def. Def's wife Lana testified that, "we found out she [DeCourcy] contacted every member of National Alliance she could...And the point of these emails and calls was to show that Will is not capable to be a chairman, we must get rid of him...And we had Kris Larson [sic], a member who she emailed." **AR177**.

Pursuing her goal of getting rid of Def. in the attempt to gain control of NA assets, Accuser wrote many long, repetitive motions, complaints, letters to the judges, and on her Internet blog, often contradicting herself. Nobody, including Defense counsels Detch and Finch, much less any investigators or prosecutors, cared to question the truthfulness of DeCourcy's writings. Had they looked critically, Accuser's obsession with Def. and her craziness could not have gone unnoticed by any of the Pocahontas Court Officers. All of them, excluding Magistrate Kelley, seemed to prefer to just give Accuser what she demanded to shut her "motor mouth" and avoid her complaints to the numerous higher State and federal agencies that she claimed to be in touch with. That 3,634 word "Affidavit" with the description of the alleged incident was one of several other similar documents that Ms. Finch rejected since she claimed "the Accuser's motive is not relevant." **RB17**.

6

SR4(2), SR5(2) What Special Prosecutor (SP) Via, Judge Dent, and Ms. Flanigan considered "most telling" was testimony of Def.'s wife Lana who " DeCourcy told [her] Petitioner had choked her." First, Mrs.Williams quoted Accuser as saying, "He *tried* to choke me. Her voice sounded like it was a joke, like there was a big smile on her face." **AR173**. All three above-named court officers conveniently ignored that first part of Lana Williams testimony: "Garland answered the phone and I asked her standard questions, 'how are you, what's up? And she started telling me what's going on. She told me several news and she was talking about Will, but she didn't say one word that something abnormal just happened." **AR172**. That goes to show the Accuser hadn't had time to concoct her so-called "attempted homicide" story that soon after it supposedly happened. On Judge's question: "was she communicating to you that she had been the victim of a violent crime?" Mrs William answered: "At the very end, very shortly...she wouldn't tell me if I wouldn't ask her to tell Will he should call me...We were about to hang up." **AR174**. The fact that in about half hour after being "beaten up" by a large man, for 20-25 minutes conversation, Mrs. Williams "didn't notice any difference whatsoever in her mood, in her voice, compared to our regular conversation," **AR173,** apparently didn't raise any suspicions about Accuser's claims from the court officers. Yet the idea that Accuser, who had been lying and contradicting herself during her entire testimony, could easily lie to Mrs. Williams that Def. only "*tried* to choke" her didn't seem to raise reasonable doubt about Accuser's reliability among them.

Does it not look strange that Accuser had never mentioned a brutal incident to Def.'s main witness Fred Streed who had been staying on the same property and didn't leave for Oregon until three days later, on 3 October 2015? Mr. Streed's sworn affidavit: "On September 30th, 2015, Mr. Williams told me he and Garland had just had a heated conversation. I talked with Mr. Williams right after it happened. He was calm and didn't appear angry. I also talked with Garland and Mr. Olanich [Oljaca's alias] soon after my conversation with Mr. Williams. She seemed very exited and angry but made no mention of an assault on her. I didn't see any bruises on her throat or other signs of a physical altercation." **AR320**.

7

Though Def. cited Streed's Affidavit at least twice on **PB8, 29**, Ms. Flanigan has not commented or even acknowledged that most important defense document evidence in her SR.

Petitioner was rushed, preparing his long Brief by the deadline for filing it, and accidentally left out an important paragraph in the INEFFECTIVE COUNSELING Section. Def. and his wife discovered that inadvertent oversight only after Brief had already been mailed, so include that paragraph here now:

Def. has another vital witness, NA Media Director Kevin Strom, who informed Def. about Accuser's phone calls to him after she had already started her campaign to oust Def. as NA Chairman, but neglected to inform Def. in time that there were two calls to him from Accuser on the day of the alleged incident, 30 September, 2015. In her first call Accuser just said that Williams had lost his temper and yelled at her. A few hours later that same day she called again and said that Williams had been choking her. Mr. Strom said that he then concluded that Accuser's story was so inconsistent that she was lying. Def. learned Accuser's two 9/30/15 calls to Mr. Strom only after Strom had arrived in Marlinton, WV, from his home in Pennsylvania, a few hours before the 8/14/18 trial. Ms. Finch informed Def., that it was too late to add Strom to the witness list. Defendant informed Finch after the lunch break, and after Accuser's testimony that morning that Strom had witnessed Accuser's testimony of the alleged battery in court and that it was wildly inconsistent with the versions she had related to him nearly three years previously on the day of the "argument." Def. asked Ms. Finch to make a *strong* point about his new important witness in her motion for a new trial at Def.'s final sentencing. Finch made this point in her motion for a new trial, but as weak and ineffective as she could have possibly made it. **AR311 #4.**

To return to Mrs. Williams testimony that was considered "most telling," Def. considered his wife's email to Accuser that was sent on 10/5/15 – almost 2 months before Accuser filed her complaint – as essential evidence. However, Ms. Finch failed to read that email and use it properly. There is a short description of the alleged incident that is consistent with Def.'s description to Trooper Brock on 10/31/15, **AR223,** and with Def.'s trial testimony. **AR125,126**. Yet Ms Finch completely ignored that

8

valuable description in Mrs.Williams' email. If to read the whole email it's obvious that such email could not be written and sent after a brutal "attempted homicide." Even supposing Def. might give a false description of the alleged incident to his wife, as NA Chairman he would never give his approval for her to write DeCourcy and give her a final warning to help her. If there was a brutal fight as DeCourcy was describing, it would be inconceivable that the Accuser and the Accused would ever work together again after what she described several times as the alleged "attempted murder."

Lana testified: "Will, when he told me what happened at site, 'I don't see how to work with her. I will never be able to speak with her after hearing her and seeing her insanity'...but I say, Garland used to be a good worker....She will probably apologize. But we should give her one notification. He said, 'if you want to you can do, but I am not able to communicate with her.' And I wrote her long email." **AR175**. Description of the alleged incident from Lana's email to DeCourcy is on **AR214.** It says "you [Accuser]... needed to be and were stopped... under your chin." In her letter to the Court as an attachment to AMENDMENT to Motion To Use Three Documents During Appeal, that was not admitted by this Court, Lana explained that the tip of Accuser's chin, being between Def.'s thumb and forefinger, as Def. showed her in about five hours after alleged incident, is "under chin" in her "Russian vision." English is not Lana's first language; Russian is, and "on chin" was expressed as "under chin," but not as "stopped on your neck." In her email description Mrs. Williams wrote "...you would lie to me that Will was 'choking' you." **AR214**. Lana didn't quote Accuser's real statement "*tried to choke*" precisely, because she was directly accusing DeCourcy of her "choking" lie. Also Lana and her accused husband could not have imagined back on 9/30/15 that what amounted to a two-second episode of touching the aggressive Accuser's chin to establish a boundary, and prevent her from getting closer, would ever be a subject of discussion about "battery" in a courtroom three and ½ years later. On 10/26/15 Def. added a short, hand-written letter to Accuser, **AR221**, along with the Termination of Contract document, **AR219**. It is not believable that this expression of good will by Def. could have

9

been written by one who had recently "attempted homicide" on the person he sent it to.

SR4(3): In writing about Trooper Brock's testimony Resp. ignores the fact that he contradicted Accuser's lie that on 10/31/15 he prepared the written report with her version of the 9/30/15 altercation outside her presence and forced her to sign it, promising that after getting her signature he will stop "ongoing crime" against her. Def. presented this fact with citations. **PB26.** The point of this proven lie was mentioned in Ms. Finch's short closing arguments. **AR181,182.**

SR4(4): As usual Resp. is presenting mostly arguments that are favorable for the State while ignoring important facts favorable for the Accused that would lead to justice. While writing about Def., stating that he wasn't feeling threatened Resp. ignores the exact quote from Def. testimony: "Q: You think she was going to hurt you? A: "Not until she jumped up and got in my face. Q: "How'd she get in your face with the desk between you?" A: "With her finger." Q: "Did you feel physically threatened by that?" A: "I am not afraid of her. But I was being advanced on by this screaming lunatic. And I was trying to talk to...my other employee [Oljaca] who was sitting next to [me], not outside the room as Accuser lied. I told her to shut up. Actually, I probably cussed a little bit in there."**AR141.**

It is significant to Accused's defense that SP admits this exchange between him and his Accuser occurred across a desk. To choke someone across a desk, whether with one or with both hands is impossible. The quotes above show Def.'s scrupulous honesty and is consistent with his statement to Brock on 10/31/15. **AR223.** A guilty, deceptive Def. would most likely lie about feeling threatened to protect himself. It should be obvious that a reasonable person would instinctively react by bringing up his arm to block a fast approaching aggressor from getting any closer. DeCourcy could have spit on Williams' face or scratched it with her fingers. She was out of control, screaming and shaking her finger in his face aggressively, provocatively.

Def. denies the whole STATEMENT OF THE CASE section in Resp.'s SR as a misrepresentation.

The determination of guilt

SR5(2): "...DeCourcy's testimony to be credible to the extent it was consistent with her statements

10

[proven to be wrong in **RB4-6**], the photographs... were consistent with the type of injury [proven to be wrong in **RB3-6**]...statement to Trooper Brock were consistent with DeCourcy's testimony [proven to be wrong in **RB4-6**]; and found DeMarais's testimony corroborated DeCourcy's testimony"[proven to be wrong in **RB2-4**].

While Def. wasn't found to be lying about anything even once, Accuser was proven in PB and RB to have lied numerous times, while under oath. Counsel Finch, in her short, futile closing argument, even mentioned several examples of Accuser's lies **AR200-204** – all ignored by Ms. Flanigan.

Judge Dent could not honestly say in her verdict that she found Accuser's testimony unconditionally credible, but only that "to the extent it was consistent with her statements."**AR208**. However Def. reasonably showed above the obvious inconsistencies and contradictions in "her statements." **RB3-6**. By this standard Judge Dent's conclusion suggests that the Accuser, a documented scammer, can make a false claim of a "crime," that is poorly investigated, then just be consistent with this questionable claim in order to prevail, despite having been caught in several lies throughout the trial of her Accused.

Def. insists that there was judicial and prosecutorial bias in Pocahontas Court and that Ms. Flanigan, representing the higher authority of the State of WV, in her Summary Response is no less biased. Def. alleges in **PB13,17** that at some point before the end of his trial counsel Finch was also working for the Court rather than for her client. Additional argument for this by Def. will be added below. **RB15-17**.

Mr. Kiser, though representing the State of WV, came across in phone conversations with Def. as a fair and impartial party who showed patient consideration with a *pro se* Def., seeking justice. While giving no legal advice Mr. Kiser encouraged Def. to ask him general questions about the appellate process and provided helpful guidance. He stated that he always tries to be objective and that if he sees the State made errors he wouldn't cover for them. That's what Def. and anybody else appealing what they see as a wrongful conviction should expect the State to do. Defendant had confidence his appeal to WVSCA would finally lead to proper justice after three and ½ years in Pocahontas courts, hand-cuffed and led to jail three times, and falsely labelled a "woman beater." Def.'s confidence for an

11

impartial appeal dimmed after reading the SR of Mr. Kiser's "last minute replacement," Ms. Flanigan.

The Sentencing

SR5(3): Def. objects that CC "dealt with the *ex parte* communications as required and didn't

consider them," and explained his view on this in **PB13, 14**. Besides the points he gave in PB,

he is going to refer to Ms. Finch's Motion to Unseal, point **#3**, confirming "additional security"

request. **AR325**. In her **#6** of that motion Finch wrote that the Office of Prosecuting Attorney (PA) of

Pocahontas County (PC) "sought appointment of a special prosecutor due to allegations contained in

the ex parte communications from the complaining witness."**AR326**.

Accuser's demand for a SP in those illegal letters was considered and satisfied by *disqualifying* PA

of PC Office, **AR11**, and appointing a SP. **AR19**. Accuser's defying the judge's order not to send her

more *ex parte* letters, **AR17**, is usually considered a serious ground for contempt of court, or even

dismissal of the case. Accuser was *not* punished, but was actually granted the SP she had demanded.

SR6(2): Def. shortly wrote about his first and only opportunity to speak freely at his final

sentencing hearing, when he "listed many grounds showing due process wasn't provided to him." **PB7**.

He cited **AR351-362**, hoping his speech, on the record, would eventually be read and considered. As

usual, Ms. Flanigan ignores those important statements by Def. that would lead to justice. Instead she

promotes the Court's conclusions without question. Evidence of SP Via and Judge Dent contradicting

themselves about unsealing of the *ex parte* letters for later use by Def. will be presented on **RB16**.

Serious grounds for a new trial that were denied by Judge were presented in **PB7, RB8**. Def. insists that

denial of the request for hearing for VIS questioning was in violation of *§61-11A-3e*. *The court shall,*

upon motion by or on behalf of the defendant, grant the defendant a hearing, whereby he may

introduce testimony or other information related to any alleged factual inaccuracies in the statement.

While giving Def. less than full opportunity to respond to VIS, Dent was insisting that Def. should

respond only "to the questions that are allowed by statute [§61-11A-3b]" and to nothing else. **AR354**.

Def. asserts that since Accuser went well beyond questions allowed by §61-11A-3b he had a right to

12

150

respond to each and every "factual inaccuracy" leveled at him in her unhinged, 14-page VIS. **AR281**.

SR6(3): Alcohol/drug testing in a case where neither was involved is not a "usual condition." **PB36**.

Def. asserts that Via's and Dent's comments and conclusions on each of the three legitimate post

trial motions, **AR334-351**, and after Def.'s speech, **AR362-369**, clearly show their obvious bias, the

possible reasons for which were mentioned in **PB1,7,10,** and for possible obstruction of justice. **RB20**.

The appeal

While repeatedly quoting Rule 10 regarding its requirements for petitioners, Ms. Flanigan doesn't

follow the requirements for respondents in the same rule.

SR6(4): In her SR Resp. fails to comment on *six* of the nine errors she named. Those ignored

errors are 1,2,3,5,6 and 9. Eight errors named in the ASSIGNMENT OF ERRORS of PB don't match

precisely the names of the chapters in ARGUMENT section, but are well explained by Def. in the body

of ARGUMENT, with proper citations to AR pages. As Petitioner reads Rule 10, Ms. Flanigan's failure

to respond to *any* assignments of error signifies that she agrees with Petitioner's view of *those* errors.

II. STANDARD OF REVIEW

Def. is *pro se* and not competent to argue against Ms. Flanagan's legalese, and her citing of case law,

and claiming such things as a "two-pronged standard of review" and an "abuse of discretion standard."

III. ARGUMENT

SR7(3): Def. denies "the substantive deficits in [Def.'s] brief in regard to the assignments of error

and argument." This accusation seems to be Resp.'s main argument that has been repeated many times

throughout her entire SUMMARY RESPONSE -- for example, in **SR9(2), SP8(3)**.

 Providing long quotes for each of nearly 100 citings of AR pages, as well as quoting authorities,

would greatly exceed the 40 pages allowed Def. in this PB. As a layman he believed that giving just

name and number of well known judicial authorities would be enough for trained court officers to

understand without his exceeding the page limit. Def. explained *significant* number of legal errors the

best he could as a non-lawyer with the expectation of consideration by the Court for being *pro se*.

13

SP8(4): Def. "does not cite the Appendix demonstrating where he raised the issues below..." *This is a false accusation!* Refer to **PB5, 7-9** for Petitioner's clearly stated explanation of his arguments.

SP9(1): Petitioner can't argue with arcane citations of case law by Resp. In his Table of Authorities, **PB iii**, however, Def. provided numbers and names of 15 cases directly related to his Accuser and her "battery" claim. Eight of these name Garland DeCourcy specifically; four more name her biased "witnesses" and co-conspirators Oljaca and McLaughlin – all filed during a 3-year period. These indicate Accuser is a documented abuser of the judicial process who will file a false report of "battery" and lie under oath. A very important error: *"guilty verdict obtained by fraud,"* **PB1**, including the fact that Accuser is now a fugitive, was well explained, **PB1-PB6,** but totally ignored by Resp. in her SR.

In the same STATEMENT OF THE CASE section Def. explained the obvious motive for the Accuser's false claim -- a judicial coup attempt – which also got *no* comment by Ms. Flanigan..

SP9(2) Resp. says: "For the sake of thoroughness, Respondent addresses each section of Petitioner's argument below." Yet in her *thoroughness* (more like in her indolence) Ms. Flanigan devoted only one 13-line paragraph to counter Def.'s 10-page JUDICIAL MISCONDUCT section. **PB7-PB16**.

A. Judicial misconduct.

In **PB7-PB16** there are names and numbers of each Rule of ***Cannon 2 of WV Judicial Code of Conduct.*** Explanations under each Rule of supposed violation, citing AR pages, follow. Defendant was expecting State's comments on *each of six* presented Rules of ***Cannon 2.***
The lack of evidence to convict Def. was well presented by him in **PB23-28**, and highly questionable "credibility of DeCourcy" *does have* plenty of "basis in the record." **PB18-22, PB23-28 , RB3-6**.

Even though Ms. Flanigan mentions "law enforcement's investigation" in this paragraph, she has not even once commented on the following errors she named in **SR6(4):** *no presumption of innocence; no proper investigation; insufficient due process; unreliable witnesses;* and *significant reasonable doubt* in her entire Summary Report. Regarding Ms. Flanigan's "lack of citations" claim, Def. wrote in **RB13**.

B. Ineffective counseling

14

Petitioner provided plenty of examples of CC counsel Finch' ineffectiveness in defending her client in **PB16-PB23** and will add some more examples here in this section.

The weakness of the point about new witness Kevin Strom, **AR311**, was presented in **RB8**. As Def. stated in PB all three post trial motions, **AR311, 325, 329,** were "weak with serious faults," **PB17**.

For example, Ms. Finch failed to even mention *§61-11A-3(e)* of WV Code, **AR329,** and she mistakenly cited *Cannon 3B* instead of *Cannon 2, Rule 2.9* in her "Motion to unseal *ex parte* communications," **AR326**, which was corrected by the judge at the hearing. **AR337**.

Resp. states: "After DeCourcy authenticated the photographs, they were admitted into evidence without objection. AR54." **SR3(2)**. This means that Finch could have objected but failed to do so. Three of eight photographs, **AR247-249,** were allegedly taken by Oljaca. Finch submitted as EXHIBIT 8 Oljaca's email to Def. showing his great fear of his co-conspirators, DeCourcy and DeMarais, **AR24,** but she hardly used that essential exhibit, **AR263,** to prove that Oljaca was a corrupted witness. Def. actually read that essential part about Oljaca's fear during his testimony. **AR165**. Finch's use of Oljaca's and Def.'s email exchange was mostly just asking Def. if it was "smart to send that email [Def.'s email reply]." **AR168-170**. Defendant presented the issue described above in **PB19**. Failure to object to the invalidated photos is proof of counsel's ineffectiveness, at least, but is also likely an indication that "the fix was in," and that she *intentionally* failed to object. Def. mentioned that Finch told him in the beginning of her representation of him "that her [DeCourcy's] undated selfies are invalid." **PB16**.

It's *not accidental* that Judge Dent forbade the sharing of *ex parte* letters with the Def. "due to safety concerns because of the nature of the ex parte communication,"**AR337,** or that Finch failed to inform Def. about it. **PB16, RB16.** As Def. explained in **PB10,14** practically *all* Pocahontas Court Officers, except Dent and Via, were badmouthed by DeCourcy in those letters. Likely, Judge Dent and SP Via, who used to be her boss a few months prior to the sealing of the *ex parte* letters, **PB15**, didn't want to be badmouthed in Accuser's future letters and complaints. **RB6.** Finch knew full well that Def. insisted on using *ex parte* letters as his evidence and would have vigorously objected to sealing them.

15

PB15. If Finch had submitted *ex parte* letters as Defense exhibits and properly used them to impeach Accuser's truthfulness, it would have been impossible to find the Def. guilty in the Pocahontas Court.

At the first sentencing hearing Via stated that "the next attorney in line...would certainly have access to it [*ex parte* letters]." **AR304**. Dent also confirmed that "any new counsel would have access to it [*ex parte* communications], could request that it be obtained through unsealing the court file." **AR305**. In the next paragraph Finch says "...he [Def] intends to represent himself." **AR305.**

The fact that Judge Dent changed her mind, first granting, then denying Finch's motion to withdraw representation after a short, private huddle, off the record, in her chamber with Finch and Via, **AR306, 307,** Defendant presented in **PB12**.

On second sentencing hearing Via stated in objecting to unsealing *ex parte* letters: "We are here for sentencing... If they [*ex parte* letters] are something that might be necessary for an appeal or something, maybe."**AR335.** Dent denied the motion to unseal *ex parte* letters, **AR340,** arguing that Def. was allowed to discuss them for "purpose of litigation" with his counsel. Sealed documents can't be used as EXHIBITs, so discussions with counsel for "purpose of litigation" would not make any sense.

Both Dent and Via heard at the first sentencing that Def. intended to make a motion for a retrial and/or appeal to WVSCA. **AR308**. A few days before second/final sentencing they both also could read in an attachment for Def.'s Amendment For Motion For New Trial, "If Judge Dent denies motion for a new trial, having these [grounds] will be useful to me when appealing the verdict to WV Supreme Court." **AR317**. In the same attachment it can be seen that Finch failed to follow Def.'s requirements to submit as new evidences the Victim Impact Statement and the sealed *ex parte* letters.

The proof that "Ms.Finch never provided him [Def.] with any of the Judge's orders," **PB16**, can be seen in the Motion to Unseal. In **AR326, #11** of that motion counsel states that Def.."became concerned that the ex parte communication in this matter had been sealed" after obtaining "a docket sheet from the Circuit Clerk's office." Sealing letters were mentioned in a few more documents besides what was submitted as **AR13,15,17**. If Finch had provided Def. with copies of all those documents in time, she would certainly have objected that her client didn't know about the sealing until receiving the docket sheet "following the trial in this matter." **AR326. PB16**. At **AR326, #10**, Finch admitted her failure to object to sealing the *ex parte* letters. At **AR311, #2** Finch confirmed that Def. "requested of [her] that she cross examine the complaining witness regarding the voluminous ex parte communications, which she failed to do." As Def. stated, Finch "knew full well those illegal ex *parte* letters had been sealed, and that he was kept uninformed intentionally by her." **PB16**.

Failing to provide Def. with numerous extremely important documents and not letting him object to sealing exculpatory evidence are not only the proof of ineffective counseling, but of a serious violation of *WV Rule of Professional Conduct 8.4. Misconduct:(C, D, F)*. Via and Dent apparently violated this same *Rule 8.4(C, D, F)*. Citation of this Rule is in **RB20**.

C. Improper Exclusion of Evidence

Due to space limitation Def. shortly mentioned his points, **PB23**, after they were presented above in his PB with explanations and citations. Defendant gives further clarifications: ***1.** Def. presented his evidence in **PB13-15,16** and proved it in **RB16. *2.** was proven in **PB7, 11, AR371, RB16. *3.** *Judge's attempt to strike VIS* -- Def. can't prove based on his AR, though Def. has his wife as a witness and "there is a contemporaneous email from Def. to Ms. Finch confirming this strange request from the Judge," as Def. stated in his Notice of Appeal, **section 17, page 5. *4.** None of the documents, like the one cited on **RB6**, showing Accuser's motive, can be seen among Defense EXHIBITs, **AR24**. Def. had been insisting on using such documents of Accuser's true motive all along ***5.** Def. doesn't have access to SP Via's file, but Ms. Flanigan, if she believes that Def. might be lying about that, could easily get the proof by contacting Via. Def. knows that he was never interviewed by any investigator, except during his 5-minute interview with Trooper Brock on 10/31/15, even though he mentioned to Ms. Finch several times that he wanted to be interviewed. Fred Streed confirms that he has never received a call from any of Pocahontas Court officers, including Defense counsel Laura Finch.

17

D. Lack of Sufficient Evidence

SR11-14. Def. presented his points with numerous citations in **PB23-28**. He insists that eight undated, untime-stamped photos; five selfies, taken by the documented liar and scam autist, DeCourcy, plus three photos taken by her proven-to-be fearful, manipulated boyfriend and co-conspirator Oljaca is not sufficient evidence of a battery. **RB15**. In this section, again, Ms. Flanigan mostly cites some other criminal cases and retells the lies of her claiming witness, the documented fraudster DeCourcy.

E. Prosecutorial Misconduct.

Limited by space Def. will amend his statement in **PB28** that SP Via "never cared to have his office investigate Accuser's claim..." to add the word *"properly"* investigate her claim.. The fact that Via's office and law enforcement *only* interviewed the Accuser and her co-conspirators and "never interviewed Defendant [and] accepted every lie of Accuser as being truthful" was hardly professional, violates ***Rule 3.8 Special Responsibilities of a Prosecutor (A)***: A prosecutor *shall refrain from prosecuting a charge* [he] *knows is not supported by probable cause,* (***G***)*: When a prosecutor knows of new, credible and material evidence creating a reasonable likelihood that a convicted defendant didn't commit an offense of which the defendant was convicted, the prosecutor shall:...(**2**)(**ii**) undertake further investigation, or make reasonable efforts to cause an investigation, to determine whether the defendant was convicted of an offense that the defendant didn't commit.* Via willfully ignored exculpatory evidence: the sworn Affidavit of primary defense witness Fred Streed that defense counsel had provided to him. **AR319, PB29.** Also, in comment [1] to ***Rule 3.8*** *A prosecutor has the responsibility of a minister of justice, not simply that of an advocate. He is to see that a defendant is accorded procedural justice. Special prosecutions are taken to prevent and to rectify the conviction of innocent persons.* He should take remedial measures to correct a defect in a prosecution, according to ***Rule 8.4 Misconduct.*** Def. believes SP Via violated this ***8.4 Rule (C, D, F),*** cited on **RB20**.

§61-11A-3(e), violated by SP Via, **AR346,** was quoted on **RB12** and presented in **PB29.**

18

Fifth, Sixth and Fourteenth Amendments of the US Constitution that Def. named in **PB28-30** and described as possible violations by SP Via will be quoted on **RB20**. Def. retracts his citing the *Fourth* and *Eighth Amendments* due to his misconstrued interpretation of these Amendments as a layman.

Example of Via's misrepresentation of facts is his attempt to use Def.'s response to Oljaca "out of context." **PB25, AR148-160, 198-199**. Some examples of possible obstruction of justice by Via can be seen in **PB29, AR346.** Def. requires more space to show more examples of Via's unprofessionalism.

E. Preserving an Error for Appeal

Def. made his short conclusion on the issues that were explained by him earlier on **PB7-9, 11-15**.

G. Procedural Errors During Magistrate Court

Def. did not "sling accusations against Magistrate Wilfong." He repeated his two counsels' opinions that Wilfong should have recused herself from hearing his case for battery and he quoted the WVSCA's order that suspended her from duties as a Magistrate, without pay, for her serious violation of *Rule 2.14 of Cannon 2*. It is Ms. Flanigan who "slings accusations" at Petitioner for defending himself.

H. Unedited from Defendant's Notice of Appeal

Def.'s statement in **PB33** stands. Having been born in 1947, Def. was raised in patriarchal America. He recognizes that it is a new day and women are now treated equally, especially in the judiciary. He does not denigrate women in the judiciary any more than he denigrates unethical men. See **PB11(2).**

I. Any Assignments of Error Not Otherwise Addressed

In Def.'s **RB13,** he stated that Resp. failed to voice her objections which is probably why she chose the shorter SR option with it's 15-page limit instead of Respondent's Brief. Her choice to submit SR also indicates waiver of oral argument while Def. requested oral argument before WVSCA to finally clear his name. He is confident he is not guilty; he has nothing to hide and nothing to lie about.

IV. CONCLUSION

Def. has provided in his PB and RB more than enough proof that a "battery" never happened, that

19

157

his Accuser is a liar, a scammer, an abuser of the judicial process, and since 27 October 2018 a fugitive. Ms. Flanigan complains that Def. "didn't include the text of any legal authority." **SR14.** In addition to citations herein, other specific citations of violations of Def.'s Constitutional rights by PC Court officers are: 1) *The **Sixth Amendment**'s Confrontation Clause gives criminal defendants the right to confront and cross-examine witnesses.* (violated by Judge Dent, **PB11, RB12**, and SP Via, **PB29, RB18**). *The Assistance of Counsel Clause of **Sixth Amendment** includes:...the right to the <u>effective assistance of counsel</u>* (violated by counsel Finch, **PB16-23, RB15-17** and Judge Dent, **PB12, RB16**); *...the right to represent oneself* (violated by Judge **PB12, RB16**). 2) *The **Fifth Amendment** applies to every level of the government, including the federal, state, and local levels... in regard to a US citizen or resident of the US ...Like the **Fourteenth Amendment**, the **Fifth Amendment** includes a due process clause stating that no person shall "be deprived of life, liberty, or property, without due process of law."* (violated by SP Via, **PB29, RB18**, and Judge Dent, **PB7-16, RB17**).

Def. believes that all three Court Officers (Finch, Via and Dent) violated ***WV Rule of Professional Conduct 8.4. Misconduct: C.****engage in conduct involving dishonesty, fraud, deceit misrepresentation; **D.***engage in conduct that is prejudicial to the administration of justice; **F.** *knowingly assist a judge or judicial officer in conduct that is a violation of applicable rules of judicial conduct or other law*. **RB17.**

Def. believes that all three Court Officers performed what might be considered Obstruction of justice by elected officials as the interference with the process of justice by withholding important information. Citations/ examples on that: for Dent in RB0, for Via in RB0, for Finch on RB0.

Enormous State resources have been wasted due to Dent's, Via's and Finch's unprofessionalism.

Def. stated the desirable outcome of his appeal in his CONCLUSION section. **PB34-37.**

Respectfully submitted,

William White Williams
1XXX XXX Rd.
Mountain City, TN 37683
(423)XXX9; (423)XXX1

20

Appendix 34: Memorandum Decision of the WVSCA

**STATE OF WEST VIRGINIA
SUPREME COURT OF APPEALS**

**State of West Virginia,
Plaintiff Below, Respondent**

vs.) No. 19-0256 (Pocahontas County 14-M-AP-01(D))

**William White Williams,
Defendant Below, Petitioner**

**FILED
June 18, 2020**
EDYTHE NASH GAISER, CLERK
SUPREME COURT OF APPEALS
OF WEST VIRGINIA

MEMORANDUM DECISION

Petitioner William White Williams, self-represented litigant, appeals the February 25, 2019, order of the Circuit Court of Pocahontas County, challenging the sufficiency of the evidence underlying his battery conviction. The State of West Virginia, by counsel Holly M. Flanigan, filed a response in support of the circuit court's order. Petitioner filed a reply.

This Court has considered the parties' briefs and the record on appeal. The facts and legal arguments are adequately presented, and the decisional process would not be significantly aided by oral argument. Upon consideration of the standard of review, the briefs, and the record presented, the Court finds no substantial question of law and no prejudicial error. For these reasons, a memorandum decision affirming the order of the circuit court is appropriate under Rule 21 of the Rules of Appellate Procedure.

This matter stems from a September 30, 2015, incident that occurred on property owned by the National Alliance ("NA") in Mill Point, Pocahontas County, West Virginia. Petitioner, a resident of Tennessee and the Chairman of the NA, was charged with battery of Garland DeCourcy, who was working on the property.[1] Ms. DeCourcy alleged that on September 29, 2015, she received a personal call while at work and "[petitioner] went ballistic and started going crazy." Following this call, petitioner would not let Ms. DeCourcy leave the office. Ms. DeCourcy eventually left and returned the following day, but tried to avoid petitioner.

Per the record, petitioner came into Ms. DeCourcy's office. When Ms. DeCourcy moved to get her purse, she asserted that petitioner told her he was not done with her and came across the

---

[1] Petitioner alleges that Ms. DeCourcy was his employee, not an employee of the NA; however, that distinction is of no moment for the issues upon review.

1

room with a hand fisted, which knocked her into chairs. Ms. DeCourcy alleged that petitioner then choked her using both hands around her neck and screamed that she knew too much. Ms. DeCourcy claimed that as petitioner pushed her into a corner, she tripped over a file cabinet, and he continued to push her toward bookcases.[2]

During the incident between petitioner and Ms. DeCourcy, Michael Oljaca, a NA member, had been standing outside of Ms. DeCourcy's office, because Mr. Williams "was getting more violent" during recent visits.[3] During the incident, Mr. Oljaca came into Ms. DeCourcy's office yelling for petitioner to stop and petitioner told Mr. Oljaca that Ms. DeCourcy needed to be "shut up for good" because "[s]he knows too much." A physical altercation ensued with petitioner and Mr. Oljaca. Following the altercation, Ms. DeCourcy and Mr. Oljaca left the building through the back door.

Mr. Oljaca and Ms. DeCourcy took photographs of Ms. DeCourcy's neck following the incident.[4] Then, they left the NA premises and went to the nearby home of Robert DeMarais, where Ms. DeCourcy rented a room. They advised Mr. DeMarais about the incident with petitioner from earlier in the day. Although Mr. DeMarais advised Ms. DeCourcy to call the police, she waited to contact the police until after petitioner left town due to fear for both for her safety and the safety of Mr. Oljaca.

Petitioner was charged with battery and his charge was presented in a bench trial in magistrate court. He was convicted of battery and appealed this conviction to the circuit court. On April 14, 2018, petitioner received a de novo bench trial in circuit court.

Ms. DeCourcy and Mr. DeMarais testified at the circuit court trial. Ms. DeCourcy testified to the incident of September 30, 2015. Mr. DeMarais corroborated Ms. DeCourcy's testimony about their discussion on the evening of September 30, 2015. He described Ms. DeCourcy as being very nervous and frightened and testified that she had visible injuries to both sides of her neck, with the injury to the left side being more pronounced than the injury to the right. Petitioner testified on his own behalf. Additionally, petitioner's wife and another witness testified on his behalf.

---

[2] Petitioner concedes that he did have an exchange with Ms. DeCourcy on the date in question, but denies that he committed battery. Specifically, he confirmed that he sat behind her desk; that his hand made contact with her chin when he held out his arm across the desk to stop her from shaking her finger in his face; and that he used profanities to her, telling her to "shut the f--- up." Although petitioner later reported to the West Virginia State Police that he was acting in self-defense, he testified that he did not feel physically threatened by Ms. DeCourcy.

[3] Petitioner maintains that Mr. Oljaca was inside the office during the entire exchange.

[4] Petitioner takes issue with these photographs and contends that "the State's only evidence was eight undated, un-timestamped selfies with [a] slight pink spot on [Ms. DeCourcy's] neck, submitted by [Ms. DeCourcy] to law enforcement more than two months after the alleged [] battery."

2

160

The circuit court found petitioner guilty of battery and his counsel filed a motion for a new trial. The following day, petitioner filed an "Amendment for Motion for New Trial" without the assistance of counsel. Petitioner's motion was denied.

Petitioner was sentenced by the circuit court to six months of incarceration; however, the circuit court suspended all but twenty days of the sentence, and petitioner was credited with two days for time that he previously served. The circuit court placed petitioner on probation for eighteen months.

Petitioner filed this appeal challenging his conviction. On appeal, petitioner asserts that there were numerous legal errors including: no proper investigation, lack of sufficient evidence, unreliable witnesses, and significant doubt that the battery occurred. Inasmuch as each of these errors deal with whether the evidence was sufficient to convict petitioner, we will address them together.

Generally,

> "[i]n reviewing challenges to the findings and conclusions of the circuit court made after a bench trial, a two-pronged deferential standard of review is applied. The final order and the ultimate disposition are reviewed under an abuse of discretion standard, and the circuit court's underlying factual findings are reviewed under a clearly erroneous standard. Questions of law are subject to a *de novo* review." Syllabus Point 1, *Public Citizen, Inc. v. First Nat. Bank in Fairmont*, 198 W.Va. 329, 480 S.E.2d 538 (1996).

Syl. Pt. 1, *State v. Mechling*, 219 W. Va. 366, 633 S.E.2d 311 (2006).

With specific regard to petitioner's claim that the evidence at trial was insufficient to convict him of battery,[5] this Court has stated that

> [t]he function of an appellate court when reviewing the sufficiency of the evidence to support a criminal conviction is to examine the evidence admitted at trial to determine whether such evidence, if believed, is sufficient to convince a reasonable person of the defendant's guilt beyond a reasonable doubt. Thus, the relevant inquiry is whether, after viewing the evidence in the light most favorable to the prosecution, any rational trier of fact could have found the essential elements of the crime proved beyond a reasonable doubt.

Syl. Pt. 1, *State v. Guthrie*, 194 W. Va. 657, 461 S.E.2d 163 (1995). Further,

---

[5] West Virginia Code § 61-2-9(b) (2014) provides, in relevant part, that a battery occurs when "[a]ny person . . . unlawfully and intentionally makes physical contact of an insulting or provoking nature to the person of another or unlawfully and intentionally causes physical harm to another person[.]"

[a] criminal defendant challenging the sufficiency of the evidence to support a conviction takes on a heavy burden. An appellate court must review all the evidence, whether direct or circumstantial, in the light most favorable to the prosecution and must credit all inferences and credibility assessments that the jury might have drawn in favor of the prosecution. The evidence need not be inconsistent with every conclusion save that of guilt so long as the jury can find guilt beyond a reasonable doubt. Credibility determinations are for a jury and not an appellate court. Finally, a jury verdict should be set aside only when the record contains no evidence, regardless of how it is weighed, from which the jury could find guilt beyond a reasonable doubt.

Id. at 663, 461 S.E.2d at 169, syl. pt. 3, in part. Finally, "[a]n appellate court may not decide the credibility of witnesses or weigh evidence as that is the exclusive function and task of the trier of fact." *Id.* at 669 n.9, 461 S.E.2d at 175 n.9.

Here, based on our review of the January 7, 2019, trial transcript, we find no cause to disturb the circuit court's findings. Both the magistrate court and the circuit court made credibility determinations as to the witnesses who testified in petitioner's criminal proceedings. The circuit court found Ms. DeCourcy's testimony to be credible to the extent that it was consistent with her statements; the photographs depicting redness and swelling were consistent with the type of injury Ms. DeCourcy described; Ms. DeCourcy's statement to the West Virginia State Police Trooper was consistent with her testimony; Mr. DeMarais's testimony corroborated Ms. DeCourcy's testimony and he saw injuries to her neck; and most telling, petitioner's wife, Ms. Williams, testified that Ms. DeCourcy told her that petitioner had choked her. Despite petitioner's repeated requests, we decline to conduct a credibility determination, especially where the circuit court assessed the credibility of these witnesses. Further, we find that petitioner's conviction should not be set aside because, contrary to petitioner's assertions, the record contains sufficient evidence to support his conviction.

In the argument section of petitioner's brief he asserts that the circuit court judge displayed signs of judicial misconduct. Notably absent from the record, however, is any request by petitioner to disqualify the circuit court judge pursuant to West Virginia Trial Court Rule 17. Petitioner's claim is largely based upon his disagreement with his conviction, the sufficiency of the evidence against him, the credibility of Ms. DeCourcy, law enforcement's investigation, the circuit court's denial of various motions, and the sentence imposed upon him by the circuit court. Although petitioner devoted approximately ten pages of his brief to his attack of the trial court judge, his brief contains little more than self-serving speculation, conclusory suppositions, and considerable reference to matters outside of the appellate record. Notably, the only legal authorities cited by petitioner in connection with this argument were Canon 2 of the West Virginia Judicial Code of Conduct and the 6th Amendment, but petitioner does not address how these were violated by the circuit court. His reply, however, suggests that he "was expecting [the] State's comments on each of six presented Rules of Cannon [sic] 2."

Although leniency and latitude is afforded to self-represented litigants such as petitioner, they must still comply with the West Virginia Rules of Appellate Procedure. Rule 10(c)(7) of the West Virginia Rules of Appellate Procedure requires that

4

[t]he brief must contain an argument exhibiting clearly the points of fact and *law presented,* the standard of review applicable, and *citing the authorities relied on . . . [and]* must contain appropriate and specific citations to the record on appeal[.] The Court may disregard errors that are not adequately supported by specific references to the record on appeal.

(Emphasis added). Additionally, in an Administrative Order entered December 10, 2012, Re: Filings That Do Not Comply With the Rules of Appellate Procedure, the Court noted that "[b]riefs that lack citation of authority [or] fail to structure an argument applying applicable law" are not in compliance with this Court's rules. Further, "[b]riefs with arguments that do not contain a citation to legal authority to support the argument presented and do not 'contain appropriate and specific citations to the . . . record on appeal . . .' as required by rule 10(c)(7)" are not in compliance with this Court's rules. Here, petitioner's brief is inadequate as it fails to comply with the administrative order and the West Virginia Rules of Appellate Procedure, and thus, we decline to address this assignment of error on appeal.

Next, on direct appeal, petitioner maintains that his counsel was ineffective at the magistrate court and circuit court levels. He also asserts that the counseling he received was ineffective.[6] This Court has long held that ineffective assistance of counsel claims are inappropriate for review on direct appeal. *State v. Miller,* 194 W. Va. 3, 459 S.E.2d 114 (1995). Specifically, in *Miller,* we addressed the difficulty this Court has when reviewing these matters:

> To meet our review function, we must match applicable principles of law to the discerned facts and circumstances of the litigated case. When those facts are not properly furnished to this Court, we are denied the basic tools necessary to carry out our function. Thus, under those circumstances, we have found that issues, such as ineffective assistance of counsel, were not ripe for direct appellate review. *See State v. Triplett,* 187 W.Va. 760, 771, 421 S.E.2d 511, 522 (1992) ("it is the extremely rare case when this Court will find ineffective assistance of counsel when such a charge is raised as an assignment of error on a direct appeal").

194 W. Va. at 14, 459 S.E.2d at 125.

Inasmuch as petitioner's ineffective assistance of counsel claims are raised on direct appeal, a developed record does not exist, and this Court is deprived of the necessary tools to address petitioner's allegations. Moreover, this portion of petitioner's brief also fails to satisfy the requirements of Rule 10 of the West Virginia Rules of Appellate Procedure because it lacks citation to legal authority, fails to structure an argument applying applicable law, and largely arises from matters outside the record. Therefore, this ground for relief is insufficient, and we decline to disturb the circuit court's ruling.

For the foregoing reasons, we affirm the circuit court's order.

---

[6] As in other portions of his brief, petitioner relies largely upon assertions not contained in the record to form the basis of his argument.

164

Affirmed.

ISSUED: June 18, 2020

CONCURRED IN BY:

Chief Justice Tim Armstead
Justice Margaret L. Workman
Justice Elizabeth D. Walker
Justice Evan H. Jenkins
Justice John A. Hutchison